OCREATING OPTIMISM

A Proven, Seven-Step Program
for Overcoming Depression

BOB MURRAY, Ph.D.
AND ALICIA FORTINBERRY

McGraw·Hill

New York Chicago San Francisco Lisbon London Madrid Mexico City
Milan New Delhi San Juan Seoul Singapore Sydney Toronto

Library of Congress Cataloging-in-Publication Data

Murray, Bob.
    Creating optimism : A proven, seven-step program for overcoming depression / Bob Murray,
Alicia Fortinberry.
        p.   cm.
    Includes bibliographical references and index.
    ISBN 0-07-141785-0 (alk. paper) (hardcover) — ISBN 0-07-144683-4 (paperback)
    1. Depression, Mental—Popular works.   2. Self-help techniques.   I. Fortinberry, Alicia.
II. Title.

RC537 .M866   2004
616.85'2706—dc22

                                                      2003014426

12 13 14 15   DIG/DIG 17 16 15

ISBN 0-07-141785-0 (hardcover)
ISBN 0-07-144683-4 (paperback)

Illustrations by Anna Witsel

McGraw-Hill books are available at special quantity discounts to use as premiums and sales promotions,
or for use in corporate training programs. For more information, please write to the Director of Special
Sales, Professional Publishing, McGraw-Hill, Two Penn Plaza, New York, NY 10121-2298. Or contact your
local bookstore.

CONTENTS

⊙

PART III

VALUE HAPPINESS

Acknowledgments

⊙

WE'VE BEEN EXTREMELY LUCKY in the marvelous people who have come into our lives and helped further our mission of teaching people how to create great relationships and defeat depression.

Sophie Ozolins, a former student who is now a great friend and colleague, has been an indispensable part of the creative process from beginning to end. Her enthusiasm, technical skills, and editorial help have been invaluable.

We'd also like to thank our agent, Jeanne Fredericks, for her dedication to this project and her ongoing support. Judith McCarthy's encouragement and on-target suggestions make her every writer's dream editor.

Prof. Anne DeBaldo at the University of Southern Florida's School of Public Health and Bobbi Rose have been strong supporters of the Uplift Program™. Gregg Ferman's enduring belief in our work made all the difference.

INTRODUCTION

The Way out of Depression

⊙

AS THE LARGE, SUNNY ROOM at the University of South Florida slowly fills with the people who will attend our five-day Uplift Program™, our excitement is mixed with nervousness that has nothing to do with stage fright, even after all our years of teaching. Without taking our eyes off the students coming into the room, each with his or her unique habits and history, we reach out and hold each other's hands.

Our Uplift students, like our clients, represent a wide range of ages, backgrounds, and professions. Most are depressed and recognize this; some are unsure and want to know more. Some are here primarily because of relationship difficulties. A few are health professionals looking for new, more effective ways to help their depressed patients. A large number have tried or studied other methods and therapies. They hope we can help. But many have been disappointed or, worse, feel that they themselves have failed. For these, even coming here takes courage.

We are always somewhat awed by this trust. And it has been justified.

Ninety-four percent of our Uplift students surveyed up to two years after taking the course report that both their level of mood and their relationships have greatly improved. What's more, their lives are still getting better because the techniques they learned have an exponential effect. Many tell us that they are happier than they ever imagined they could be, and they look to the future with confidence and optimism.

And so can you.

This book will take you on an odyssey, a voyage of exploration, healing, and change. Like the explorers of old, you will venture into new waters and dispel old myths. We will provide the vessel, charts, and compass. We will share exciting personal and professional discoveries from our own passages. We will briefly recount the stories of others who, by using these instruments, have made their own successful journeys and returned transformed. We will identify the landmarks and points of orientation: studies, research, and our clinical experience encompassing much of two decades. At stages along the way, we will invite you to take your own bearings and, following the charts we provide, arrive at an undiscovered continent: yourself.

You are not your depression, or your despondency, disappointments, perceived failures, or negative beliefs about yourself. Although some of our individual characteristics, perhaps even half of them, are the result of our genes, human beings are not genetically doomed to be depressed or pessimistic.[1] Your depression has been foisted onto you by a society that lost its own way somewhere around five to ten thousand years ago. At different times around the globe, but for the same reasons (climate change and increasing population), hunter-gatherers were forced to wrest a living from the earth as farmers. We stopped living harmoniously with each other and the environment.[2]

Our species' genetic makeup has not caught up to our rapidly changing lifestyle. Gradually, but steadily, since that time we have become a misled and convoluted society that fosters abuse, trauma, and powerlessness when it should engender support, safety, and autonomy. A society that produces ignorance, materialism, and fanaticism instead of wisdom, value happiness (which we'll define later), and a true spirituality. A society that, in its actions if not its words, devalues the very things that make us most human—our connection to each other and the world around us. Instead, it reinforces isolation, violence, and emotional destruction. And we don't mean just Western or developed society; we are talking about the vast majority of our kind. During this voyage you will discover how to heal your depression. In fact, this healing will begin well before we reach the last port.

The idea that your individual pain is rooted in an abusive social environment may be difficult for you to accept at first. This concept, like a number of ideas we will invite you to examine, is ultimately as revolutionary as Copernicus's assertion that the globe-shaped earth revolves around the sun. Yet you will discover that no matter how far you venture from the shores of conventional wisdom, you will not sail over the edge of your world and drop off.

And, given the scope and pervasiveness of the problem, any solution must be new, bold, and encompassing. Here are the facts. We have a depression pandemic of unprecedented proportions. According to the World Health Organization (WHO), up to 340 million people suffer from depression worldwide (including about 20 million in the United States alone). Up to 30 percent of women in developed countries suffer from some form of depression. In 2001, WHO predicted that depression would be the major source of death after heart disease. Yet, more recent studies show that depression itself is a significant contributory factor to fatal coronary disease.

Depression lies behind a considerable proportion of the world's health care problems. Increasingly, illnesses the medical community categorized as purely "physical" are now found to be linked to depression. They include (as of this writing) diabetes, some forms of cancer, osteoporosis, fibromyalgia, chronic pain, and even eye diseases. And this does not include depression's role in addiction and conditions arising directly from a negative lifestyle such as obesity, lack of exercise, isolation, and stress.

Depression is a symptom of underlying social problems as surely as the plague of the Middle Ages was due to poor public hygiene. And depression's grasp is as pervasive within each community and far more wide reaching geographically. According to a 1998 Australian government report, no one is immune from its effects. Everyone will either feel its pain sometime in his or her own life or someone close will.

The social cost of depression is enormous in terms of work and the economy, health care, education, drug addiction, and law enforcement. In fact, depression may well be the most expensive and debilitating problem human beings now face. And yet we focus only on the surface of these issues, partially because of ignorance and vested interests.

In spite of enormous amounts of research, no one has yet come up with a treatment that works for everyone, which is probably not news to you. Many of our students and clients—not to mention Alicia herself—have discovered the hard way that the much-touted "solutions" just don't work for them, don't have lasting effects, or offer part but not enough of the answer.

Antidepressants are not the panacea they are made out to be by the drug companies and many in the medical community. From the late 1970s on, a large number of studies have shown that they work about as well as placebos (sugar pills) with far more side effects. Many of the most popular and widely available psychotherapeutic treatments have limited results because, as we'll explain, they are based on a flawed premise that depression is caused mainly, if not solely, by your thoughts and behaviors and that if you change these you can free yourself from depression.[3] This notion ignores much of what researchers now know about neurobiology and the role of childhood trauma in altering the structure and function of the brain. While new research increasingly points to a genetic factor in depression, it also indicates that these genes need to be activated by the environment.

None of these theories addresses that most essential factor in the human environment—relationships.

Despite all indoctrination to the contrary, you do not in fact heal from the inside out. You don't "pull yourself up by your bootstraps." You can't think, meditate, eat, work, exercise, or focus your way out of depression, although each of these, *done in very specific ways and within a certain context,* may help.

This book is about showing you what does work. Although you will find that you in no way caused your depression, very specific and extremely effective actions will get rid of it.

In fact, you can do this in seven simple steps. With information, insights, and exercises we will guide you to your solution and show you very concretely how to create your own healing environment and stimulate your full human potential for empowerment, optimism, physical and emotional health, and real happiness.

Of course we can't go back to living as our hunter-gatherer forebears did. We are too numerous, the woolly mammoth is extinct, and grubs (insect larvae that form a staple of traditional Australian Aborigines and other indigenous groups) are probably a taste most easily acquired in extreme youth.

But, we will teach you to incorporate those elements of the hunter-gatherer lifestyle that will enable you to forge a functional interdependence with others as well as with nature and your own spirituality.

We are a relationship-forming species, a highly social animal. We become pessimistic, depressed, and even physically ill when our relationships are dysfunctional or out of kilter. We will show you that your depression and the blocks to the life you want were set in place by relationships gone wrong in childhood, ones that reflected the trauma and emotional abuse of a highly dysfunctional society. But each of us is capable of forming truly supportive, healing relationships. And our unique, simple, and powerful techniques will make sure you do.

You will discover that you can create the essence of the safe and nurturing hunter-gatherer band even within our dysfunctional society. And within the context of that support and security you will triumph over your depression.

Having given you the basic tools to combat depression and helplessness, we will look at how to prevent relapse, further expand your personal empowerment, achieve work success, and continue to create a solid basis for happiness and healthy spirituality (a powerful antidepressant on its own).

The book follows this process in three parts. In Part I, "Mapping the Way," we vividly bring to life the elements of hunter-gatherer society that enabled our forebears to live free of depression and we will contrast these with how we live today. We then look at the eight fundamentals of happiness: connection to others; autonomy; self-esteem; competence; purpose; and connection to your body, nature, and spirit.

You may be vulnerable to depression because you are misinformed. Drawing on the latest research in neurobiology and psychiatry, we next lay bare the myths and misinformation about depression and examine what it really is and its real causes. We'll also look at how depression expresses itself through illness.

Next, we'll start you on the process of actively defeating the negative beliefs and behaviors that cause your depression and blocks to what you want from life. In Step 1, "Identify and Defeat the Inner Saboteur," you will learn how to understand and change this self-defeating mechanism. We'll explain how depression is perpetuated by trauma locked in the body and, in Step 2, "Reconnect to Your Body," we'll show you how to free your body from the past and reclaim this empowering aspect of yourself.

Step 3, "Create Healing Relationships," which encompasses all of Part II, leads you through a very simple yet extremely powerful process that is the only sure-fire formula for getting and staying free of depression. We show you how to identify your functional needs and get them met in your current relationships and also how to meet new people who are right for you. You will learn how to negotiate, set clear boundaries, and avoid harmful codependence. You will discover how to use rules, roles, and rituals to bind families, friends, and coworkers together in a healthy interconnectedness. Finally, we examine what makes a functional community and how you can become part of a supportive, encouraging, and dependable network.

In Part III, "Value Happiness," we lead you through the remaining steps to an optimistic and depression-free life. We'll help you navigate a course that avoids the false values engendered by modern society and leads to lasting fulfillment. In Steps 4, "Elevate Your Self-Esteem" and 5, "Uncover Your Competence," you'll discover the real secrets of how to feel increasingly good about yourself and achieve more in every aspect of your life, as well as how to keep your emotional immune system high.

Your life will take on a new depth and richness as you explore and enhance your unique sense of purpose and spirituality in Steps 6, "Access the Power of Shared Purpose" and 7, "Deepen Your Relationship to the Divine."

Bon voyage!

A WORD ABOUT STYLE

Since this book has two authors, we use the terms "we," "us," and "ours" as the editorial voice. We sometimes also refer to "we" or "us" in terms of the human race, and we've tried to be clear when this is the case. When talking about one of us in particular, we use our names. In the Appendix, "To Friends and Family," which Bob wrote, he uses "I."

Another stylistic issue involves the use of "she" or "he" to refer to a person when gender doesn't matter. To get around the awkwardness of writing "he or she" and "himself/herself" every time, we have used "she" and "he" (and "his" or "her") in alternating chapters.

OUR OWN JOURNEY

Before we hoist sails and set forth with you on this voyage, we would like to add a word about the navigators: ourselves. We have been practicing our method, which forms the basis of the Uplift Program™ and is called, not surprisingly, the Fortinberry Murray Method™, for nearly twenty years. We have also presented our method to the medical staff at some of the country's major medical centers, including Duke University Medical Center, Tufts New England Medical Center, New Jersey's Englewood Medical Center, California's Mt. Diablo Medical Center, and the Royal North Shore Hospital in Sydney, Australia.

Our unconventional approach arose from our own search for answers to two questions: how can we create a really close, conflict-free, and empowering relationship with each other and how can we heal depression—primarily, at first, Alicia's. Almost to our surprise, the former was the key to the latter—and all the good that has since come into our lives.

Alicia's depression, which had been diagnosed on several occasions as "treatment resistant," had its roots in her parents' alcoholism and mutual bitterness and in her early sexual abuse.

Bob's parents, although also both alcoholics, were happy in their careers and their relationship. His mother, an American by birth, was brought up in Sydney and made her way as a writer in London. His father, from an Aussie bush town, nonetheless made his mark as a mystery writer of international renown. Although Bob's parents were more interested in working and partying than child-rearing, he was never criticized and enjoyed the freedom to roam unsupervised from a young age. Later, however, after his father's death when Bob was fifteen, he was made to feel guilty for his inability to rescue his mother from her grief and alcohol-induced ill health. However, by then he had learned enough self-reliance to set out on his own.

Alicia followed in her father's journalistic footprints and became a writer and editor for New York–based national magazines. She specialized in health and psychology and later trained in the Feldenkrais Method®, which uses movement to help people reconnect to their bodies and discover new, nonhabitual patterns of physical function and learning. Bob initially delved into psychology and then, upon finding that it offered very few real solutions, left to pursue a career as a producer with the BBC in England.

Our relationship started out as exciting, passionate—and tempestuous. (Now it is still exciting and passionate but conflict free.) Bob saw Alicia as his mother, who had needed rescuing from depression. Alicia saw Bob as her father, who was a world-traveling philanderer. Somehow we managed to extricate ourselves from the misunderstandings caused by our past programming. We discovered that we really loved each other for who we were, not just as stand-ins for our parents.

However, Alicia's depression became a growing problem. Although she was fully functional in her work, it was in spite of bouts of excruciating emotional pain. Bob was driven to new efforts in his attempts to wrest a solution from existing psychological theory. When none was available, he turned to the fields that were churning out new and applicable information at a truly astounding rate—neurobiology, anthropology, and genetics. Alicia explored ways of helping clients free their bodies as well as their minds from the past.

As our lives merged more fully, so did our insights into the human condition, approaching it from all angles—the brain, emotions, the body, and spirituality. All played a vital role in Alicia's recovery, Bob's self-discovery, and the continuing evolution of our truly healing and wondrous relationship. From that great love and that great challenge came the method we have used to help literally thousands of people in private sessions, workshops and seminars, and the seed of this book.

A Note to the Reader

You will find a number of exercises throughout the book that reflect the processes experienced by many who found relief from depression and created exceptional relationships through the Uplift Program.

The exercises are an important part in your discovery of your optimal self. Different ones involve self-awareness, creativity, movement, and taking action. All are precisely calibrated to progressively create change in your brain and body as you do them. A number of the actions that you take will bring about shifts in your relationships that will in turn help you heal and develop.

Although your ultimate goal of real happiness may seem hopelessly out of reach, it isn't. Each step we suggest you take is doable, and the inevitable result is success. However, your program—that set of neural connections that hold you back from the life you want and contribute to depression and pessimism—will probably try to stop you at some point. Taking these steps will enable you to break free from the bonds of the past, which would deprive your program of its power. Most people find the exercises engaging and are further motivated by the astonishing changes that occur, sometimes starting immediately. These changes accrue exponentially.

For the written exercises, you will need a computer, loose-leaf notebook, or journal with different sections so that you can return to some processes and refine them or expand on them. You can also then keep track of what you've done and refer back.

Relationships are the key to healing and change. Some of the processes involve interacting directly with people in your life and asking that they participate. But even for the exercises that you do on your own you may want support and feedback from friends.

If you are experiencing emotional pain or are concerned about maintaining the important activities in your life, you may want a supportive relationship with a psychotherapist. The ideas and processes in this book are an extremely useful adjunct to psychotherapy.

We train mental health professionals in the Fortinberry Murray Method. Our Uplift Program workshops and support groups offer a powerful healing environment and opportunities to connect with like-minded people. For more information on these opportunities, please refer to our website, upliftprogram.com.

PART I

MAPPING THE WAY

I

HAPPINESS LOST

◉

Recent research has shown that the root causes of most people's depression are childhood trauma and abuse and the real or perceived fear of abandonment. We passionately believe that our society produces isolation, maltreatment, and disempowerment. In other words, the very way we live is abusive to ourselves and our children. In the words of two prominent researchers, the late Gerald L. Klerman and Myrna M. Weissman of Cornell University, "society itself has pathogenic effects." What's more, they say, the rate of depression has been doubling every twenty years since 1960, largely due to the increasing stresses and isolation imposed on the modern family.

In fact, according to a study headed by Jean M. Twenge of Case Western University, today's "normal" children report the same level of depression and anxiety as child psychiatric patients in the 1950s. Your social environment, on its own and filtered through the family you grew up in, is the fundamental cause of your depression.

It's not that depression and pessimism are new—far from it. They have always been around, but our Stone Age ancestors' society contained healing mechanisms, now lost, that ensured that depression, when it came, was temporary. Isolation, except in extreme circumstances, never happened. To illustrate what we mean, let's look at one family who were clients of ours. They are not untypical.

Denise, a forty-year-old mother of two, came to see Alicia regarding her increased anxiety that was interfering with her sleep. Since her husband, Jeff, had been laid off from his job as an engineer, she was the sole financial support of the family, which included fifteen-year-old Jason and ten-year-old Jessica. Her job as an advertising executive had its own stresses, including long hours and no control over her work schedule. Her major concerns, however, involved Jeff and the children, all of whom had problems of their own.

Denise felt that somehow as a working mother she was to blame for these problems: her husband's depression and anger, both of which had escalated since his layoff nine months ago; Jason's truancy, suspected drug use, and fights; and Jessica's withdrawal from friends and outside activities coupled with increasing weight gain, probably signaling depression. Jeff and Jason seemed to get into heated arguments whenever both were in the house, yelling at each other and, in one instance, breaking valuable dinnerware.

Denise's anxiety is one aspect of an underlying depression. This condition is also behind much of the family members' symptoms: overusing food, drugs, and alcohol; rage; and perhaps even the ADD/ADHD and violence Jason has displayed since early childhood. Alicia explained to Denise that her and her family's depression was the by-product of a society out of control. And so were her work stress, Jeff's unemployment, and their financial burden.

Denise's family, like most of us, is cut off from nearly all of what makes them truly human—a network of supportive people; work that does not interfere with other aspects of their life and is pleasurable, empowering, and socially rewarding; frequent interaction with nature, including other animals; and a connection to the sublime. In his book *The Human Zoo*, Desmond Morris says that we are like animals living in an urban zoo, subject to psychological and physical stressors our minds and bodies were never meant to cope with.

In many ways Denise's family—and most if not all of us in some way—resembles laboratory rats in an overcrowded cage, deprived of the "natural" (genetically suitable) habitat, and subject to traumatic, bewildering, and unpredictable events over which they have no control. Such rats, as experiments have shown time and again, stop behaving like rats. They violently turn on each other, abuse or ignore their offspring, and become ill.

THE LOST TRIBE OF US

So what would we be like in our natural environment, in hunter-gatherer times? Humans are fairly adaptable and have survived in most climates and surroundings. Beside the basic requirement of edible plants and game, the most important aspect of our environment was a closely knit, mutually supportive "band."

Let's look for a moment at how a family of four, resembling Denise's family in age and gender, would have lived in an environment that was congruent with their nature. Anthropologists tell us that all hunter-gatherer societies had many similarities.[4]

Denise and her family would be part of a group of thirty to fifty people. They would rarely encounter other humans and would have little to fear from them if they did.[5] In fact, they would be excited to share information and skills and to intermarry (a woman would join her husband's band—maybe *that's* why women are better communicators), thus ensuring genetic variation.

The nuclear family was not isolated or beset with stresses, as it is today. It would not have been the major economic unit, since every member of the band who could walk would have contributed to the economy of the group. Food was shared, and possessions, what few there were, were mostly communal. Forget territory disputes. When you are basically a dot on the landscape, whether you're nomadic (usually within a specific territory, like lions and our cousins the chimpanzees) or stationary, the idea of "owning" land is laughable.

Even natural disasters—storms, drought, floods, and so forth—would have been less stressful for the family. Modern research has shown that people who live in closely knit communities can survive such stresses much better than those in more developed but alienated societies.

Therefore, Jeff and Denise's anxiety about providing for themselves and their children would have been unwarranted, except perhaps in times of drought or climactic change. Then the group would have moved on to more abundant pastures, unimpeded by borders, work permits, professional licenses, or moving vans. They would not have had to keep up with the bills, the mortgage payments, the car payments, the insurance premiums, or the Joneses.

Food and shelter were in most cases easily available. We tend to look down on the lives of our remote ancestors as being, in the words of the seventeenth-century English philosopher Thomas Hobbes, "nasty, brutish, and short." But this is far from the truth. To start with, research has shown that hunter-gatherers lived surprisingly long lives. As Dr. Anthony Daniels, consultant psychiatrist, points out in the June 27, 1999, edition of Britain's *Sunday Telegraph*, when humans civilized themselves their health deteriorated drastically and their life expectancy at birth nearly halved. Not until the end of the nineteenth century did we start living as long as our hunter-gatherer forebears.

Scholar John Hayward has described hunter-gatherers as having "the first affluent society." Of the !Kung people of the Kalahari he writes, "They are able to provide all the basics of life for themselves by about two to three hours work a day, depending on the season. The rest of the time is spent on leisure, either gossiping and socializing, telling stories, playing games or resting. This compares very favorably with the modern affluent lifestyle in which commuting, shopping, cooking and household chores must be added to a forty-hour 'working week' before leisure can begin."

Work, therefore, would not be the all-encompassing safety issue it is for Jeff and Denise. Jeff would not have been laid off. (With very few people and no technology, who could be unnecessary?) As a young man, Jeff would have hunted with his male friends, thoroughly enjoying the camaraderie and the rush of adrenalin and dopamine (the happiness, or reward, neurochemical) that accompanied this pursuit. They would have brought back their catch to the admiration and delight of the others. They would have cooked the game they'd caught while the women prepared the vegetables and roots for a feast. (Much like the modern barbecue, where the men tend to grill the meat and the women prepare the trimmings.)

Although the men would have been silent during the actual hunt so as not to announce their presence to predators and prey, they would have spent the next days or weeks around a campfire happily talking about their prowess and the woolly mammoth (which no doubt got bigger with each telling) that got away.

In many bands, the men would not have married until they were in their forties, when they could be counted upon to be a stable mate and survive. Jeff would not have married when he was young and inexperienced and the monumental stress of having to care for his family without a wide support system wouldn't have existed. Without that stress he wouldn't have been triggered into raging at his family.

Denise would not be in anything like the position she's in. Confident in the protection of the men of the band, she and the other women would have looked after the children together. Gathering and hunting small game would have been an enjoyable opportunity to share news (i.e., gossip). Although she would probably have married at puberty and learned how to manage a family under the direction of older women, during her life she might have up to about four husbands. As she grew older and wiser her value as a wife would have risen.

IMPACT ON CHILDREN

In this context, Jason and Jessica would have borne little resemblance to the unhappy youths we introduced you to. First of all, they would have been sheltered from the vicissitudes of their parents' stresses and relationship difficulties. From infancy, they would know only the loving arms and laps of women who had plenty of time for them. As the children got older, if their parents argued or were ill, they would have been welcomed at another campfire among people they knew well and trusted. Child raising really was a communal endeavor.

Children helped bring in and prepare food from an early age, often able to catch small game by reaching with tiny hands and slipping nimble bodies into places adults could not. In a society that spends so few hours a week on "work," we are not talking unfair child labor practices. Young children learned to take pride in their accomplishments through praise and to make decisions that impacted not only themselves but others. They picked up their skills by watching older members of the band (including older siblings), who also provided a wide range of role models. How different all this is from what happened to Jason and Jessica (and probably you and the children you know)!

Most modern children aren't given an economic role, which provides the primary source of recognized importance within our society. (In places where children do bring in income from a young age, this is usually a debilitating hardship.) With schoolwork taking up more and more time, even chores are becoming a thing of the past.

Jason and Jessica have been made to feel entitled to a certain standard of living, while being given no chance to contribute meaningfully to it. In terms of society, their only importance lies in their future contributions.

Young men like Jason hunted because they are neurobiologically primed to do so. The three elements of the hunt that trigger the release of the happiness chemical dopamine in the young male brain are the danger and uncertainty of it, the intense pleasure at a successful outcome, and the particular kind of companionship involved. In this sense it's not unlike a football match, which is as close as we come to male hunter-gatherer "work."

David Goldman of NYU School of Medicine and others have shown that achievement, danger, and uncertainty are very important for adolescent and young adult males. Jason is genetically programmed[6] to go forth and kill the mighty mammoth and brave the saber-toothed tiger, yet he's still living at home under his parents' thumbs and either sitting in a classroom or bagging groceries for allowance money. Jason's physiology is primed for risk and danger, and the law says he has to wear a bicycle helmet and can only take his skateboard to designated areas.[7]

But Jason had problems long before adolescence. His diagnosed ADD/ADHD may have had a lot to do with being made to sit still at an early age in school[8] and the stress of the household pre- and postnatally.[9] (A mother's stress and anxiety can be passed on to her unborn infant via a sharing of stress hormones, making the infant hyperactive from birth.) Plus, with few other role models around, Jason had taken on his father's rage as the only way he knew of coping with stress.

Jessica is also strongly affected by the family's tension and distress. Since her older brother got his attention through rebellion, she had to find another niche. She became the "goody-goody," mother's little helper in the kitchen, and the earnest pupil. In a family with very little time or affectionate attention to give (unlike the hunter-gatherer band), Jessica's strategy hasn't worked all that well. She's retreated further and further into depression to dull the pain of guilt and the fear of abandonment.

The guilt started when she was little and, like all young children, believed she was the center of the universe and the cause of everything. In her eyes, something was very wrong. Mommy was tired, strained, and unhappy; Daddy was mad all the time and they fought. What could it be if not her fault? No one ever pointed out to her the fallacy of this belief, which is now ingrained.

Plus, she's got to deal with her body (which, according to researcher Paul Kaplowitz of Virginia Commonwealth University School of Medicine and others, is developing much faster than that of a girl her age even a few decades ago). She has never looked like her Barbie doll or the girls and young women on TV or in the teen magazines. Her classmates are wearing makeup and talking about boys. She's afraid of boys because Jason has been cruel and abusive. (In a hunter-gatherer band, this abuse would have been detected and not tolerated.)

Denise's modern family lives in an inner suburb of a large city. Their world is that of highways, cement, and glass, rather than the sound of trees in the wind, the smell of wet or parched earth, the sight and calls of animals, and the feel of grass beneath their feet that would have enveloped their ancient counterparts.

The hunter-gatherer band would have been closely bound together by spiritual beliefs, storytelling, dance, song, and rituals both religious and other. Denise's family members barely speak to each other. Communal meals, which Denise tried to provide when the kids were young, have given way to busy schedules and fast food. The family enjoys no structured interaction with their neighbors and no joint worship. (Virtually all recent research has shown that the old adage "the family that prays together stays together" is true.) The family, like the nuclear unit itself, is a lone ship in the night, and it is sinking.

THE MISMATCH

How did the way of life that provided all we needed to thrive get lost? What happened to the "lost tribe of us?"

In the Bible, Genesis describes how humans were expelled from the Garden of Eden for partaking of the forbidden fruit or, to put it another way, for attempting to change from the way we were designed to be. To us, this has always been a marvelous analogy of what really happened to humans about ten thousand years ago, almost a folk memory written many thousand years closer to the event.

What is recalled, perhaps, is the time when our ancestors were forced to give up their ancient ways and become farmers and herders because of a Stone Age population explosion coupled with a change in the earth's climate. Prior to that, our evolutionary forebears had followed much the same hunter-gatherer lifestyle for some two and a half million years.

During this vast period, we developed a whole string of genetic characteristics that helped us survive the dangers and exploit the opportunities we faced. Most of the attributes were social. Humans' social cooperation enabled us to survive and made up for our lack of other advantages, such as sharp teeth, long claws, size, and speed. Biologists declare that a creature who lives as long as we do takes about 50,000–100,000 years to evolve in any significant way. Genetically, we are still those hunter-gatherers.

Evolutionary psychologists and theorists of evolutionary medicine call this divergence between our species' inheritance and our modern lifestyle the "mismatch." This theory holds that we are genetically programmed to live in a certain way, that of traditional hunter-gatherers, and that any significant deviation from this way of life creates both mental and physical stress. The result, writes Robert Wright in *Time* magazine, is the "evolution of despair."

Once we began farming, we were forced to make many changes to our technology and economy, which negatively impacted our social and family life. Now "tied to the land," as the saying goes, we had to "wrest a living from the soil," suggesting a very different relationship to nature and subsequently to each other. We were forced to live in a way that we were not—and still are not—well adapted to.

The plight of the isolated and unsupported nuclear family has worsened over the years at an increasingly rapid pace. First, we lost the communal hunter-gatherer band to the extended family that worked its own patch or herded its own flock. The subsequent industrial society needed and produced a small and increasingly vulnerable economic unit supported by a wage earner who would work for very little in the factories. The information age hasn't been any better, forcing more uncertainty, relocation, and isolation on families.

These days, even a two-member nuclear family is an endangered species, with divorce and the rise in single- (or no-) parent households. In the following chart, we've outlined some of the basic aspects of the mismatch, most of which you saw at work with Denise's family and their imaginary precursors.

HUNTER-GATHERER	MODERN SOCIETY
Nuclear family part of band	Unsupported, stressed nuclear family
Interdependent	Isolated and alienated
Cooperative	Competitive
Nonhierarchical	Hierarchical
Band of 30–50 members	Mass society
Relationships a priority	Work a priority
Social and technological stasis	Rapid societal and technological change
Individual empowerment and autonomy	Disempowerment and loss of self
Consensus decision-making	Loss of decision-making power
Work 5–10 hours per week	Work 40–60 (or more) hours per week
Roles defined and valued	Roles confused and devalued
Little specialization	Great specialization
Early responsibility and economic role	Late responsibility and dependence
Communal child rearing	Insufficient adult supervision
Little or no child abuse	Prevalent child abuse
Rituals around most activities	Few rituals
Pervasive spirituality	Fragmented or lost spirituality
At one with nature	Separate from nature

Clearly we are caught in a social system that does not meet our human needs and over which we have lost control. We are forced to work too much, change too fast, and socialize and chatter too little. Worse for the future, we spend less and less time caring for and teaching our own children. With each step away from the lifestyle to which we are evolutionarily adapted, we become more stressed, less happy, and more prone to depression.

ISOLATION, ABUSE, AND DEPRESSION

When examining depression, the most salient and destructive aspects of our society are isolation and abuse. One dictionary's definition of *abuse* is "to change the inherent purpose or function of something or to use improperly." Our society constantly tries to make us into something we are not, with purposes and functions that are not congruent with our real selves. The way we are forced to live is abusive. (According to Dr. Scott Weich of the Royal Free Hospital School of Medicine in London, even apartment living, with people raised above the ground and packed on top of each other is abusive to its occupants in the way that a cage is to a lion. The higher up you live, he says, the more depressed you are liable to become.)

Much has been written on the link between disempowerment and spousal and child abuse. According to prominent forensic psychiatrist Dr. Gary J. Maier, constant, pervasive stress creates abusive individuals. For example, Jeff—under the unremitting strain of conditions that go back to his childhood and the recent loss of the means to fulfill his role as a man as he understands it—rages at his son. Jason in turn strikes out at and seeks to dominate the one person at *his* mercy, his sister.

Childhood abuse is recognized by most researchers as the leading cause of adult depression and pessimism. Abuse literally changes brain chemistry and structure. But according to researchers such as psychologist Kristi Williams of Ohio State University, we are not naturally an abusive species. The deliberate infliction of harm upon children is quite foreign to our nature. Child, sibling, and spousal abuse is not generally observed in present-day hunter-gatherer societies, so presumably it didn't occur that often in the distant past either. In his book *The Forest People*, Colin Turnbull states that the worst he observed in three years of living with hunter-gatherer pygmies was "a healthy sprinkle of spankings and slappings" when the children put themselves or other members of the group in danger.

If a young child is abused—hit, criticized, threatened with abandonment, sexually molested, and so forth—she will believe that she is bad. She won't blame the abuser, especially a family member, but rather herself. She will feel that because of her wickedness, she deserves punishment and that she may well be abandoned. (For a child in a hunter-gatherer band, ejection from the band meant death.)

This child will be dogged by anxiety, shame, and guilt throughout her life and will be vulnerable to depression and low self-esteem. In technical terms, she will feel that her status, or social attention holding power (SAHP), will go down. SAHP is largely subjective; our SAHP rating involves what we think other people think of us. Shame and guilt are associated with lower SAHP, as is depression.

In his book *Human Nature and Suffering*, Paul Raymond Gilbert says that SAHP is a measure of an individual's ability to hold attention and attract investment from other members of the group. In hunter-gatherer terms, a man with high SAHP will have more wives and more of his children will survive.

Every member of a hunter-gatherer band was vital to the group's prosperity. Because ongoing depression hampers a person's level of function, hunter-gatherers would rally around the depressed person and give her the emotional and physical resources that would enable her to recover. Her sense of isolation and fear of ostracism would diminish and she would get better. In our society, this mechanism doesn't exist, and the depressive reaction can enter a downward spiral of deepening helplessness and despair.

WORK OVER PLEASURE

Alarmed about the problem of *karoshi* (sudden death due to overwork), the government of Japan is trying to get its workforce to reduce the number of hours worked per year from 2,124 to 1,800 by 2005. Studies show that overwork leads to mental and physical illness, which lower productivity.

Contrast Japan's plight—or even the forty- to sixty-hour workweek of most Americans—to the fifteen or so a week that our minds and bodies are "built for" to allocate to food and shelter. Overwork is one of the main causes of stress and thus abuse and depression in our culture.

For hunter-gatherers, cooperation and social bonds were the primary focus and the prerequisites for survival. For women in traditional bands, gathering was largely an opportunity to socialize. Bob observed women gathering in modern hunter-gatherer societies in southern Africa, and he was struck by the singing, talking, and laughing that went on. It reminded him more of a mother's group than any workplace in the developed or developing world.

In the modern workplace—where socializing is discouraged—much of the intrinsic pleasure of work (along with its neurochemical rewards) is removed. Women are also separated from their children, relationships are rigidly hierarchical, and tasks tend to be repetitive and disconnected from their outcome. Yet we feel defined by work and so are forced by social pressure, threat of isolation, and economic factors to do too much of it. These aspects of modern life lead directly to depression.

CHANGE VERSUS STASIS

As humans, we are creatures of stasis. Rapid change is stressful and a depressant. For millions of years, we followed essentially the same lifestyle. Change came slowly, giving us a chance to integrate it. The more rapid the shifts to which we are subjected, the more stressed we become.

Of course, hunter-gatherers were constantly on the move, going from one foraging area to another or moving with the seasons. Their peripatetic lifestyle has been used as an argument by those who say that change is natural to humans and that therefore they *ought* to be able to cope with rapid technological, organizational, and employment change. This school of thought also holds that the education system should prepare pupils for a life of constant change.

However, if you look closely at the life of hunter-gatherers, you will find that the changes they faced were within the context of stable technological, economic, and social circumstances. The whole band moved together and relationships were stable, providing emotional security. (More profound shifts were unusual, the results of climate change or population growth.) It is abusive to force rapid change on a stasis-loving creature.

DECISION-MAKING AND DISEMPOWERMENT

One of the greatest differences between today's society and that of our ancestors lies in the individual's right to make decisions concerning her life. That right ensures our autonomy and control over our environment. Without the capacity and opportunity to make decisions, disempowerment and depression are inevitable.

In the small hunter-gatherer band, every adult had a say in vital decisions. Everything was cooperative, even justice. Colin Turnbull, who studied the pygmies of central Africa in the 1950s, noted that all their decisions required unanimity. For example, when the band had to choose where to go next, the adults discussed the various options until they reached an agreement. Responsibility was a communal matter. In other hunter-gatherer societies, like those of the Australian aborigines, major decisions were left to the elders, but again, a final decision required unanimity. The only prerequisite for joining the council of elders was to reach the age of about thirty-five.

In our society, most of us have a minuscule—if any—say in what happens to us. Jeff didn't choose to lose his job; his wife didn't choose her colleagues, boss, clients, or work hours. There are just too many of us for a pygmy-style process of consensus in many companies or in politics.

By the age of about twelve, a hunter-gatherer youth was regarded as an adult. Yet today, because of rising housing costs and increasing job shortages for young people, ours are staying home longer and longer. Some are kept in a state of childish dependence until their midtwenties or even later. The lack of significant control over one's life is a major factor in low self-esteem and low rank. Those who perceive their rank to be low tend to seek to impose their will on others.

LOSS OF ROLES

The devaluation of traditional roles is another significant source of stress and depression in the modern era.

In the hunter-gatherer world, both economic and social roles were clear. From a young age, men hunted and protected the band and women gathered and helped take care of the children.

In modern Western society, the man experiences enormous psychological pressure to ensure that the family is safe and provided for. Yet, job security is lower than it has ever been. Many men still feel threatened by women who are finding their stride and successfully competing for jobs, even though the workplace is often not conducive to optimal functioning for women.

In our clinical experience, and this is substantiated by research by Prof. Richard Price of Michigan University and others, the fact or fear of not being able to adequately provide for one's family is one of the causal factors in adult-onset depression in men. The distortion of a man's role from carefree hunter and sage to encumbered householder was bad enough. Society then made the role of provider more difficult and insecure, with longer work hours, the threat of job loss, and lower pay relative to purchasing power. (According to economists, it takes two salaries to maintain the same standard of living as one did in the 1950s.)

While roles are changing, studies show that at the moment men and women still get their self-esteem differently. Men, more so than women, tend to fall into depressive episodes when their self-perceived status declines. Major depression triggers for men include losing a job (among men suicide is highest among the unemployed) or car, feeling snubbed by other men, and losing a mate to another man.

Recent research seems to indicate that to a woman, the loss or devaluation of her traditional roles is of more importance than loss of employment. A woman is five times more likely to have a depressive episode following a crisis involving children, housing (including household finances), and reproduction. Since hunter-gatherer times, these areas have been part of her domain. Unfortunately, over the last few millennia the importance that society attaches to these roles has been downgraded to the point that they are not seen as "work" and therefore not valued.

If you look at a woman's role in a hunter-gatherer band, you'll see that these domestic roles were combined with her economic role. Her work in this sense was equally important to that of a man, if not more so. She was the provider of about 70 percent of the food (including protein from small animals), she made most of the clothes, and she looked after and reared the children.

With the development of agriculture, all that changed. The increased emphasis on physical strength and other more masculine traits, such as single-mindedness needed to defend territory, led to a demeaning of women's roles. This process of social disadvantagedness increased as the centuries rolled by.

The more women as a whole became lower in rank, the more their SAHP fell, and the more they tended to behave as if they were of lower status. Increasingly, they became the more depressed and isolated gender.

Men retained their traditional groupings. The hunting band became the military unit, sports club, or office. Women on the other hand became increasingly cloistered and confined to the home. This isolation was reinforced by the idealization of the "traditional mother" whose job was to run the home, bring up the kids, and "stand by her man." This absurdly limited view of women's roles was heaped with praise and declared, at least by conservatives and religious scholars, to be beneficial to society at large.

Yet increasingly, the only escape for women has been into a male-dominated and male-structured workforce. In the corporate world, the need for the social company of other women and the exchange of personal information that usually characterizes women's conversations can be a drawback. Women are largely denied the opportunity to work in their way, to fulfill both their economic and child-rearing roles in a manner that makes them happy.

Thanks to the mismatch, depression among our elderly is one of the fastest-growing problems in the developing world. Most are stripped of their role at retirement, deprived of a community that values them, and often cast into a nursing home. Each one of these losses is a depression trigger.

According to recent research by Lynanne McGuire and others of the Johns Hopkins School of Medicine, those older people who are institutionalized show greater depressive symptoms and a lower immune system when compared to those who remain in the community. Although it evolves, a hunter-gatherer never loses her role. Elders' knowledge of past conditions, skills, and lore were vital for the band's survival. This may be one of the reasons that humans are one of the very few species (along with whales and elephants) to care for their elderly and infirm.[10]

Depression need not automatically accompany old age. Researchers have found that when older people feel that they do have a significant role within a supportive community, their incidence of depression is much less than in the general population of elderly.

GUILT

Like so much else about ourselves, guilt worked when we lived in small hunter-gatherer bands with clear, consistent, and unquestioned rules and taboos. It was a powerful deterrent to acting against the best interest of the group. In our modern world, with its jumble of cultures and the breakdown of institutions such as churches and schools offering shared moral values, guilt is increasingly losing its effectiveness as an inhibitor to wrongdoing. In fact, more often than not, it serves only to promote suffering and depression in the wake of events over which we have no control, but for which we continue to punish ourselves.

Lack of decision-making, disempowerment, isolation, overwork, abuse, and guilt are but a few examples of how the mismatch has deprived us of the happiness that is our genetic inheritance and driven us to anxiety and depression. We've lost the tribe that was us. Of course we can't go back to the days when our distant ancestors roamed the planet; there are too many of us now and the herds we followed have gone.

However, solutions exist, even for Denise's family. We worked with the whole family and individual members until a cohesive unit formed that offered mutual respect and support. Slowly, a chaotic and heartbreaking situation came under control, and the individual members began his and her long road to healing.

The first step of their journey was for each family member to understand that the predicament was not his or her fault. This came as a great surprise to Denise and to Jeff, who was also racked with guilt over his "failure to provide for my family as a man should."

We can use the lessons of the past to help us cure the depression of the present. We can all form a supportive "tribe" around us that can mitigate and even undo the effects of our abusive society. Together, we will explore just how this can be done as we go on.

However, first, let's look at happiness. What is it? What can you do to reclaim this birthright?

2

Reclaiming Happiness and Optimism

◉

You are wired for happiness. This may come as a surprise to you, but it's the truth. In an amazing example of nature's push for the survival and procreation of life itself, we, like every other species, are geared toward doing that which will help us survive. And, at least in a natural state, doing these things is guaranteed to give us satisfaction and pleasure.

However, to those who are depressed, happiness can seem like an unreachable shore. This hopelessness can foster a "what's the use" attitude that saps your motivation to combat the illness. Even when you attempt to look beyond the horizon of your own difficulties, you see a world beset by poverty, strife, and violence. You hear pundits pronounce that this is the natural state of humankind. Religious leaders cry that earthly life is a trial; we must somehow lift ourselves above our "animal nature" and look for our reward only in heaven. The nonreligious as well may feel that personal happiness is somehow frivolous or not for them, even while they seek it desperately.

But what really *is* happiness? Happiness and depression are not simply opposite sides of the same coin. This is obvious if we look at these states in terms of the brain. Depression involves, as we'll see, a structural lack of development in certain areas of the brain as well as a complex chemical imbalance. Happiness primarily depends on levels of one neurochemical, dopamine. But the most recent research shows that the same elements that can prevent and alleviate depression also lead to happiness and optimism.

The natural state of hunter-gatherers was not unremitting bliss. They faced early death in childbirth and hunting accidents along with droughts and other natural conditions. Perhaps they competed for status and mates and experienced brief anxiety or depression that caused the loser to back down. But the band was always there to offer support—emotionally and physically, as studies of modern hunter-gatherers have shown—and provide the human fundamentals of happiness.

THE EIGHT FUNDAMENTALS OF HAPPINESS

In the last few years, researchers have devoted a lot of time to the topic of happiness, and they largely agree on what brings it about. According to Prof. Stephen Reiss of Ohio State University, it's important to make the distinction between long-lasting, "value-based happiness" and the more transient, hedonistic, "feel-good happiness." In a recent article in *Psychology Today* he wrote:

> Feel-good happiness is sensation-based pleasure. When we joke around or have sex, we experience feel-good happiness. Since feel-good happiness is ruled by the law of diminishing returns, the kicks get harder to come by. This type of happiness rarely lasts longer than a few hours at a time. Value-based happiness is a sense that our lives have meaning and fulfill some larger purpose. It represents a spiritual source of satisfaction, stemming from our deeper purpose and values. Since value happiness is not ruled by the law of diminishing returns, there is no limit to how meaningful our lives can be.

Pleasure that does not contribute to our sense of relatedness often turns against us. In a hunter-gatherer society, "feel-good" pleasure, including lighthearted exchanges and sensory experience, added to the already-existing relatedness among band members and between individuals and nature. Lacking this support and interconnectedness, modern humans often seek happiness in ultimately unfulfilling and potentially harmful ways. These include misusing food, drugs, sex, and power; addiction; and rampant materialism.

So what is it that makes us happy?

According to the research and our experience, there are eight fundamentals of value happiness: relatedness or supportive connection to other people; a sense of autonomy (characterized by personal independence and control); self-esteem; a sense of competence; a sense of purpose; functional connection to your body; connection to animals and nature; and spirituality.

Five of these (relatedness, self-esteem, competence, autonomy, and a sense of purpose) were highlighted in a recent large-scale study by psychology professor Kennon Sheldon and others of the University of Missouri involving some six hun-

THE EIGHT FUNDAMENTALS OF HAPPINESS

1. Connection to others
2. Autonomy
3. Self-esteem
4. Competence
5. Purpose
6. Connection to your body
7. Connection to nature
8. Spirituality

dred individuals in both the United States and South Korea. The Missouri study was cross-cultural, which is important because it shows that these keys to happiness are likely to be innate to us as a species, part of our evolutionary inheritance. To the surprise of the researchers, wealth, luxury, and other hedonistic pleasures were way down the list.

Other studies have shown that happiness also involves all aspects of connection: to your body, to nature (including animals), and to spirituality, which all serve to enhance the most important link of all—to each other.

Connection to Others

As a human being, you are a relationship-forming creature. Evolution designed you so that whatever you do, you do the best in the company of supportive people. Relationships are at the very heart of your being. As Paul Martin has shown in his book *The Sickening Mind*, relationships govern your immune system, largely controlling what diseases you get and how soon you will recover from them; they determine how you feel about yourself and the world in general; and they dictate your mood and your behavior patterns.

If your relationships are supportive and fulfilling, you can be healthy and happy, you can free yourself from depression, and become optimistic. If your relationships are anything less then the reverse happens: you become ill, happiness is impossible, and you can sink into profound pessimism.

The more disconnected you are from good relationships with other people, the unhappier you become. The ability to cooperate with others was the main reason we survived as a species among well-endowed predators. Functional relationships are now essential to protect you from being controlled by the abusive forces in this society.

The very size of the human brain has less to do with our much-touted cognition and tool-making than with the need to form alliances and to interact at a complex level with other members of our kind.

According to Prof. Robin Dunbar of the University of Liverpool in England, apes developed larger brains than monkeys because they had to cope with bigger and more complex social circles. Human bands had still more numbers (up to fifty) and sophistication than our chimpanzee relatives, requiring even greater brain mass. In fact, our brains are so sizable and multifaceted that they account for 20 percent of our entire metabolic activity. According to Prof. Dunbar, most of this brainpower is taken up with relationships.

Our modern societies, however, are too large for even our expanded brains. If you have to relate to more than fifty people, you will have difficulty in forming functional connections, and you will become stressed.

Chimps make connection through grooming each other. In the larger human group, grooming would take too much time, so, according to Dunbar, we developed language as an alternative. Most of what we communicate is gossip. So-called "serious topics," such as planning projects or avoiding danger, take up a very small part of our communicating time. Exchanging personal information in small groups about our interests, lives, and experiences and those of others makes us happy, just as grooming does with chimps. But to get the real benefit of connection, to be truly happy and secure, you need *specific kinds* of relationships.

Much of this book is devoted to helping you create the particular kinds of relationships that will bring you happiness and optimism and help you combat depression. Here are some of the basics. Your relationships must meet your fundamental human needs for physical safety, emotional security, attention, and importance. The people you connect to closely must largely share your interests and beliefs, including spiritual ones, and strive for a common purpose.

In other words, to increase the sum of your happiness, those connections must be as close to those of our Paleolithic ancestors as possible. With supportive, loyal, and like-minded people around you, you don't fear exclusion and you can become optimistic, positive, and emotionally healthy.

Happiness Tip: Make a list of friends you haven't contacted in a while but would like to, and call them.

Autonomy

Autonomy is a feeling of independence and a sense of being in control of your relationships and destiny. It's about being an individual within the context of a supportive group. Like everything significant in your life, autonomy depends on the quality of your relationships. Without it, security is difficult, which makes happiness impossible.

In our present society, very few people have autonomy. In a sense, we all have an identity crisis. We are in grave danger of losing our individuality. Losing your autonomy is easy and the process can be pernicious. Just consider:

When was the last time you went out of your way to shop in places where the merchants know you and pay attention to your individual requirements? Where people have the time and interest to talk to you or ask after your mother, dog, or health and inquire whether you want the "same order as before"?

When did you last insist on talking to a person, not a machine? Do you try to deal with those businesses that have replaced their computerized voice-mail systems with live human beings (as some have begun to do)? Or bought your airline ticket from your local travel agent rather than shopping anonymously on the Web?

How well do you know your neighbors, and how much do you socialize with them? Doing so gives you a sense of being watched over and protected. Would you consider taking a pay cut to work for a small outfit whose boss you know and who will value your input in decisions affecting you? All of these things will increase your web of connections and relationships and will contribute to your safety and sense of control over your life—and your autonomy.

Research shows that loss of autonomy leads not only to pessimism and depression, but also to violence. Autonomy is sometimes confused with cutting off from society, with a tendency for people to become "loners." And certainly the need for control over one's life does drive some people to seek separation from an overcontrolling or overcomplex society.

But you don't have to be a hermit to feel independent. Having autonomy means that you are given input—and a veto where necessary—over all decisions that affect you or your relationships. It means knowing what you need from other people in your life and what they need from you. Autonomy means being aware of and insisting on your boundaries. It means that other people see you as an individual with needs and rights as well as a member of groups such as "patients," "consumers," "parents," or "children." When you become a number, statistic, or generalization, you lose your autonomy.

The less control we have over our lives, the more frightened we become. We become controlling and fear that the autonomy of others is a direct threat, or we become fearful, submissive, depressed, and pessimistic. But the process can be reversed when you assert your autonomy in functional ways.

Happiness Tip: Go to as many local establishments rather than chains as possible and strike up a conversation with the proprietor or service people.

Self-Esteem

You can't be happy or optimistic if you don't feel good about yourself. And you can't feel good about yourself in a vacuum.

Self-esteem is a function of your perception of how other people view you. It will rise when you're praised, treated as important, or given appropriate attention. It will fall when one of these doesn't happen. Society has a vested interest in your lack of self-esteem. If you feel bad about yourself, you'll work harder (although less effectively), stand up for yourself less often, and you'll buy more unnecessary stuff. Real self-esteem comes from the support, praise, and encouragement you get from people around you. These enable you to overthrow the negative beliefs about yourself planted in childhood.

Happiness Tip: Try to catch yourself every time you make a self-deprecating comment.

Competence

A sense of competence is part of your self-esteem and relates to how well you feel you function. Some people feel competent in certain areas but still have a sense of low self-esteem overall. But without a belief that you perform certain tasks really well—and that these abilities matter to the people around you—you won't have either self-esteem or happiness.

Genetic inheritance may factor in your abilities and your choice to specialize in certain areas, but as French neuropsychology researcher Stanislas Dehaene has shown, your upbringing and schooling probably have more influence.

Your sense of competence then derives from two elements—your interests (probably the genetic part) and the encouragement and praise you got from others. One recent study by social psychologist Dr. Marianne Miserandino of Arcadia University concluded that by the time children reach third or fourth grade, they have a pretty fixed idea of their own competence (which may well be wrong), which in turn influences how well they will do at school.

However, it's never too late to enhance your sense of competence. We'll show you how to create an environment that supports you in doing what you do best; turn the people around you into allies, not critics; and garner praise that enables you to shine.

Happiness Tip: Ask the people in your life to tell you when they think you've done something well.

Purpose

It's very dispiriting to ask "why am I here?" and find you have no answer. Of course, a hunter-gatherer wouldn't even ask the question. He would have a lifelong purpose within the band, an economic or wisdom role for which he was valued. But in our abusive society, people are made to feel that their only purpose is to make money or, particularly if they are women, be caretakers. Even these roles are sooner or later stripped from them because of age, physical or emotional illness, or corporate or governmental downsizing. Without a sense of purpose, you risk sinking into depression and pessimism.

Your mood, optimism, health, and very survival depend on countering this vicious societal broadside. Remember that to your ancestors, work was only a small part of life; you must seek out a life purpose separate from your economic or even caretaking role. And you *can* develop a fulfilling and meaningful sense of lifelong purpose, one that will bind you to others and stimulate your genetic inheritance for happiness.

Happiness Tip: Ask your friends and acquaintances (in fact, anyone you can) to describe what they see as their purpose beyond making money or caring for others.

Connection to Your Body

To a hunter-gatherer, viewing his body as separate from his self would have been as ridiculous as seeing himself outside the context of the band.

Sensing a breeze on bare skin, running, lying down, feeling the warm sun or cool water, throwing a well-directed spear, experiencing sex or a supportive arm to aid faltering steps all provide an unquestioned source of well-being and happiness. For some, these and other bodily experiences still do.

Many, however, have lost the full capacity for direct, unfiltered contact with physical experience that is so vital to our complete sense of self and to our capacity for pleasure and happiness.

Sedentary work and schooling, dysfunctional exercise, shame around sex and bodily functions, chronic stress, trauma, and abuse all play a role in separating us from this vital aspect of ourselves. As if all that isn't bad enough, the media seem to be competing with themselves in bringing us more unrealistic, air-brushed, and computer-enhanced versions of what we should look like.

We will show you how distorted body image, trauma, and abuse play a particularly potent role in depression. We will then help you reclaim your body and rediscover physical experience as a source of empowerment and happiness.

Happiness Tip: Throw out all your magazines that feature impossibly perfect-looking men or women on the covers.

Connection to Nature

We've all experienced a sense of awe, serenity, and contentment in nature. Its permanence amid change, its beauty, and its power are just some of the things that draw us in. Whether among trees or in a desert or beside a mountain creek, we feel close to our origins, close to the natural "us."

Strong evidence suggests that humans become more pessimistic as they watch the despoiling of the natural world. Your potential for hopelessness and pessimism increases with each highway through a national park, each high-rise or shopping center where a meadow once flourished, each news item about the destruction of old-wood forests or the extinction of some species of animal, even if you've never heard of it before.

Research by Washington University psychology research professor Peter H. Kahn (among others) has confirmed that ecological destruction is one of the causes of our increasing rate of depressive illness. Equally, Prof. Kahn says, evidence suggests that depression can be alleviated if we become involved in animal rescue or the preservation of our natural home. Even bringing plants into our office or home or sharing a communal pet can lift our mood.

Nature isn't just about trees, the oceans, or endangered species. One aspect of nature is as close as our living room or the nearest park. Companion animals, particularly dogs, have kept us company over the eons. Many studies have shown that pet owners live longer and are healthier and you are less likely to have a heart attack if you own a dog. Contact with an animal is a marvelous antidepressant.

Our brains are forged to live in small, mutually supportive communities in close contact with nature and animals. The further you get from this ideal the more stressed, depressed, pessimistic, and unhappy you become. When you structure your relationships according to your needs—and your life so that you are in contact with the natural world—you become happier, more confident, and less depressed.

Happiness Tip: Walk in a park or other natural area for twenty minutes each day. Pat at least one dog and talk to its owner.

Spirituality

You are neurologically geared for spirituality. We believe, and many researchers confirm, that without a solid grounding in spirituality there can be no happiness. Of course, spirituality does not necessarily imply belief. It is a feeling of being able to commune with, or even to rely on, something greater than yourself. An ability to lose yourself in that greater Is. Sometimes spirituality takes the form of surrender and letting go, and at others it becomes a powerful incentive to action. But whatever aspect it takes for you, spirituality, like a sense of purpose, is a powerful weapon against depression and pessimism.

Many forces in society prevent you from having truly empowering spirituality. Controlling cults or religions; fear of ridicule by colleagues, friends, or family; a pervasive sense that science and spirituality are enemies (which is simply not true); and in some cases governments that support a particular form of belief to the exclusion of others interfere with our attainment of true spirituality. The all-pervasive materialism of our economic system is the largest obstacle we face. Our society sometimes seems founded on the assumption that the powers greater than us are General Motors and Coca-Cola.

Even if you are filled with doubt, anger, or despair you can discover your own functional spirituality. And by now it will come as no surprise that others can help you do so!

Happiness Tip: Make a list of all the things you believe in that give you comfort.

GETTING TO OPTIMISM

Happiness and optimism go arm in arm. It's very difficult to be optimistic if you're unhappy, and difficult (but not impossible) to be happy if you're not optimistic. You want to be optimistic—to "look on the bright side of things." You want to see the glass half full and be primed to take advantage of the good times around the corner. What holds you back?

In part it may be your genes. Probably between 30 to 50 percent of our basic optimistic/pessimistic outlook is genetic. Some of us are born with a bias toward optimism and some in the other direction. This makes sense for hunter-gatherers, who lived in small bands and, as children, shared many of the same experiences. People with naturally different outlooks were needed to keep the balance between risk-taking and risk-avoidance.

The balance is out of kilter in our present society, which creates what is called "learned pessimism." The early abusive or traumatic events in your life are compounded by a relentless media barrage of images of war, terrorism, famine, and natural disasters that teach you to be pessimistic. Society is fermenting depression, and depression begets pessimism no matter what your genetic disposition.

Along with most researchers, we believe that the transition from pessimism to optimism is possible. It is also possible to get to what Prof. Martin Seligman in his book *Learned Optimism* calls "flexible optimism." The flexible optimist can take in both the pessimist's reality and the optimist's knowledge of opportunities and a bright future.

According to researchers led by assistant professor Ian Brissette of Rutgers University, you can set up the conditions for optimism by surrounding yourself with a tribe or band of supportive people. If you are prone to believing that the worst is bound to happen, your outlook will be tempered by others' optimism, as would have happened naturally in a genuine hunter-gatherer band. If this relationship nexus meets your basic human needs, it will provide a buffer against the negative impact of a pessimistic society and a safe place to explore your emerging optimistic self.

3

THE TRUTH
ABOUT DEPRESSION

◉

Sandi sits in Alicia's office, her eyes red and puffy from crying, her hands shredding a tissue. A PR consultant for the fashion industry, she's in her late twenties, stylishly dressed, and overly thin. Although most wouldn't notice this, it seems to Alicia that the structure of one side of Sandi's face is less clearly defined than the other, as if the bones were damaged in very early childhood.

Sandi can remember what she now knows were bouts of depression since her early teens, although the diagnosis only came five years ago. She alternates between eating and sleeping too much and too little. When the depression is absent she overworks. But when she goes down again, it's hard to even get to work and she isolates herself from others. She is subject to frightening nightmares. During these depressive incidents, she cries a lot, is irritable, and is absolutely clear on one thing: nothing will ever get better. Her latest bout, triggered by the breakup with a boyfriend, is the worst episode yet.

Sandi also suffers from chronic pain throughout her body, which has been diagnosed as fibromyalgia. No amount of massage, chiropractic, kinesiology, or any of the other methods have made any difference.

Sandi's a smart and determined young woman; she tried psychotherapy as well as bodywork and medication. With one therapist, she identified many of the negative thoughts that accompany her depression (which was somewhat helpful) and attempted to re-experience and release her "birth process" with another (which wasn't). Recently, her physician told her, "It's in your genes. Since antidepressants don't seem to be helping, there's really nothing you can do." Finally, a friend told her about the Uplift Program, and she came to see Alicia for an initial consultation.

"What's wrong with me?" she asks, half angry, half pleading. "Why, after all I've done, can't I get better?"

The short answer to Sandi's questions is, "There's nothing wrong with you intrinsically, but lots of wrong things have happened to you." In therapy, Sandi unearthed a number of traumatic incidents in early childhood—including being slapped and constantly criticized by her mother and approached sexually by her father—and was able to link patterns in present relationships back to those events.

The first part of healing Sandi's depression—and probably yours or the depression of those who are important to you—is to throw out most of what you think you know about it.

You aren't alone in your confusion and misinformation about this rapidly proliferating problem. Perhaps no illness today is getting so much attention, yet scientists still know relatively little about how to cure it. What they think they know changes almost daily and is under attack from other researchers. And even the important bits that the experts do know and are agreed on aren't filtering down to the person who really needs to hear them: you.

So let's take a hard look at what depression really is and why Sandi (and, perhaps, you) are in such pain and, until now, haven't found any real solution. We'll start with the basics.

THE DEPRESSION SPECTRUM

Depression is not new to humankind; some form of the illness has always been around, but it was usually a short-lived experience and it served a particular purpose. Hunter-gatherer bands needed a few individuals to be depressed, and thus submissive, at any one time to maintain equilibrium and to prevent conflict. Depression was also a way of coping with loss, forcing members of the band to stop struggling against the situation and thus finally accept it. But this was mostly reactive depression and very different from what we experience now. Today's depression is a pandemic, needlessly clutching at victims in all societies throughout the world.

Thirty percent of women, 46 percent of teenagers, and 10 percent of all people in developed countries suffer from depression. This condition also underlies many of our most prevalent illnesses.

Depression involves a slowing down of some mental activity, especially in the prefrontal cortex of the brain—the command and control center. It is characterized by pervasive pessimism, hopeless thoughts, inability to experience pleasure, disjointed sleep and perhaps eating patterns, unpleasant dreams, dissociative episodes (in some people), an inability to concentrate, dysfunctional body patterns, and physical illness. This much is agreed. Controversy and misinformation creep in when you look at what falls under the category of depression and what causes it.

Depression is the most researched and, perhaps, least understood of all psychiatric illnesses. Researchers point to a whole range of disorders that are associated with depression, although there is heated debate about where one disorder begins and another ends, and whether they are really separate at all. General anxiety disorder, bipolar disorder (manic depression), social anxiety disorder, various dissociative disorders,[11] post-traumatic stress disorder (PTSD), and obsessive-compulsive disorder are just a few.

We believe that many of these conditions are part of the same family of disorders. They are all different expressions of the depression spectrum. Depression can also take the form of "physical" illness in a process known as somatization, probably the cause of Sandi's fibromyalgia.

Depression is cyclical by nature. It comes and goes, though the bouts may last longer as the sufferer gets older until it may seem constant. It can also cycle between different expressions of the disorder. Depressed people might alternate between "depression" and "anxiety" or even "depression" and "physical illness." Some people experience occasional bouts of major depression and others a seemingly constant low-level form of the illness called *dysthemia*. Still others are plagued by a mixture of the two.

What we do know is that many of the conditions associated with depression have similar root causes in childhood experience, brain development, and, perhaps, genetic predisposition. The causal relation between these factors is complex, and the emerging research has profound implications for those seeking to rid themselves or others from depression and related problems.

RELATIONSHIPS GONE WRONG

Various experts have pronounced that long-term depression is caused by a genetic disorder and/or a chemical imbalance, dysfunctional behavioral patterns, maladaptive thoughts, self-destructive beliefs, and early life experiences. In our opinion, many of these, such as behaviors, thoughts, and beliefs are *symptoms* rather than *causes* of the disorder.

The underlying cause of lasting depression is almost always a failure of relationships, usually between adults and children in early childhood, which is what makes our depression different in kind from that of the hunter-gatherers. These relationship failures are the result of the mismatch between how we live now and how we are genetically programmed as a species to structure our lives.

Virtually every recent study has linked depression to childhood trauma and abuse. That does not mean that every person suffering from depression had a traumatic childhood; just that, given our dysfunctional society, the majority probably did.[12]

When we speak of childhood trauma and abuse, we are not just talking about physical or sexual abuse. Rather, we follow the definition of abuse given in a 1992 report called "The Psychological Maltreatment of Children" from the American Academy of Pediatrics (AAP), which defines it as "a repeated pattern of damaging interactions between parent(s) [or, we presume, other significant adults] and child that becomes typical of the relationship."

Maltreatment, in other words, is that which makes a child feel worthless, unloved, endangered, or as if her only value lies in meeting someone else's needs. Examples cited in the report include "belittling, degrading, or ridiculing a child; terrorizing a child by committing life-threatening acts or making him or her feel unsafe [including threat of abandonment]; exploiting or corrupting a child; failing to express affection, caring, and love; and neglecting mental health, medical, or educational needs." Childhood trauma can also include witnessing domestic, community, and televised violence.

Is Depression in Our Genes?

What about Sandi's physician's statement that her depression is genetic and there's nothing much she can do about it? What about the thorny issue of nature versus nurture?

Sandi's mother was depressive, and one brother was diagnosed as such. Depression does run in families, which has led some researchers to speculate that a particular gene is responsible for depression.[13] Even if someone does find an inherited gene that predisposes people to depression, not everyone who has the gene will get the disorder.

At present, we know very little about genetics in relation to mood and behavior. The best guess of researchers is that our genes influence about 50 percent of what we do or feel. It is known that a mother's neglect early in life can actually change the way genes behave and set a child up for a number of psychiatric illnesses, including bipolar disorder. Presumably the same is true of other forms of abuse as well.

Prof. Charles Nemeroff of Emery University School of Medicine is one of the leading authorities on the neurobiology of depression and is convinced that genes aren't the whole story and that abuse plays a significant role. He believes that abuse fundamentally alters brain chemistry through the agency of an amino acid neuropeptide called corticotropin-releasing factor or CRF. If you have been abused, your brain produced too much CRF, and you become depressed.

According to Nemeroff, depression is not the only disorder caused by early childhood neglect and/or abuse. These factors, he says, particularly in the presence of a genetic susceptibility, permanently alter the neurons (brain cells) that specialize in CRF, resulting in hyperactivity (ADD/ADHD) and PTSD as well as depression.

Meaning that even if you have a family history of depression or anxiety, you will probably not become a victim of depression unless something seriously untoward happens in your childhood to trigger it.

OR FAULTY THINKING?

A psychotherapist told Sandi that her belief system caused her depression. You've probably come across this theory: depression is due to faulty thinking, beliefs, and (say some) actions. Change these and all will be well. Unfortunately, this explanation is incomplete and thus misleading. As we'll show in the next chapter, your beliefs are the *result* of your childhood conditioning, they are *part*—but not *all*—of the process that led to your depression.

If simply changing your beliefs and/or behaviors could defeat depression, then all of the therapy that Americans and others in the developed world have engaged in since Freud would by now have banished the disorder.

It's not that your beliefs and actions cause your depression, although they perpetuate it. Your beliefs and behaviors spring from the same childhood experiences that helped cause your depression. Each of these traumatic experiences involved relationships.

Relationships with significant adults in your childhood led you to adopt negative self-beliefs and to behave in self-defeating ways. These keep you trapped in the past, forever acting out negative behavioral patterns and attracting people and circumstances that mirror your childhood experience. This in turn retriggers the trauma of the past to perpetuate depression in the present.

Like any system—functional or dysfunctional—depression is self-reinforcing. It uses your pessimistic and self-deprecating beliefs and your self-destructive behaviors as barriers against positive change.

Yes, it's important—indeed vital—to identify the negative beliefs and behaviors that keep you stuck in the past and retrigger trauma and depression. You need to challenge them and go against anything they want you to do. But you can't do this and maintain the results entirely on your own or even with just the help of a therapist. Your childhood "programming" was put in place by your early experiences with other people, and you will need to enlist other people later in your life in the process of getting rid of them.

Just changing your thinking and behavior won't create the conditions necessary for healing your brain.

Or Is It Serotonin?

When Sandi was prescribed antidepressants, she was told that her depression was due to her brain's diminished capacity to "uptake [properly process] serotonin." Despite the articles in professional psychiatric journals that have regularly appeared for years—and more recently in the media—this is what most people are told. And yet, in the words of the song from *Porgy and Bess*, it "ain't necessarily so."

Ever since Peter Kramer published his book *Listening to Prozac* in 1987, it has been accepted in lay and psychiatric circles that depression is caused by the brain's failure to uptake the neurochemical serotonin. Provide a pill, the conventional wisdom had it, that prevents neurons from "reuptaking" (that is, refusing to allow serotonin in) and all would be well. Prozac was but the first of a long line of selective serotonin reuptake inhibitors (SSRIs) designed to do just that. And it's probably true that the brains of depressed people don't process serotonin very well.

However, recent research—particularly studies using powerful brain-imaging equipment—have shown that brain chemistry (serotonin in particular) is by no means the whole story, and may not even be a very important part of it. In terms of the brain, long-term depression seems to be the result of misdevelopment in a number of crucial areas of the brain.

If you're depressed, and a scan is taken of your brain, you'll find some interesting structural anomalies when compared with the brain of a nondepressed person.

These anomalies, which are most pronounced in victims of childhood abuse, have a dramatic effect on how the brain functions. This recent discovery has forced the experts to change most of what they thought they knew about depression. Probably the most significant of these abnormalities involve the hippocampus and amygdala in the limbic system, and the frontal lobe of the cerebral cortex (see Figure 3.1).

If a person suffers from long-term depression, the hippocampus, a crescent-shaped part of the brain that deals with learning and forming new memories, is smaller than in people without the illness. It has fewer neurons. The hippocampus allows a rat, for example, to remember where it was when it got an electric shock and what was going on around it at the time. Such contextual learning helps the poor rodent avoid dangerous places in the future. A depressed or anxious person may not be so good at remembering, and thus avoiding, the circumstances that trigger depressive or anxiety-provoking episodes.

FIGURE 3.1 BRAIN REGIONS INVOLVED IN DEPRESSION

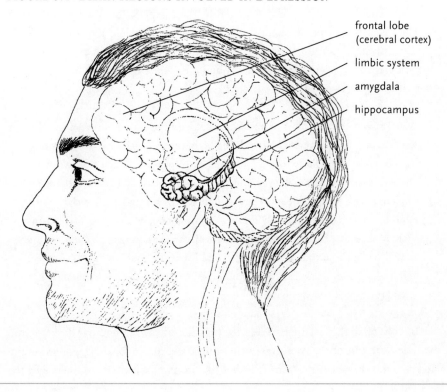

frontal lobe
(cerebral cortex)

limbic system

amygdala

hippocampus

The walnut-sized amygdala is a key area of the limbic system and helps process emotions. Its job is to alert you to signs of stress or danger. It does this by passing almost instantaneous messages to the hippocampus, the frontal lobe (part of the command and control center of the brain), and the central nervous system. It activates the automatic flight, fight, or freeze reactions. The amygdala is not designed to be accurate—just fast. If you suffer from anxiety or depression, this area of the brain is more active and enlarged—sending out more emotionally charged messages—than that of someone not afflicted with depression or anxiety.

Finally, there's a problem with the frontal lobe, the brain's decision-making area. Recent studies using Functional Magnetic Resource Imaging (fMRI) have shown that if it doesn't work as it should, then making decisions—even simple ones, like getting up in the morning—may be difficult. In a depression sufferer, this area remains undeveloped and it works more slowly than it should. In particular, it is slow to switch off the alarm signals coming from the amygdala, leaving the sufferer stuck in the "down," low-self-esteem, submissive mode typical of depression or the tense state of anxiety.

Like Prof. Nemeroff's CRF imbalance, these structural problems are directly related to early trauma or abuse. Apparently, these experiences abort proper brain development in the frontal lobe, prevent neurogenesis (brain cell growth) at a critical time in the hippocampus, and enlarge the amygdala. The effects of this damage are elegantly summed up by neurobiologist Martin Teicher, writing in the journal *Cerebrum*:

> Whether abuse of a child is physical, psychological, or sexual, it sets off a ripple of hormonal changes that wire the child's brain to cope with a malevolent world. It predisposes the child to have a biological basis for fear, though he may act and pretend otherwise. Early abuse molds the brain to be more irritable, impulsive, suspicious, and prone to be swamped by fight-or-flight reactions that the rational mind may be unable to control. The brain is programmed to a state of defensive adaptation, enhancing survival in a world of constant danger, but at a terrible price. To a brain so tuned, Eden itself would seem to hold its share of dangers; building a secure, stable relationship may later require virtually superhuman personal growth and transformation.

In light of all this, we believe that the inability of the brain to uptake serotonin is a side issue, one of the *symptoms* of the structural problem of the depressed brain. Taking an SSRI antidepressant is rather like taking aspirin when you've got the flu—it may make you feel a bit better, but it doesn't cure the disease. In fact, a number of researchers, including David Burns, M.D., are adamant that serotonin deficiency may not be the problem at all.[14] In an article published in 2000, the *Psychiatric Times* reviewed recent studies, and Burns and others wrote: "There is no persuasive or consistent evidence that a deficiency of brain serotonin causes depression or that an increase in brain serotonin relieves depression."

Another problem for the *Listening to Prozac* lobby is that antidepressants, according to a 2002 Royal College of Psychiatrists report, only work for about 60 percent of people at best, and that placebos (sugar pills) work just about as well. Furthermore, research indicates that the drugs' effect wears off quickly. According to a study by Prof. Giovanni A. Fava of the University of Bologna and others, which was done with long-term antidepressant users who were slipping back into depression (as most do), four of five patients responded to a larger dose of the drugs, but all relapsed again within a year.

Many studies (few of which have found their way into the mainstream press) have shown that even the so-called "safe" SSRIs, such as Prozac, have some very nasty side effects ranging from sexual dysfunction and heart disease to suicide.

Despite all this, we are not saying that no one should take antidepressants. We sometimes encourage clients to get a medical opinion regarding going on antidepressants (and always to get medical supervision when coming off them, which can be problematic). Some of our clients have received short-term benefits from taking antidepressants. Whether their relief is due to the placebo effect is neither here nor there when someone is in pain.

Some "natural" antidepressants, such as St. John's Wort and SAM-e, have been shown to work, but only in cases of mild depression. Even then, their efficacy is no greater than SSRIs.

Like many drugs that went through awkward development stages, in the future antidepressants may provide safe and more focused answers to at least some of the most difficult symptoms of depression. If so, we'll encourage our clients to look into them, as well as working on underlying issues.

MOSTLY IN THE MIND

OK, if antidepressants, herbal or otherwise, aren't the answer, what about talk therapy or a combination of drug and talk therapy? These are the usual trio of possibilities facing people with depression and, like Sandi, you've probably tried some if not all of them.

Somewhere between 250 and 500 types of therapy involve talk. The one most commonly used to treat depression and anxiety is cognitive behavioral therapy (CBT). Such therapies seem to work on brain chemistry in much the same way as antidepressants, though obviously without the same side effects. In a study by Dr. Lewis Baxter at the UCLA School of Medicine, reported in *The New York Times* on August 27, 2002, patients with depression who responded to either a reuptake inhibitor like Prozac or CBT over ten weeks showed virtually the same changes in their brains.

Although this may seem surprising at first, it makes sense when you think about it. We tend to perceive thoughts as having no physical substance, but that's far from true. A thought is in fact a physical thing, involving the exchange of neurochemicals and electrical energy. The dialogue between you and a therapist affects your neural circuitry just as a drug would,[15] and the brain's reaction to it is similar to the brain's reaction to a drug—or a placebo. Interestingly, the effects of CBT, like antidepressants, also tend to wear off.

So why do both drug and conventional talk therapy work (when they do), and why don't their benefits always last? To get an answer, we have to remind ourselves of the most powerful and defining aspect of human beings—relationships. We believe that relationships are the secret ingredient in all successful treatment.

When antidepressants and placebos work, it's because of the relationship between the prescribing physician and her patient, aided by the brain's propensity for self-fulfilling prophecy. If you believe it will work, it will (at least for a while).

This was a point made by Simon Wessely, professor of psychiatry, Kings College London, in a 1998 *New Scientist* article "Mostly in the Mind." Wessely was one of the first to throw doubt on the claims of the drug companies about the efficacy of antidepressants in a study he did in 1977.

Humans are programmed (for reasons we'll go into later) to put great store in authority figures and tend to believe what they are told. When you consult a therapist or a physician, you are strongly predisposed to believe what that authority figure says.

Many studies have shown that it's not so much the therapeutic method, but the relationship between client and therapist that determines which treatments will be most successful. Talk therapy works best when this connection is strong and supportive and is liable to be effective only as long as the relationship remains so. When the client ceases to visit the therapist or stops believing in and trusting her, the old problems may resurface.

Even before then, if the external environment continues to reflect the abusive patterns of the past rather than replace them with constant support and encouragement, the old feelings will probably come back.

We'll get to the elements that, in our experience, really do work in a moment. First we'd like to take a brief look at a disorder that is related to depression (some say it's the next step along the continuum of mood disorders in severity). Post-traumatic stress disorder (PTSD) has become much more prevalent in the wake of the terrorist incidents of September 11, 2001.

PTSD and Depression

PTSD was only accepted as a separate psychiatric disorder as recently as 1980. It was first noticed among veterans after World War I but was only taken seriously as a distinct illness after the Vietnam War. The disorder was "post-traumatic" because the symptoms—including increased anxiety; avoidance of stimuli associated with the event or events; agoraphobia; vivid dreams related to the trauma; and frequent recall of the past experience—would frequently appear some time afterward.

Interest—and even more controversy—surrounding PTSD soared when a number of researchers began to notice that the same symptomatology was evident in survivors of rape, natural disasters, auto accidents, and childhood abuse. Some, more traditional, psychologists declared that PTSD didn't exist and that it was simply a misdiagnosis of other disorders. Yet by the mid-1990s, PTSD was found to affect nearly 8 percent of the American population, making it one of the most prevalent psychiatric disorders. Since then the numbers have gone up considerably.

Not everyone who experiences traumatic events develops PTSD: only 30 percent of Vietnam veterans became sufferers of the condition. What distinguishes people who get PTSD seems to be that they were victims of previous traumas.

Research and Bob's experience of working with Vietnam veterans point out that early trauma predisposes the sufferer to the disorder. The later incident (war, rape, or witnessing a violent crime) provides the trigger in a process known as "retraumatization."

Millions of television viewers experienced retraumatization when they witnessed jets slamming into the World Trade Center buildings over and over again in the aftermath of the terrorist attacks of September 11. Incredible as it may seem, according to the psychiatric bible *Diagnostic and Statistical Manual of Mental Disorders* published by the American Psychiatric Association, watching such events can be as traumatic as being a victim. According to a study carried out by Prof. Roxane Cohen Silver of the University of California at Irvine and colleagues, more than 17 percent of the U.S. population living outside New York exhibited signs of PTSD after September 11. The majority of those who fell victim were women and those with a history of depression.

We ourselves noticed that many of our students and clients exhibited PTSD symptoms after September 11—even those in Australia. Again the same pattern emerged—those who had a prior history of abuse or trauma and who suffered from depression were more likely to develop PTSD or its close cousin, acute stress disorder.

Recent neurological studies confirm that PTSD and depression are very similar in their effects on the brain. Moreover, the two disorders share a number of symptoms, including a tendency to avoid social contact, to suffer from nightmares associated in some way with traumatic events, and to be hypervigilant.

The point here is not to quibble about diagnostic criteria—labels have never cured a person of anything, and in some cases simply make matters worse. But it seems to us that not only do many depression sufferers probably have some form of PTSD, but thinking in these terms helps clarify the nature of depression itself.

CREATE YOUR OWN ENVIRONMENT

In Chapter 1, we outlined the social background of depression as rooted in the mismatch between the way we're genetically programmed to live and the society we have created for ourselves. We believe that the modern pandemic of depression is largely a result of this mismatch.

In a hunter-gatherer society, abuse such as Sandi suffered could not have taken place. There would have been other protective adults around to observe and prevent it.

In global terms, the cure must be a social one. But while society and the medical profession seem stumped, you can immediately take some steps to get rid of your own depression and lack of optimism. Depression need not be a life sentence. But getting free does mean changing your life, and, in particular, it means changing the basis of your relationships.

After taking the Uplift Program, along with some one-on-one sessions with Alicia, Sandi emerged from her depression. She came to see that it was not the result of any choices she had ever made or beliefs she had actively adopted. It was not her fault. That alone was a big relief and deprived the negative voices within her of a lot of their power.

She also discovered that her early emotional and physical abuse had set in place the conditions for depression and anxiety, and the beliefs and actions programmed in at that time triggered and retriggered the ensuing mood disorders. She was able to identify how she had re-created negative relationship patterns from childhood in her adult love life, with friends, and at work.

She began to build relationships with people (including a new boyfriend) she could count on to support her and meet her needs by using the relationship techniques we'll show you later. Instead of pulling her further into depression and anxiety, they became the mechanism for healing and transformation.

In the meantime, she started to mend a relationship she'd lost a long time ago—with her body. Using our Repatterning Movement exercises™ (RPMs) she learned to listen to that aspect of herself and regain a functional mastery of it. Slowly, the trauma of the past, and the accompanying physical pain, let go of her skeleton and muscles. Exercise, particularly in a natural environment, became a very important part of Sandi's recovery. She began a walking schedule that she maintains to this day.

She used her new relationship techniques, together with other new skills, to enhance her self-esteem and sense of competence, especially in the workplace. Since this had been a major source of her feelings of helplessness and failure, her new career success did much to turn her state of mind around. As the work progressed, she began to feel that she was getting a new strength and serenity. These enabled her to meet challenges and make decisions she couldn't have earlier. She started to explore spiritual ideas, recapturing a sense of connectedness that she lost many years before.

SEVEN STEPS FOR A DEPRESSION-FREE LIFE

1. Identify and defeat the inner saboteur.
2. Reconnect to your body.
3. Create healing relationships.
4. Elevate your self-esteem.
5. Uncover your competence.
6. Access the power of shared purpose.
7. Deepen your relationship to the Divine.

Many people have experienced the same dramatic healing that Sandi did using our unique method. We will lead you through the necessary steps that follow to fully free yourself from depression and anxiety. These steps will be achieved through a series of actions and exercises.

One small first step you can take (literally) to begin immediately to improve your physical health, stimulate your brain, and go against depression is to begin a walking regime, as Sandi did. Taking a friend along can greatly improve the anti-depressant power of this exercise. We suggest you keep a Walking Log as a record of the experiences that bring you closer to nature, your body, and others.

Exercise 1 Walking Log

Take time every day to go for a walk. Aim for twenty or thirty minutes, though you may enjoy it so much you may wind up walking more. The goal is to enjoy the process of walking, rather than focusing only on the benefits. We suggest you invite a friend along whenever possible.

In a spiral notebook or on a computer, keep a daily record of each walk, noting the date, duration, and the route you took. List new and unusual things you notice on your walk. What, perhaps, do you see regularly that you experienced differently today? Note any colors, scents, and pleasant sounds. If you went with a companion, what thoughts and feelings did you share? What new sensations and changes do you notice in your body?

4

STEP 1: IDENTIFY AND DEFEAT THE INNER SABOTEUR

◉

So far, we've seen that depression is the result of a number of factors, all having to do with relationships gone wrong in a dysfunctional society. The unsupported, troubled nuclear family is a breeding ground for trauma and, in the broadest sense of the word, abuse. These experiences alter the structure and chemistry of children's brains and, along with possible genetic factors, predispose them to depression and its associated disorders, anxiety, and PTSD.

We've also seen that none of these changes is irreversible; you are not doomed to depression. The first step in peeling back the layers of depression is to see how you have re-created the very circumstances that will retrigger earlier traumas. These conditions keep you captive to and even exacerbate the illness. You don't do this on purpose; in fact "you" don't do it at all. These self-defeating beliefs and behaviors are learned and can be unlearned. They are not you, but they are part of a self-reinforcing system that has a life of its own. Its goal is to maintain your depression. We call it the *inner saboteur*.

How Did I Get to This Point?

When forty-five-year-old Peter walked into Bob's office in San Jose, California, he was dressed in a smart suit and was wearing freshly polished shoes. He looked as if he were about to attend the board meeting of a major bank. His voice was cultured.

Yet Peter started the conversation with "I'm a complete loser!"

"What makes you think you're a loser?" Bob asked.

"I have a job I don't like, that pays very little, and that I can't seem able to leave. I have no relationships and I don't know what to do with my life. I feel totally pessimistic and blocked from making any progress."

Peter's tone of voice, which was alternately flat and irritable, would have given away his depression even if the words hadn't.

"I'm not even sure exactly why I'm here. I'm not sure I believe you can really help me. I certainly know what's wrong with me. God knows I've been through enough workshops and therapy to have learned that. I just don't know what to *do* about it."

Many people who come to see us for private sessions or to the Uplift Program believe that they understand their problems but are stuck on making changes. However, they often find they aren't as clear about their self-defeating patterns as they need to be to combat them.

Several years before coming to see Bob, Peter divorced his wife of ten years. She was the driving force behind their successful accountancy software business. Brenda was also critical and controlling and had been having an affair for most of their marriage. Peter moved into an apartment nearby, got a low-paying job in city government, and saw his daughter only on weekends.

"How did I get to this point?" he demanded of Bob.

A PHYSICAL PRESENCE IN THE BRAIN

We know that by the age of six our brains have been "programmed" in certain ways. This program governs everything we do, think, remember, see, dream, like, dislike, and feel. Our "personality" is largely formed by that age; it has been programmed in. But it can be changed.

For example, a New York City police crime report shows how the program works. A mugging had occurred on West 54th Street in broad daylight in view of four people. The first witness described the assailant as a tall, thick-set black man. The second swore that the mugger was white and of medium height. The third was convinced that the criminal was Asiatic, but wasn't sure how tall he was. The fourth witness was positive that the mugger was a woman disguised as a man. The villain was never caught.

Each of these witnesses was telling the truth: they really did "see" what they reported but it was filtered through the prism of their program. They saw what they were programmed to expect. This prism makes eyewitness accounts the least reliable testimony, even though they are the most relied upon in court.

To understand how our brains can trick us into perceiving a very narrow and often misleading view of reality, we need to go into a bit of gentle neurobiology. What we refer to as the *program* is, in terms of brain mechanics, a series of synaptic connections in various regions of the brain.

When we look at pictures of the brain, we see the "gray matter," which is where the main brain activities take place. The gray matter is made up of more than a trillion neurons, or brain cells (see Figure 4.1).

At the center of the neuron is the cell's nucleus, where all the processing that the neuron does takes place. Stretching out from the cell are feelers that look like the filaments of a spiderweb. These feelers are of two kinds: *axons*, which carry information from one cell to another, and *dendrites*, which receive that information and transmit it to the receiving cell.

When one cell wants to convey information to another, it reaches out with its axon and fires neurochemicals at the dendrite or the cell wall of the receiving cell through a small extension on the axon called a *synapse*. Connections between neurons are called *synaptic connections*.

FIGURE 4.1 BRAIN CELL AND SYNAPTIC CONNECTIONS

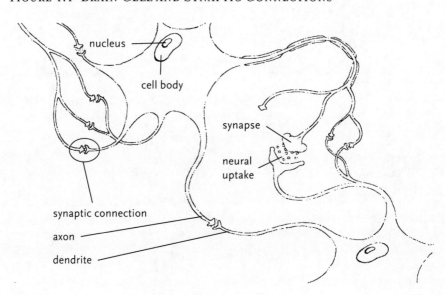

Learning, thinking, remembering, and tying one's shoelaces are all made possible because of the connections between neurons. Each neuron has the ability to make about 100,000 connections, which gives our brains a fantastic amount of raw computing power and an almost infinite capacity to learn.

This processing takes place in different regions of the brain. Our brain is divided into three major areas: the *cerebellum*, the *cerebrum*, and the *central brain* (see Figure 4.2). The cerebellum is the least important part, as far as mood disorders are concerned, since it mostly regulates the motor functions of the body. The cerebrum is where the "higher" functions of thinking, remembering, and motivation take place. Near the center of the brain is the *limbic system*, the seat of our emotions and our arousal. This area also controls the central nervous system.

Scientists tell us that when we're born, the cerebrum is pretty much free of connections, although the other areas have been working away for some time. How-

FIGURE 4.2 PRIMARY BRAIN AREAS

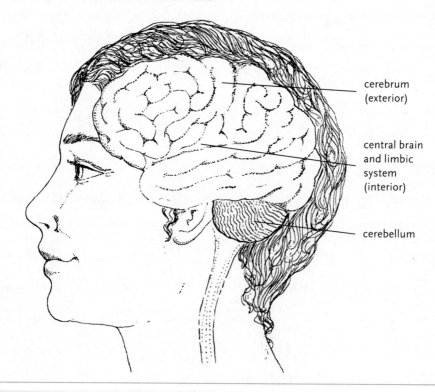

cerebrum
(exterior)

central brain
and limbic
system
(interior)

cerebellum

ever, as soon as we're born, it begins its work. The cerebrum starts making connections that enable us to react to our environment, breathe, see, experience pain and pleasure, and relate to other human beings. Some of these early connections will remain with us throughout life and have profound influences on our behavior.

When a baby is given to its mother, for example, they make eye contact. A link is formed between eye contact and love and safety, which is unique to humans. Through breast- or bottle-feeding, the infant makes a connection between food and safety and love. This is why asking someone you find attractive to dinner is such an important part of a courtship ritual, and why the old saying that "the way to a man's heart is through his stomach" is so accurate.

These connections form part of our programming, particularly in regard to relationships. Studies of adults who had been born prematurely—in the days when "preemies" were whisked away and put in an incubator without early eye contact with their mothers—showed that their relationship-forming abilities had been severely compromised. We are programmed by our human genetic inheritance to need eye contact and gentle touch just as we are to need food and air. The deprivation of any of these contacts can have profoundly negative consequences.

Each time the baby is fed or eye contact is made, the established neural connections are reinforced as more cells get in on the act. You can think of this process in terms of a muscle building up strength. Exercise stimulates muscle cells to make connections with each other, and, as they do, the muscle increases in mass.

If a child is brought up in a Spanish-speaking home, then connections will be made between love and safety and Spanish. The child—and subsequent adult—will feel safer and more at ease among Spanish-speaking people. Similarly with music, a particular kind of music played in the home will be associated in the child's mind with all the positive aspects of family. In fact, to a young child, all aspects of home are "positive."

So if a child is born into a dysfunctional household, one where there is abuse, anger, alcoholism, or other damaging factors, then he will associate these with home and safety as well. This is why a battered woman will most often stay in an abusive relationship or, if she does leave, find another abuser.

We refer to these negative aspects of the program as the inner saboteur. It is a self-perpetuating system of connections between cells, a neurological presence that seems so intrinsic to us that we're not usually conscious of its influence. You did not install the inner saboteur; it's the result of what happened to you.

It may be difficult to unlearn what you have been taught, but it is possible. Going back to the analogy of the muscle; if you stop using it, if you cease to do the exercise, the connections between the muscle cells will wither. So it is, we believe, with the various sabotaging aspects of the program. Once you identify and arrest these behaviors and ideas, the connections between cells will wither, and corresponding aspects of the program will fade.

Anything that can be changed is not essential to you. The program is not you. The real you—optimistic, nondepressed, and able to form really supportive relationships—is waiting to be programmed in.

PETER'S PROGRAMMING

Bob discovered that Peter's father had been a country-town shopkeeper whose business had failed. His dominating mother was severely critical of both Peter and his father, describing them as "ne'er do wells" who only survived because of her reliable job in local government.

The only other major figure in Peter's early life was his uncle George, his father's older brother. George lived in a small shack and made a precarious living driving the town's only taxi. Unlike his brother, however, George read widely and could talk with some knowledge on topics as diverse as astronomy, philosophy, and mathematics. George did not care about material things; his sole love was of books. He never married and was a loner.

In his early years, Peter would often sneak over to George's shack to escape his mother's tongue and her not-infrequent physical assaults. His uncle would read to him and talk about things unrelated to the daily grind of shopkeeping or local politics. Later, his mother forbid Peter from visiting his "worthless" uncle. Whenever Peter neglected a chore, she would make the ultimate threat: "You'll turn out just like George." Peter's mother also criticized his playmates and refused to allow them in the house. Since no one met her standards, neither of his parents had many friends.

Peter's parents were also pessimistic in their outlook. In the rare event that his father added a new range of products to the store, he would mutter, "It'll probably never sell, but nothing else works." Peter could not remember his mother ever making a positive remark, even about herself.

Probably because of George's encouragement during his early years, Peter did well at school and went on to study mathematics at CUNY. He discovered an interest in systems analysis and after leaving college he headed out West and took a series of jobs in computers. He always quit before he could rise within the firm, just as he left his successful business to Brenda.

Peter's program, the root of his self-perceived failures, is made up of four components: *neural specialization* (how our brain makes us "specialize" in certain behaviors), *idealization* (and thus the lifelong emulation of childhood authority figures), the *meeting or not of needs*, and *social influences*. And so is yours.

Neural Specialization

As explained earlier, the child's brain learns through a process of making neural connections. With each experience, a set of connections is made or strengthened. If unenforced, these connections wither fairly rapidly. However, when the experience is repeated a number of times the connection grows stronger. The brain becomes specialized in certain behaviors. The inner saboteur is born.

The infant tries to come to grips with each new event and his brain attempts to devise a strategy for coping with it. Some of these coping strategies work and are retained. For example, if he is criticized by his parents, the coping strategy may be to act "bad," since this is the only way he can make sense of the situation. He will develop "bad" behaviors to make his parent right. A child who is ignored may find that he gets attention when he is ill; thus illness or accidents will become an unconscious coping mechanism.

In this way, Peter "learned" to be a failure, accept criticism, be overly docile, and have unsupportive relationships. These strategies may have worked in childhood to blunt his mother's anger, but they are dysfunctional in an adult. However, they are his "specializations," developed to cope with the particular set of circumstances that he found himself in as a small child.

Anyone with a specialty (say a doctor with a specialty in tropical medicine) will, subconsciously, look for environments in which that specialty can be used. For the physician, it could be very warm climates; for an abused child, the environment could be a climate of abuse, criticism, or abandonment.

If Peter were to list the self-defeating behavior patterns that developed from his coping mechanisms, it might look like this:

"I assume I'm going to fail, so I don't try."
"I act as if nothing good will happen to me."

"I find it hard to trust anyone."
"I criticize people and expect them to criticize me."
"I find it hard to make friends with anyone."
"I reject people who are good to me or try and help me."
"I avoid confrontation and situations in which people may judge me."

In almost every situation, Peter will use one of these behavioral strategies. They will hold him back and prevent him from having good relationships or a worthwhile career. Peter, like all of us, was born with the capacity to learn an almost limitless set of behavioral responses. However, the neural specialization formed by his reactions to situations over which he had no control severely limited his options.

Behind these standard responses of his lie a set of beliefs, most of them unconscious:

"People will not like me (at least, no one who's worth anything)."
"Nothing will really turn out well."
"Everything I do is wrong."
"No matter what I do it's never good enough."
"Only intellectual pursuits are worthwhile."
"I really am a failure."
"People who are nonjudgmental or nonabusive are boring."
"I deserve to be punished for my failures."

Take a moment to consider some of the behavioral patterns and beliefs that tend to sabotage you.

EXERCISE 2 BEHAVIORAL PATTERNS AND BELIEFS

1. Write a list of your self-defeating behaviors. You don't need to state every dysfunctional habitual pattern, just a few will do. You can add to this list later.
2. Write down a list of negative beliefs you have about yourself.

Idealization

We take on many beliefs and behaviors from the significant adults in our childhood. Children under six possess an innate, powerful drive to believe what their elders tell them. A small child needs to assume that the adults around him can do no wrong. To trust in them absolutely, and therefore learn without question, he must idealize them.

Recent research has shown that this idealization usually lasts for life in one form or other. As adults, we emulate our early authority figures and even marry or have relationships with their surrogates (people who have similar relationship or behavioral characteristics). Thus we tend to re-create the same relationship environment in our adult life as we had when we were small. We even act out their roles, behaving like our mother with our partner, for example, and like our father with our boss. Or we may regress to playing ourselves as a child and cast other people in the role of our parents.

The templates for all our adult relationships are created in childhood. We may have only a very few such role models compared to the hunter-gatherer child living in a band. And so we may be forced to seek out only those people who fit the molds planted in our brains. Or else we try to squeeze everyone we meet into these limited slots.

According to a 1996 American Psychological Association (APA) report, adult abusers and abuse victims almost always come from abusive homes. In our experience, people who were subjected to criticism in childhood almost always choose critics as their partners, bosses, or friends. Of course those who came from warm, supportive environments tend to re-create these as well.

Your programmers are not just your parents, though they are usually the major influences. Your older siblings, your kindergarten teacher, a relative who lived with you, your nanny, the neighbors you spent time with, your older or more dominant playmates, even television personalities, all could have had a hand in writing elements of your program. Very young children are totally vulnerable to all these adults.

We don't just idealize "good," supportive people; a young child is unable to distinguish between "good" and "bad." And once the behavior or belief has been programmed into the brain, the individual continues as if on automatic pilot. Peter, for example, idealized both his parents and his uncle and adopted characteristics of each.

How were *you* programmed and by whom? Who installed the inner saboteur?

In the exercise Significant Adults, take a moment to identify these early authority figures. This will be the list of characters in your own drama, the possible roles that you can play, and the number of people whose surrogates you can have relationships with. Some will have been a positive influence, some negative, many both. Later on we'll find out who were the most significant programmers, but for now let's cast our net wide.

And remember, you aren't blaming anyone. Your understanding of what happened is essential to your recovery; it's not about them.

EXERCISE 3 SIGNIFICANT ADULTS

Write a list of all the important people from your early childhood. Note that these significant adults must have been:

1. With you before the age of six.
2. Older than you (to a four-year-old, a five-year-old is an adult).
3. With you a considerable amount of time (living with you or having regular contact over a period of at least six months).

If you can't remember some of these people, ask family members, neighbors, and friends.

Needs

Peter would like to believe that he doesn't need anything from anybody. However, the truth is that we are all desperately trying to get certain needs met. The self-defeating way he went about doing so was the problem.

When we talk about needs, we're talking about those that get met through relationships. We're not talking about the primal drives—to feed, flee, mate, and so forth—that you share even with reptiles who are incapable of making relationships.

In our view, only four basic categories of need exist: *physical safety, emotional security, attention,* and *importance.* We are not the first to come up with a set of basic human needs. However these are, we believe, the simplest and the most useful in creating supportive relationships.

If a child is brought up well, all of these will be met in functional ways. However, in our society the unsupported nuclear family is under enormous stress and struggles to achieve this most fundamental of tasks. Often parents simply do not have enough time to give to children. The kids are forced to adopt dysfunctional strategies to get what they need.

In a family with more than one child, each will take on different characteristics. One will become the scholar, one the clown, one the rebel, and so on. Which attributes a child adopts depends to a large extent on which niches are already occupied. If one sibling becomes the scholar, then that position is filled. The next in line may become the athlete, the "loser," or the "stupid one." Also, to some extent the child will adopt the behavioral strategy he thinks his parents expect him to take.

However the characteristic came to be adopted, the object is the same: to get physical safety, emotional security, attention, or importance. Even being the black sheep of the family will get attention of a kind, and any attention is better than none.

Social Influences

Your family conditioning is itself formed, and reinforced by, society. Our culture can keep us depressed and make us pessimistic. It can reinforce the negative aspects of the program, and it can have a damaging effect on our sense of self.

When we talk of societal influences, what exactly are we talking about? "Society" is not a uniform voice, it is an amalgam of disparate voices: of churches, schools, the media (including advertising), politicians, various business interests, our peers. Each can be subdivided and some have more influence than others.

The two aspects of society that influence our program most as we develop in childhood and adolescence are our peers and the media, and one is affected by the other. The media, of course, are not confined to radio, the press, and TV. The media also encompass films, video and computer games, the music industry, the Internet, and so forth. A person's mood is very much affected by what he reads, listens to, or views. Watching a film with an uplifting or inspiring ending makes us feel optimistic—*Field of Dreams*, for example, or *Star Wars*. As Paul Martin points out in *The Sickening Mind*, a film that makes us laugh raises our immune system, as well as our mood.

On the other hand, according to a 1993 report from the APA, television violence accounts for about 10 percent of kids' aggressive behavior. Is that a big effect? It's about as big as the link between smoking and cancer.

Constant viewing of violent or depressing films, TV, or video games can also instill pessimism and depression into a young mind, particularly if one or more of his parents is depressed.

The influence of peers begins early—though in the first six years it's not nearly as significant as that of parents—and is shaped by them. Families that contain secrets, such as Peter's did (his father's and his uncle's failures), tend to discourage socialization. In our experience, children of these families become shy and withdrawn or socially maladroit, which sets them up to be shunned by their peers and for a downward spiral of further rejection. In many cases, this leads to violence and aggression. Also, if parents don't adequately encourage social activity by their off-spring, the children will take on the message that the outside world is inherently dangerous and they will set themselves up to be rejected. Just like Peter. Whatever the cause, feeling shunned by other kids is one of the prime causes of both depression and pessimism later in life and can also foster aggression and impair intelligence and reasoning ability.

As we get older, we tend to be increasingly influenced by our friends, although, of course, we select them on the basis of our early conditioning. An abused child, for example, will gravitate toward an abusive group.

As adolescents or preadolescents, we're even more directly influenced by social messages. We try to conform to what society teaches us and seems to expect. If we can't meet these ideals—because our bodies aren't the right shape or we don't have the money to buy the right clothes—we feel rejected and pessimistic.

EXPOSING THE INNER SABOTEUR

As they say about alcoholism in AA, the inner saboteur is "cunning, devious, and powerful." It wants to keep you confused and in the dark about its workings. It hides its own motivations, origins, and influence. It encourages you to bury the reality of your early experience under the myth of a perfect childhood. But by truthfully examining your programming, you'll expose its machinations and begin to break its power. And you don't need hours of complicated and lengthy psycho-analysis to do this.

To help you understand your own program better, let's take a closer look at Peter's.

Clearly Peter's mother was dominant in the family and the major influence in his early life—the significant adult who was his chief programmer. Her criticism and pessimism were the main internal voices driving him. Peter would seek out critical, controlling bosses and friends who he felt were impossible to please. If they weren't like that at first, he would often provoke them into these behaviors and then leave.

Peter tended to make everyone he came into contact with a surrogate for his mother, even his daughter. He tried desperately to please her and allowed her to criticize him. During his therapy he tried a number of times (unsuccessfully) to get Bob to criticize him, to confirm his mother's opinion.

He was also apathetic about work and pessimistic about his ability to advance himself. He was stuck between needing to be good enough to at last win the praise of his internalized mother (an impossible task) and yet needing to prove her right.

On the surface, Peter shared his mother's low opinion of his "slovenly" uncle, yet in reality Uncle George was also a role he came to play as an adult. The escape from his mother's criticism and pessimism was to intellectualism—to books, to collecting, to his uncle. Peter also took on his uncle's ineptitude at relationships and his reclusiveness. This was reinforced by the example he had of his parent's unhappy relationship, which was reproduced in his own marriage. Brenda was critical and overbearing, constantly putting him and his interests down.

From his father Peter got his sense of hopelessness and failure. Peter thought that no worthwhile boss would want him and that he would be unable to keep any well-paying job. To put it simply, the childhood roles relating to early idealized figures and being played out in Peter's drama were:

Peter = George (the intellectual) + Father (business, career failure)
Brenda, Daughter, Boss, Friends = Mother

EXTERNALIZE NEGATIVE BELIEFS

The key to understanding your habitual patterns is to recognize the true origin of your negative assumptions about yourself. These beliefs are the real blocks to optimism and self-fulfillment. For many of our clients, the hardest thing to take on board is that the notions they hold about themselves are not theirs.

The controlling beliefs may not be conscious. They may only be discovered through the self-derogatory remarks we make about ourselves. In this way, Peter's assumption that "I'll never amount to much" is both highlighted and reinforced by phrases such as "I'm a complete loser!" Each time he says such a thing and it's not contradicted, he reinforces his unconscious belief system. The inner saboteur's insidious damage remains undetected and unexamined.

Bob was able to get Peter to see and externalize these beliefs by helping him find the significant adults behind them.

Bob: Tell me how the interview went on Friday.
Peter: Oh, you know. The same. I do the same stupid . . .
Bob: Stupid?

Peter: Yeah, stupid.

Bob: Who called you stupid?

Peter: No one, I am stupid.

Bob: Who made you *feel* stupid?

Peter: In my early life? Everybody!

Bob: Who is everybody?

Peter: Mother!

Bob: How did she make you feel stupid?

Peter: Said I never got anything right. She said the same thing to Dad as well. Never actually used the word *stupid* that I recall. But that's what I felt all right. Stupid, just damn stupid.

Bob: So it's her voice.

Peter: Yeah, I guess. But I really do do stupid things.

Bob: Yes, to make her right.

Clearly Peter's beliefs that he would always fail at a career and that he couldn't make friends came from his mother's constant criticism of his father (a "failure") and from her remarks that Peter would "turn out just like" him. Although he tried to make these beliefs come true, they were lies.

Behind every belief there's a voice. Identifying this voice and attributing it to someone in your past is a powerful tool to distance yourself from negative beliefs. As Peter rightly says, his mother might not have used the words "you're stupid," but criticism, a tone of voice, an expression, an action, a silence, or even an omission—the lack of praise or encouragement—all these speak loudly.

ARREST THE INNER SABOTEUR

The following actions will start you on the path to freedom from the dictates of the inner saboteur:

THREE ACTIONS TO ARREST THE INNER SABOTEUR

1. Identify your program.
2. Recognize how your habitual patterns show up day to day.
3. Make choices that counter the program.

Action 1: Identify Your Program

This action has two stages. First, identify and externalize the negative voices from childhood. Second, look at the program overall.

The exercise Identify the Sabotaging Voice will help you discover the voice behind one of these beliefs and the self-defeating behaviors that stem from it. We suggest that you do this exercise at some point for each of your negative beliefs.

EXERCISE 4 IDENTIFY THE SABOTAGING VOICE

Write down one of the self-defeating beliefs you are aware of. This may be a belief you listed earlier. Answer the following questions to help you discover where it came from (i.e., whose voice it really is) and how it influences your behavior:

1. Which significant adult(s) in early childhood said this or made you feel they believed it?
2. Which of your behaviors might stem from this belief?

Your program is at the root of almost every difficulty in your life. The exercise Identify Your Program (on page 61) is an extremely effective tool for recognizing the issues underlying every block or problem in a way that makes it easier to resolve. This written exercise plays a pivotal role in the Uplift Program, which Peter attended after his private sessions with Bob.

To help you respond to the following questions on your own, we'll share Peter's answers. One problem Peter worked on was his inability to find and keep a well-paying job.

1. **What are some of the self-defeating actions associated with the difficulty?** "I find critical bosses who make me angry and undermine my sense of competence. Instead of confronting them, I use their behavior as an excuse to leave." "I don't work on a résumé for a better job or network with people in my real field of expertise to find out where to look for a good one." "When I do get job interviews, I try to prove that I'm intellectually superior to the interviewer or give the impression that I don't really want the job."

2. **What are some of the beliefs behind these actions?** "I'll never be much good, so why try?" "I'm wasting my time since only very intellectual pursuits are worthwhile." "Even if I did do a job well it would never be good enough for the boss."

3. **Which significant adult(s) in your early childhood believed or seemed to believe these things about you, themselves, or someone else?** "Dad always felt he was a failure." "Uncle George saw anything except intellectual pursuits as beneath him." "Mother made sure everybody knew she thought Dad and Uncle George were failures. Mother was sure I'd be a failure just like Dad and George."

4. **Which significant adult(s) engaged in similar self-defeating actions?** "Dad never seemed able to get anything right at the store." "George hung out in his shack and didn't try to better himself." "Neither of them formed functional relationships at work or anywhere else."

5. **What childhood actions or behavioral patterns are similar to the self-defeating behaviors around your current difficulty?** "Fled Mother's criticism by escaping into books—and I still do." "Never tried to achieve anything because it would make me vulnerable to Mother's criticism and abuse. I'm still afraid to take risks." "Left a situation or relationship before I was kicked out or abandoned. Like in all my jobs and even with my wife." "Never said what I wanted or needed because that brought more problems. Still don't with anyone, look at how I let my daughter treat me." "Stayed away from friends and even George so Mother wouldn't get mad. I still don't have any friends."

6. **Which significant adult(s) are you acting or thinking like now? Whose role are you playing?** "I've become my father in failing—or thinking I have." "I've become George in not trying." "I've taken on Mother's belief that I'll never amount to anything. I do things unconsciously that prove her right."

7. **Who are the people involved in the current difficulty (e.g., wife, child, friend, boss, interviewer, client, and so forth)? And which significant adult(s) do these people stand in for (remind you of)?** "Any potential boss is my critical mother and so I don't want to have anything to do with this person."

8. **How can you summarize your program around this issue?** "My program around my difficulty in finding the kind of work I want is to defeat myself by not trying very hard to find a better job. This is due to my certainty that I'm going to fail anyway and to my attitude that no job is worthwhile unless it's very intellectual (and I don't look for jobs that are). I find bosses who are like my mother (critical and controlling) or else I goad them into being so. I'm unconsciously fulfilling my mother's disparaging remarks that I'm a 'failure' just like my father and George.

I don't stand up for myself, explain how I feel, or ask others how they really feel about me or my work. Until I do this, nothing much will change."

You might want to do this exercise yourself now. Don't worry if you can't think of the "right" answer to any question immediately. We're just getting your brain used to thinking this way. You can return to this exercise at any time and make changes or additions.

When you've completed this exercise, you'll understand much better how your program works against you regarding one issue. Obviously, you may find a number of problems, triggers, and blocks that you will want to understand in relation to your program. You will need to do this exercise for every one of them to defeat the program. We suggest that you return to this exercise often until you feel that you can see clearly the program's influence on every troubling aspect of your life.

You may want to write out your summary of the program as it relates to each issue on an index card, on your PDA, or even as a pop-up on your computer. Whenever you feel stuck or in doubt about a decision, you can get a lot of clarity by reading the appropriate program summary. These index cards (or electronic versions) are a prime weapon against the inner saboteur.

EXERCISE 5 IDENTIFY YOUR PROGRAM

Write down a current difficulty in your life, something you feel triggers your depression or blocks you from being happy or doing what you want. Answering the following questions will help you identify your program around this issue:

1. What are some of the self-defeating actions associated with the difficulty?
2. What are some of the beliefs behind these actions?
3. Which significant adult(s) in your early childhood believed or seemed to believe these things about you, themselves, or someone else?
4. Which significant adult(s) engaged in similar self-defeating actions?
5. What childhood actions or behavioral patterns are similar to the self-defeating behaviors around your current difficulty?
6. Which significant adult(s) are you acting or thinking like now? Whose role are you playing?
7. Who are the people involved in the current difficulty (e.g., wife, child, friend, boss, interviewer, client, and so forth)? And which significant adult(s) do these people stand in for (remind you of)?
8. How can you summarize your program around this issue?

Action 2: Recognize How Habitual Patterns Show Up Day to Day

It's helpful to know how your inner saboteur works in general, but to arrest it and stop the harm it does, you need to pinpoint its daily activities. This may not be easy at first.

Remember what we said about the program being the distorting prism through which you view everything that happens in your life? Most of our reactions to people and events are quite automatic. And so are the choices we make, even when we think we know what we're doing. To make an informed decision you have to first know what your programmed response would be.

So, for example, it's one thing for Peter to realize he avoids looking for jobs that would suit him because his program wants him to be unhappy in his work and ultimately fail (just like Dad). That's a great first step. Now he has to notice when and how, for example, he procrastinates looking for a job he might want.

In the Uplift Program it was suggested that Peter keep a Daily Program Log of his actions and beliefs concerning issues that troubled him. In Peter's log (spread over several days) he wrote:

Saturday: Bought newspaper to scan the help-wanted column to see if there would be a job in computer sciences that would suit me. Read the news first, then the science section (program reaction: avoiding looking at the classifieds to see what jobs are going). Decided I'd be more up for making calls after lunch (program reaction: delaying). Never actually got around to the classifieds.

Wednesday: Went for job interview. Went in believing I was too old for them to be interested in me even though they had asked me to come (program belief: nothing good will happen). Spoke at length about things not relevant to the position (program reaction: sabotage real prospect of getting a job I'd like, need to show off intellectual ability like George).

Friday evening: Met a woman at the swimming club. She seemed to like me. However, I didn't feel she was intelligent enough for me (program belief: 1. relationships are doomed; 2. she failed the "uncle" test by not being an intellectual). I didn't ask for her phone number.

As you may remember, Peter originally thought he understood everything about his problems. He was astounded by the extent of the parallels between his childhood and his current life that came up when he first did the exercise Identify Your Program. But it was what emerged from his Daily Program Log that really bowled him over. "That damn program is so insidious!" he exclaimed. "It just sneaks in everywhere. No wonder I've felt defeated. But now that I know what to look for, I won't be so easily bushwhacked."

The Daily Program Log is also very useful in helping to avoid addictive behaviors, because it helps spot the feelings, thoughts, and triggers that often precede them.

The good news in all of these entries is that Peter had become aware enough of his dysfunctional patterns to be able to spot program-driven actions and beliefs and start to change them.

We suggest you begin a Daily Program Log of your own. At this stage the entries may, like the ones in Peter's, be mostly negative. That's OK. Catching the negatives is a marvelous first step.

EXERCISE 6 DAILY PROGRAM LOG

Keep a record of all the program-driven actions and beliefs you can identify on a daily basis. Also record anything you do that breaks the mold of your program.

Make sure you note the situations and people who seem to trigger your self-defeating patterns. Note how these habitual responses influence the decisions and choices you make.

We suggest you keep this log for at least a week. Doing this will help you identify your inner saboteur at work in many different aspects of your life. As you become more practiced, you will learn how to make choices that go against the program.

Action 3: Make Choices That Counter the Program

The inner saboteur was put in place by a constant repetition of events, circumstances, and remarks during the first six years of life. It must be counteracted every time it shows up now.

You are now armed with enough information to begin to go against each instance of the program, to make small changes that open your life to different influences and exciting new possibilities. Slowly, you can build an environment calibrated to create exactly the new neural connections that you need. After prolonged lack of use, the old circuitry will be replaced by a new one.

Going against the program involves looking at each self-defeating choice your program wants you to make and making another one instead.

Peter, for example, realized that it wasn't true that he couldn't make friends; he never gave himself a chance by cutting himself off from the company of anyone he might enjoy. To counter this aspect of his program, he joined a book discussion group where he met a number of people who shared his passion for reading, including an attractive woman who edited a newsletter of book reviews. The second time the group met, he screwed up his courage and asked her out. To his great surprise, she accepted.

In another onslaught against his habitual isolation, Peter joined a group of colleagues for lunch. He was pleasantly surprised to discover that his workmates shared many of his interests, and he was invited to join them frequently.

Some aspects of his program did not give way so easily to Peter's new resolution. He still resisted going to job interviews or even looking at the employment section of the newspaper. At Bob's suggestion, Peter approached Jim, a new friend from the book discussion group who seemed sympathetic and easy to talk to, about his problem and asked for help. His friend agreed to ask Peter at least weekly what new job prospects he'd circled in the paper and how many calls he'd made to set up interviews. Once Peter started going to job interviews, Jim would debrief him, sometimes pointing out his self-defeating behaviors.

After a number of interviews, Peter did get a well-paying job as a systems analyst, even surviving a big layoff.

To begin to go against your program, consider the following questions: What decisions did your program make for you today that you could do differently tomorrow? What actions could you take this week that would begin to counter the program? What support would you need to change these behaviors, and who could you enlist to help? What would they need to do, and what information about your program would you need to share so they can assist you?

Congratulations. You have begun to take some very effective steps to arrest the inner saboteur. Throughout the rest of the book, we'll show you how to build on this awareness and create a new environment that will in turn combat your depression and nourish the real you.

5

STEP 2: RECONNECT TO YOUR BODY

◉

In the mid-1990s a number of universities and medical centers became interested in our techniques for working with both emotions and the body in a truly integrated manner.

One rather dramatic demonstration of our theories occurred when we were guest speakers at Tufts University New England Medical Center's innovative and nationally acclaimed Orofacial Pain Center in Boston. After our morning talk to the multidisciplinary staff, including surgeons, a neurologist, and several dentists, we were invited by the head of the Center, Prof. Noshir Mehta, to join members of the group on their teaching rounds.

At one point the group, which included more than half a dozen specialists and students, crowded into a small room where a middle-aged woman sat in a dentist's chair. She had suffered for many years from a problem with her jaw known as TMJ, making it almost impossible for her to open her mouth without pain. She had come to the Center after unsuccessful treatment elsewhere. After Dr. Mehta explained the case to his colleagues and students, Bob asked if he might very briefly speak to the woman.

"You don't have to answer this question, and I'd more than understand if you don't feel comfortable in this setting," he said to her. "But I'm curious. What is it that you cannot say? What is the secret?"

The woman looked at him, blinked, then broke into tears. Her mouth opened as she sobbed. Finally, she began to speak of her past, which included sexual abuse and her father's threats if she told anyone. She still had not told her husband, who was not unlike her father in some ways, and she feared he would leave her if he knew about the incest.

"Tell me about the pain now," Bob asked gently.

The woman furrowed her brows and moved her jaw, tentatively at first, then more. "There's hardly any," she said finally.

The woman's body had tried to make sure that her father's command was carried out by making it painful to speak. The fact that eating was also painful may have provided a "secondary gain" for the program, since she was thus punished for the incest that she unconsciously perceived to be her fault.

It may also be that her previous dental procedures, some of which were possibly uncomfortable, functioned as a reenactment of the abuse by an (unwitting) authority figure.

Dr. Mehta later told us that he and his colleagues planned to incorporate some of our techniques as part of their standard intake.

Depression is an illness of the body as well as of the mind. In fact, the brain and body are inseparable parts of your physical being—your *soma*. Yet, the body aspect of depression is often minimized or entirely left out of therapy and self-help books.

The body is programmed for depression much as the brain is. In his book *The Body Reveals: How to Read Your Own Body*, Ron Kurtz says, "Deeply ingrained habits of thought and feeling . . . originating in our earliest years . . . will be inevitably translated into a body statement. Indeed, the body has no choice. It displays the total dynamics of the individual. The circuitry of the nervous system, when so organized, restricts and contains the available options for response. To this extent we are preprogrammed."

Trauma, the root cause of most depression, lodges in the body and sets up a self-reinforcing system. Trauma and depression manifest themselves in the body in three ways. First, many physical problems, such as illness and injuries, can be directly associated with or caused by a mood disorder. Second, childhood trauma imprints itself on the body as poor posture and maladaptive movement patterns. Finally, childhood abuse and dysfunctional social messages combine to create faulty body image, low self-esteem, and a range of related disorders.

DEPRESSION AND PHYSICAL ILLNESS

Researchers have identified depression as an important factor in a whole slew of physical illnesses—and the list seems to grow weekly. They include heart disease, some forms of cancer, diabetes, eye disease, irritable bowel syndrome, Alzheimer's disease, Parkinson's disease, and many more. These are in addition to ailments that have long been linked to emotional difficulties, such as chronic fatigue syndrome, fibromyalgia, and chronic pain.

Sometimes depression and anxiety can masquerade as a physical illness, displaying all the bodily symptoms but with no physical basis. This is called somatization and can be just as debilitating as any other disease. Somatization differs from "psychosomatic" illness, such as a peptic ulcer, which is brought on by an emotional state but involves an underlying pathology.

People used to dismiss psychosomatic illnesses as being "hysterical," "just in the mind," and therefore not "real" or worthy of respect. Now we know better. Two 1987 studies found that up to 80 percent of all people who consult physicians do so because they suffer from what are called "functional complaints" (so-called because they are a function of a psychological process, such as depression, and not a product of a structural change in the tissues of the body).

There are three possible scenarios for the dance physical illness and depression do with each other. First, you can be ill and depressed (illness itself can lead to depression). Second, you can be depressed and feel down in your mood but well in your body. And third, you can be depressed and feel upbeat in your mood but physically ill.

SOMATIZATION

So why does a mood disorder somatize? Most researchers agree that for some reason the sufferer represses her emotions and does not allow them to be expressed openly. For example, anger—which itself can be a depressive symptom—stimulates blood flow to muscles and elevates heart rate and blood pressure to prepare for fight or flight. Once one of those actions has been taken, blood pressure drops, the muscles don't require so much blood, the heart rate goes down, and the person can relax.

If the emotion is repressed or denied, it can't be expressed through action. The body continues to respond to the feeling, even though the mind refuses to acknowledge it. This is how anger, anxiety, or depression can lead to heart disease, for example. Once the heart adjusts to beating at the anger rate, it may reset itself to a faster level of functioning that becomes independent of the emotion that originally caused it. Even if the psychological problem is resolved, the cardiac system will not necessarily return to normal and may be permanently damaged.

The same is true of any organ, including the lower intestine. An early experience of abuse leads to acute anxiety and a resulting tightening of the bowel. After a while it remains tight and doesn't relax even when the anxiety-provoking situation has passed. According to studies by researchers such as Prof. William Whitehead of the University of North Carolina, a history of sexual abuse is present in more than half of all irritable bowel sufferers.

Certain cultures and family systems inadvertently cause their members to be prone to somatization. In these environments, physical illness is considered more acceptable than psychological problems or negative feelings. Uplift participants and clients often report that in their families of origin they could express "any emotion as long as it was a happy one." Anger, fear, pessimism, and depression were simply not allowed. But these negative emotions don't just go away.

The brains of these depressed children, particularly those with a genetic or biological vulnerability, subconsciously learn to express negative feelings as a physical malady.

Somatization in these cases follows a predictable pattern. Significant adults punish (physically or emotionally) the child for her "bad feelings." At the same time they reward her for being ill by criticizing her less and giving her more attention, and perhaps importance. Illness thus becomes a dysfunctional coping mechanism for getting needs met. It can even provide physical safety. An Uplift student with a history of childhood illness told the group that the only time his father did not hit him was when he was sick in bed. His immune system learned to welcome illness.

Most families mobilize to deal with an illness and do everything possible to ensure that the stricken member recovers. Some dysfunctional families, however, do everything possible to maintain the illness. The crisis allows everyone to focus on something other than the real issues that lie below the surface. The sick child, who in such an environment is probably depressed as well, becomes the focus for the family's classic codependence. Long into adulthood, illness will remain a subconscious behavioral reaction to certain stressful situations.

This dysfunctional coping mechanism is then reinforced by the medical profession, whose members are geared to take "physical illness" more seriously than "psychological" problems. Alarmingly, according to a number of studies, some 50 percent of doctors are unable to properly diagnose depression, especially somatized depression. The attention many physicians give their patients increases in proportion to the severity of the diagnosis. This interest is itself a reward, reinforcing the idea that it's OK to be ill but not depressed.

TRAUMA IN THE BODY

"Trauma is the frightening experience of the destruction of all self-nurturing functioning resources," writes prominent psychiatrist Joerg Bose, M.D., in the *Review of Interpersonal Psychoanalysis*. "Trauma . . . shatters the self." It also fractures our connection to our bodies, making them agents of retraumatization rather than healing.

A traumatic event, or series of events, locks itself into the body as a somatic pattern. A child who is hit or slapped around the head or upper body might adopt a raised shoulder, a sort of boxer's stance, to ward off blows. (Even the threat of such abuse, such as a hand raised in anger, can have this effect.) After a while the shoulder remains in this position quite independent of the abuse. The central nervous system becomes permanently geared for blows.

The defensive posture is both an outward manifestation of the inner anxiety and a constant reminder to the brain that danger is near. The anxiety and depression are constantly invoked, as if the trauma is, as we call it, an "ongoing energy event" that resurfaces at any hint of the original circumstances.

Conscious recollection can be hampered by an overwhelming emotional response. This sometimes happens when a child is severely abused at an early age by an idealized older person in the family. Faced with the possibility of admitting that the adult has done something wrong, the child's brain simply erases the memory from consciousness. But the somatic footprint remains.

The imprint of trauma in the body not only maintains the sense of vulnerability and victimhood within the person but communicates this to others as well. Research shows that criminals can spot a likely target in seven seconds through their submissive, downward-gazing posture and awkward, uncoordinated movement. In the same way, someone programmed to criticize and control will seek out people whose slumped posture suggests that they will accept this kind of behavior. The victim, in turn, may be drawn to the controller, whose bullying demeanor reminds her at some level of the childhood abuser. The relationship itself will then constantly retrigger the trauma and reinforce the depression.

A NOTE ON RELEASING TRAUMA

It's not uncommon for emotions to come up when your body is relaxed and letting go of defensive patterns. This may occur, for example, during bodywork sessions.

Some people may find themselves feeling angry or even crying for no apparent reason. They usually feel much better after releasing these pent-up emotions, and it's important to have such an outlet. Sometimes people even shake or tremble and may experience involuntary movements. This simply indicates that muscles are letting go of tension and is also a good thing.

It's very important to have someone you can be with or talk to when these feelings come up. A good friend may be enough, but if you continue to feel troubled, you may want to work with a mental health professional who is highly skilled in psychotherapy. A professional who is well-trained in both emotional and body-oriented therapy can be particularly helpful in enabling you to feel safe during these releases and will integrate them into your therapeutic process.

Finding such a practitioner isn't easy. (You might want to search for a Fortin-berry Murray practitioner.) The most important thing, however, is to be with someone you trust and feel really understands you.

If you are thinking of seeing a physical therapist, bodyworker, or somatic teacher, ask whether she is comfortable with clients expressing emotions. You might also request that you be told what she plans to do and asks permission before you are touched. If the individual isn't a trained psychotherapist, it's important that she acknowledges her limitations and doesn't try to impose her ideas onto your experience. Remember that no one ever touches just your body—they touch *you*. And keep in mind that your brain will inevitably experience any practitioner as an authority figure.

We recommend that you avoid any method that emphasizes cathartic release of trauma or uncovering buried memories.[16] If these things occur spontaneously in a safe environment, that's fine.

DYSFUNCTIONAL BODY IMAGE

Pass any magazine rack and you'll be bombarded by hundreds of images of men, women, and babies that share one thing in common: they aren't real. These "photos" have been stretched, airbrushed, retouched, and sometimes even combined with others (a nose from one picture, a chin from another, breasts from yet another) to match an industry ideal. Yet most of us don't look like that, never have and never will. In a society that values youth and a very narrow definition of good looks over just about everything (except possibly money, and money and image are inexorably linked), we've lost the race before we even began.

And that leads to loss of self-esteem and, in some cases, contributes to a sense of self-loathing so acute that people destroy themselves with extreme diets and weight-loss pills, compulsive and unending plastic surgery, and punitive exercise regimes. And, of course, suffer depression and anxiety.

But the impossibility of living up to an artificial social ideal is just the tip of the iceberg of our detachment from our bodies. A child learns about her body from interactions with the environment. This includes everything from the way in which she is touched and held to her freedom to explore the terrain and objects around her. If she is held appropriately, encouraged verbally, and given room to move and play freely while supervised, her experiences will stimulate her body and brain to develop optimally. As the various stages of cognitive and movement functions click into place, she will gain a sense of self-esteem, competence, and autonomy over her body and her emotions. She will have a true "body image."

Any form of trauma will hamper this delicate process to some degree. This includes everything from being yelled at or criticized to being confined indoors because it's too dangerous to go out to play or being forced to sit rigidly in chairs for long periods at school. Trauma and abuse can lead to diminished bodily awareness. In some cases, the loss of awareness of parts or all of the body is so extreme, it becomes a form of dissociation.

Without awareness, movement is hampered; without free movement, safety, self-esteem, and competence are compromised. If you don't have a clear connection to your body or accurate idea of how much space you take up, you are far more prone to injury and to self-destructive behavior.

Sexual abuse is especially pernicious in causing dissociation from the body, distorted body image, and related disorders. And it is surprisingly prevalent. According to an August 2000 report from the American Psychological Association, "There is evidence that as many as 34 percent of American women, and 20 percent of men, experienced some form of sexual abuse as children (usually by a family member or family friend)."

Sexual abuse gives the survivor the message that her only worth is in her body, at the same time taking away her comfort, ease, and control in relation to it. Sexual abuse, and the bodily shame and fear of loss of control it engenders, is a common factor in anorexia and bulimia. It has also been linked to body dysmorphic disorder (BDD), a form of severe body image distortion.

Thus, trauma becomes imprinted in the body, leading to physical illness, low self-esteem, distorted body image, and dysfunctional somatic patterns, all of which perpetuate both depression and anxiety.

Healing the Body

It's difficult for verbal therapy alone to break this cycle of mind-body interaction. No matter how hard, for instance, a therapist works with someone to raise her self-esteem, nothing much is going to happen while she remains slumped over herself in a frightened, defeated, and withdrawn posture. The message is just too strong, to herself and others, that this is who she is and that nothing will change.

The same is true for those trying to alter physical patterns without shifting emotional ones. No matter how hard some people, even movement professionals, have worked on their bodies, some somatic echoes will remain until they address their feelings about themselves—and improve their relationships.

Once you notice that you're holding emotional tension in your body, you probably want to be free of it. You may also discover, if you haven't before, that a bewildering number of methods and techniques purport to help you feel better in your body, improve your posture, strengthen muscles, and release trauma. How do you find a way that works for you?

Two requirements need to be met for you to counteract your somatic programming and reclaim your body: (1) relationships that make you feel safe and within which you are free to express emotions and feelings, and (2) awareness of your movement patterns and exploration of more functional options.

When these conditions are met, you can largely if not wholly erase trauma's signature from your body. When they aren't, no method or technique will create lasting, beneficial change, and may in fact do harm.

Using the Body to Teach the Brain

One of the most important modern discoveries is that not only can the brain affect the body, but the body can teach the brain. Alicia was particularly excited by the ramifications of this idea during her four-year Feldenkrais professional certification training.

The Feldenkrais Method was introduced to the United States several decades ago and paved the way for this realization. Using very gentle, small, and pain-free Feldenkrais movements, either on their own or assisted, stroke victims began to report gains in recovering lost function that had been thought impossible before. This went far beyond building up or limbering muscles; it indicated a whole new area of learning. Clearly, the flow of information regarding physical function was not simply from the brain to the body via the nervous system, as most people had thought, but the other way around as well.

What's more, athletes and even piano students have since confirmed another tenet of Feldenkrais: practicing a skill *in one's imagination* is as powerful as actually carrying out the movements repeatedly.[17] Obviously, thought (visualization) and action are one and the same to the brain.

Gradually, new neural imaging techniques began to explain this phenomenon and as they did so, to shed light on the very nature of learning. When a person learns something conceptually new, cells in the brain form connections around the idea or behavior or experience.

What's more, learning different concepts (like a sport or language, but not additional information about a subject you're already familiar with) stimulates the brain to keep on learning fresh things. New learning has, in fact, been shown to keep the brain active and to ward off Alzheimer's disease.

Moshe Feldenkrais believed that enhancing people's ability to function optimally in their bodies and thus stimulating their capacity to learn would increase their self-confidence and give them tools to solve any problems. As a tough Israeli who, as he once told Alicia, had walked out of Russia at the age of twelve and aided British Intelligence during World War II, he had little patience for psychotherapy or for focusing on emotions and relationships.[18]

We took his ideas a step further. We wanted to encourage the brain to open up to new options for thinking, feeling, and relating. We began to use Feldenkrais and other forms of movement to subtly release somatic patterns caused by trauma, to gently stimulate the brain to seek out more functional options in all areas of people's lives, and to challenge the person's limited system of beliefs and behaviors— the program.

We now address muscular-skeletal, emotional, behavioral, and cognitive patterns as basically the same thing. We teach people to use one to become aware of, and then change, the other. We bring movement into the Uplift Program and, when appropriate, hands-on work into one-on-one Fortinberry Murray sessions.

Working with the body was a vital aspect of Gina's recovery from depression. A single woman in her early thirties, Gina suffered from head and neck pain and fatigue as well as depression. Her desperate need to succeed at everything she did— from sports and grades in her youth to her current position as head of personnel for a large Manhattan consulting firm—contributed to her problems along with her feeling that nothing she ever accomplished was good enough.

When Gina first came to the Uplift Program, her favorite part was Repatterning Movements (RPMs), some of which are similar to Feldenkrais Awareness Through Movement® lessons. She found it an enormous relief simply to lie on the floor with her eyes closed and focus only on Alicia's voice directing her through movements that were relaxing, intriguing, and pleasurable. She also enjoyed the more active and playful group RPMs, which entail laughter as well as learning. It was a totally new experience for her to follow her own comfort and curiosity rather than worrying about meeting other people's standards.

After each RPM, Gina felt a dramatic improvement in her ability to move and a decrease in pain. Over the several days of the Uplift Program, her body began to let go of its habitual rigidity, especially around the neck, jaw, and shoulders. The severity and frequency of her headaches decreased and she had more energy. She began to feel a deep sense of letting go and of new possibilities for living based on pleasing herself instead of others.

Heartened by her physical improvement, and excited by these new thoughts and experiences, Gina began to pay more attention to other aspects of the Uplift. She allowed herself to look honestly at her past without idealizing it. She came to see how her parents' criticism, coupled with unrealistic expectations, played a significant role in her depression and sports injuries.

Gina also remembered her parents fighting, sometimes screaming at each other and even throwing things. At these times she would hide in her room, curled into a small, tense ball. Since her parents sometimes argued over her, she was especially prone to imagining that all the fights were her fault. If only she had somehow been good enough, perhaps brought home even better grades or more wins, her parents would have loved each other more.

During the Uplift, Gina largely freed herself from the somatic imprint of the trauma. She also came to realize that, in spite of her unconscious guilt, the problems at home were really not due to any failure on her part. She began asking herself what she wanted rather than what the internalized parents would have demanded.

Gina kept in touch with us after the Uplift and reported her progress over the next six months. She told us that the relationship techniques she'd learned enabled her to make a number of new friends she could confide in and relax with. She was spending fewer hours at work but, to her surprise, seemed to be getting more done. She'd even gone on a few dates and managed to enjoy herself.

Gina began and maintained a routine of RPMs and walking in Central Park in the mornings and on weekends with a woman who lived nearby. Throughout the day, she tried to stay aware of when she tightened certain muscles or stopped using her body fully and freely. Her physical pain and depression were mostly gone, and on the few occasions that she relapsed, she knew what to do to pull out of it.

REPATTERNING MOVEMENT

We developed Repatterning Movement exercises to enable your brain and body to explore nonhabitual ways of moving, feeling, and being. Unlike most exercise, they are not about strengthening muscles or improving aerobic capacity.

Like Feldenkrais Awareness Through Movement lessons (ATMs), RPMs clarify communication between your central nervous system and your muscles so that you find yourself moving more easily, comfortably, and well. RPMs are also powerful tools for relaxation, emotional awareness, and meditation.

The short and simple RPM included here offers a safe and gentle way to begin to explore and change your somatic program. It is designed to help you walk with more ease and pleasure and without fatigue or injury. You can do this RPM any time you wish to relieve stress and enhance your connection to your body.

You might want to do this exercise once before going out for your daily walk so that you can notice the difference it makes. After that, as part of your regular walk, take a moment to remember how it felt to rotate your pelvis and shoulders in opposite directions during the RPM. For the first five minutes of your walk, take careful note of how much movement you feel in these areas, and whether increased movement helps you walk more efficiently. If you find yourself stiffening up again, make a mental note to redo the movements in full. You may want to note these continuing observations about your body in your Walking Log.

One RPM will get the ball rolling, but if you want to continue to reprogram your brain and body, you'll need a variety of these kinds of movements. Several series of longer RPMs covering a full range of functions and areas of the body, as well as emotional and meditative themes, are available on audiotapes made by Alicia.[19] Or look for a Feldenkrais ATM class in your area.

Exercise 7 Repatterning Movement for Walking

Before you begin this exercise, you might want to record the instructions and play them back for yourself. If you do so, be sure to rerecord steps 12 through 20 (for the left side of your body) and steps 2 through 11 (the body scan, which is done near the start and again near the end).

- **Prepare a space.** Find a surface to lie on that's firm but comfortable, such as a carpet or an exercise mat. If you feel you will need a pillow or towel under your head or knees because of neck or back discomfort, have these on hand.

- **Stay within your comfort.** If you feel any strain or discomfort, take one of these four actions: (1) Stop and rest. (2) Make the movements smaller or do fewer. (3) Find a way of doing the action that eliminates the problem. (4) Do the movement in your imagination. If you are still uncomfortable after doing 2 and 3, stop and rest. Rest whenever you need to. If you find your breath getting shallower and faster, you are trying too hard.

- **Slow down.** Most of us do everything too fast, as if we were trying to please an impatient parent or teacher, which makes it harder to really feel what you're doing. Try these movements slowly at first. Then you can experiment and find your own pace.

RPM

1. Take a moment to walk around a bit. Walk more slowly than you normally do and notice what you feel. Do you feel light and easy or heavy and encumbered? How loud or soft are your footsteps? Can you feel your hips and upper body moving? Do your arms swing? Do your shoulders move as well?

2. Lie down on your back with your arms at your sides and your legs outstretched. Note your emotion as you prepare to pay attention to your body. Notice as well any thoughts that arise about your body. If they are critical or judgmental, you might ask yourself, "Whose voice is that?" Notice what you feel about the room: Does it feel large and you small or the other way around? Is it dark or light, warm or cool, friendly or entrapping? Notice the level of comfort or tension in your body: do you allow the surface to support you fully or at only a few points of contact?

3. Follow your breath. Is it long and deep or shallow and fast? Are you breathing mostly in your chest, your abdomen, or somewhere in between? Experiment with bringing your breath into different areas and changing its rhythm and depth.

4. Now bring your attention to your head. At what point does it make contact with the surface? At the center of the back of the skull or to one side? Closer to the top of the skull (so your chin feels closer to the ceiling than your forehead) or to the bottom (so the chin seems slightly tucked into your neck)?

5. Notice your neck. Where do you feel it begins at the base of your skull and where does it merge with your back?

6. Where do your shoulders make contact with the surface? How is this different for one shoulder than the other?

7. Where do your arms make full contact with the floor, and where are there spaces? Are your palms up, down, or somewhere in between? How is this different on one side than the other?

8. Follow the line of your spine, noting how the different areas of your back touch the floor or curve away from it: the upper, middle, and lower back. If you note a space between the lumbar area and the surface, where does it start and end, and how high does it feel?

9. Notice your pelvis and buttocks. Do you feel more pressure against the floor on one side than the other?

10. Moving down the body, note any space under your thighs, knees, calves, and ankles. Does one leg touch the floor differently than the other? What about your heels? Is the pressure directly behind the heels or to one side?

11. Think of one side of your body. Does it feel heavier or lighter than the other? Darker or lighter in color? Does it feel more supported by the surface or less? Is there a change in your pattern of breathing? What are your thoughts and emotions regarding your body now?

Awareness Tip: If you notice critical or judgmental thoughts, ask yourself, "Whose voice is that?"

---

12. Now roll onto your left side in a comfortable fetal position with your legs bent and one on top of the other. Place your head on your arm or, if necessary, on a pillow.

13. Begin to rock gently forward and backward, so that your right shoulder and hip roll first slightly toward the floor, then backward. This should be a small motion, perhaps a light jiggle, as if you were a child being rocked to sleep. Is this movement comforting? Experiment with the rate of movement until you find the most pleasant way. After a while, stop and rest on your side. Note any thoughts or emotion.

14. Now begin to rock again. After a few moments, stop moving the shoulders and upper body but allow the pelvis to continue to move forward and back. Don't worry about getting these movements "right." Just follow the instructions to the best of your ability without strain. Rest on your side.

15. Return to the rocking motion. After you've done this awhile, stop moving the pelvis but continue to move the upper body forward and back. Does this feel awkward or smooth?

16. Roll onto your back and rest. Which side feels closer to the floor? What has changed on the right side? On the left? Check your emotions and thoughts.

17. Come once again to your left side. Bring the right shoulder forward and at the same time bring the pelvis back. Bring both back to the upright (neutral) position. Do this a few times, slowly and gently.

18. Reverse the action, bringing the right shoulder back and the pelvis forward and then bring both back to neutral. Stop and rest.

19. Now combine the movements: bring the right shoulder forward and the pelvis back, then move the right shoulder back while bringing the pelvis forward. Explore this movement. What is the expression on your face? Smile.

20. Stop and rest on your back. Notice any changes. Which side feels closer to the floor? Heavier, fuller, darker, or lighter and airier? Which side feels more you? Notice your thoughts and emotions and compare them to the start.

Awareness Tip: Ask yourself, not "Is this right?" but "Is this the most effective and pleasurable way for me?"

---

21. Repeat these movements on the other (right) side (steps 12 through 20).

22. Rest and repeat the full body scan (steps 2 through 11).

23. Slowly—very slowly—come to sitting and then standing. Notice any differences from before you lay down. Do you feel taller or shorter? If you do notice a physical change, is there an accompanying emotional shift?

24. Now begin to walk, slowly. Do your shoulders and upper body move more than they did before? Does your pelvis rotate? If your shoulders move, do they rotate in the same direction as the pelvis or in the opposite direction? Do you feel lighter or heavier on your feet? What kind of sound do your feet make now? Is there an emotional feeling attached to this way of walking? Don't worry about whether you are walking "the right way" or not. If you are even a little bit more aware of your body, you are doing very well. If there's any internal criticism, ask yourself, "Whose voice is that?"

TAKING CARE OF YOUR BODY

It's well known that exercise not only helps keep you mentally fit but can be an antidepressant as well. In fact, according to a study by James Blumenthal, Ph.D., of Duke University, a brisk thirty-minute walk around an athletic track three times a week may be just as effective in relieving the symptoms of major depression as the standard treatment of antidepressant medications. That's why we suggested earlier that you get started on a walking regime right away.

Walking isn't the only exercise that's good for you, of course. Bicycling and swimming, for example, tend not to cause injuries. However, according to Alen Salerian, medical director of the Washington Psychiatric Center, walking may well be the best. After all, it's what our bodies were made for. Hunter-gatherer women walked and carried children, food and firewood. Their men stalked prey for long distances, then sprinted for the kill.

Research has also shown that even moderate walking can have dramatic effects in terms of keeping the brain young. How much should you do? A half hour or more of walking a day is optimal. "Even a little is good but more is better," Dr. Kristine Yaffe, a neurologist at the University of California, San Francisco, told "BBC News Online."

Despite what you may have heard or read, you'll find no magic diet or food cure for depression and anxiety. However, oily fish such as salmon, mackerel, and sardines have been found to have some benefits.

If you suffer from hypoglycemia, which is not uncommon for those with depression and anxiety, you will probably find that eating a number of small meals rather than two or three large ones will reduce or even eliminate hypoglycemia-related discomfort and mood swings. Since hunter-gatherers were mostly "grazers" rather than "gorgers," this is the way our systems digest most easily. This mode of eating can also be beneficial for irritable bowel syndrome, which often accompanies depression.

On the whole, however, the best diet for overall health is balanced and varied, with an emphasis on fresh and whole food. As with everything else relating to your body, you need to learn what works best for you.

THE BODY AND RELATIONSHIPS

As we've seen, you can do a lot to free your body from the past and make it an agent of healing rather than retraumatization. But the most important factor in this, as with all things for a human being, is relationships. Your body tightened up and adopted defensive postures in response to unsafe (unpredictable, unhappy, and so forth) childhood relationships; it can only let go of this holding in the context of safe and nurturing ones.

Every interaction you have with someone, from your spouse to your boss to a sales clerk, affects your body as well as your emotions. Remember, you have only a small number of relationship templates, and so your brain tends to slot everyone you come across into a role from the past. If you perceive a person as critical, threatening, or dismissive, your muscles and nervous system will gear up for action in the same way they did when some authority figure in your past acted that way.

If you work or live with such a person or see them frequently, these defensive patterns will be constantly reinforced. Many people can't seem to lose weight—subconsciously they see the extra body mass as a physical boundary, one that they need in the absence of more functional ones. (We'll be helping you to erect functional boundaries instead of dysfunctional ones.)

In the presence of someone you feel is gentle and supportive, on the other hand, you will probably begin to let go of your physical defenses. Let's look more closely at how to create that healing relationship environment.

MEDITATION: LOVE

Relax with me just awhile. Let me sit with you.

You tell me that there is no love for you, that there never has been. You say that all there has been is darkness and pain. You say that reaching out is pointless, for there is no one to reach out to. Your history has consisted of small and large acts of betrayal.

You tell me that your parents loved you but had no way to show it. That they protected you but knew not what protection meant.

And now you sit alone, in your room, in your chair, in your body, in your mind. No human but only the clatter of despair to keep you company.

Relax with me just awhile. Let me sit with you.

Let your mind form around the word *love*. Picture the word. Give it no characteristics. Let it be just a word, a floating image of letters, large or small, in whatever type or color you fancy.

Now, slowly picture a person who would love you. Picture a smile. Picture eyes that shine for you.

Picture a puppy who has not yet learned to fear. Picture acceptance.

Picture a flower offering its beauty to you. Picture acceptance.

Picture now a figure offering you strength and protection. Picture acceptance no matter how great your pain. Picture a firm hand to lead you.

Relax with me just awhile. Let me walk with you.

Picture now a high place to which you are gently led. Picture the wind gaining momentum as you climb. Feel it rush through your hair. Allow exhilaration. Allow yourself to reach the top of that high place. Feel your chest swell against the power of swirling currents of air. Feel safe, even here, for the hand remains in yours. Acceptance is still there.

Picture what you see looking out from that high place. Are there mountains? Is it a plain stretching to the horizon? Are there cities? Or is it dark with a sky filled with stars?

Can you feel love in this place? Can you cry your pain to the wind and demand love in return? Can you, at last, ask for love, here, in this high place where only the wind can hear you?

Your pain is the absence of love. If the wind can hear you, it can take your pain. If the wind can hear you, you can be loved.

Relax with me awhile. Let me stand with you.
Picture accepting the puppy's love.
Picture accepting the flower's beauty.
Accept the one who loves you and the smile that is yours forever.
Relax with me awhile. Let me sit with you.

PART II

STEP 3:
CREATE HEALING
RELATIONSHIPS

6

HEALING FROM THE OUTSIDE IN

◉

W e'd like to let you in on a fundamental but far-reaching secret. Once understood and put into practice in very simple and specific ways, it will trans-
form your life. *A relationship is the mutual satisfaction of need.*

The problem is that most of us don't know what our real needs are. Or if we
do, we are afraid to tell others. As a result, many of us find ourselves in relationships that do not fulfill our basic needs, and leave us feeling disempowered, isolated, frustrated, and depressed. Lacking clear boundaries and concrete guidelines
for communicating our needs, we may cut ourselves off from the very source that
could prevent and heal depression—a supportive relationship environment.

"But what if I can't make relationships?" cry some when they first hear this. "I
can't even seem to meet nice people!" The answer is that *anyone* can make good
relationships. Aside from the extremely rare exceptions of people with serious neurological or particular psychiatric problems, if you are able and motivated to read
this book, you can connect with other human beings to your mutual benefit.

However, this is something you have to *learn* to do. While we are all born with
the desire to love, be loved, and to belong, we aren't hard-wired with the skill to
make this happen. Like Peter (whom you met in Chapter 4), many of us seem to
have missed Relationships 101—and the information out there is limited and often
misleading, anyway. It's as if we are expected to instinctively grasp advanced alge-
bra or quantum physics. Plus, our inner saboteur is invested in keeping us alone
and feeling unlovable. So every time we make a mistake or get rebuffed, we say to
ourselves, "There! I *knew* I couldn't do it!"

Peter felt that way, but he found to his surprise that he actually could form supportive relationships. He put himself in circumstances where he was with other

people who shared his interests, and then he used our simple techniques to form friendships and professional networks. And so can you.

In this section, we cover the basic principles and the nitty-gritty of forming relationships that make you happy, enable you to overcome the negative programming, and conquer your depression. To start, we're going to look at someone who seemed trapped in a bad relationship and saw no hope of turning it into a good one.

Marty, a thirty-four-year-old former nurse, came to the Uplift Program after years of depression and severe chronic back and neck pain. Her attractive features and luxuriant dark hair were counteracted by her facedown, hunched-over stance and a tendency to wrap her arms around her waist. Although she had been athletic as a younger woman, she was now in so much physical pain that often she didn't leave the house at all. She had quit nursing two years earlier, after burning out on an understaffed psychiatric ward. Since then, she hadn't felt strong enough to return to work or enter training to qualify her for a new career. She'd lost contact with the friends she used to have.

Marty's husband, Stan, seemed to compete with her when she was working and criticized her for not earning money when she wasn't. He tended to raise his voice and wave his arms during arguments, which triggered the childhood trauma Marty had experienced when her father yelled and on occasion hit her mother. Marty's mother was critical, cold, and uncommunicative, expecting Marty to work hard around the house from a very early age. She made it clear that she believed her daughter was stupid and would never amount to much. When Stan was threatening, he reminded Marty of her father; when he was critical and dismissive, of her mother.

The situation was worsened by Stan's inappropriate dependency on his elderly parents, who lived nearby and made constant and unreasonable demands on both him and Marty. When they were on vacation the couple enjoyed each other's company, but when Stan re-entered his parents' ambit, his temper and need to control resurfaced. Marty's resulting sense of powerlessness and hopelessness were major factors in her depression and physical symptoms.

Like so many people, Marty did not believe she had the right to ask those around her to change. Instead, she wanted what we call the "I am a rock" solution (referring to the old Simon and Garfunkel song, "I am a rock, I am an island"). "Make me strong enough to withstand their criticism and control!" she pleaded when asked what she wanted from the Uplift.

RELATIONSHIPS AND THE BRAIN

Marty was in for a bit of a shock. One of the themes of the Uplift Program, of course, is that no matter how strong you are, you can't remain unaffected by how others treat you. Your brain responds chemically, structurally, and in terms of synaptic connections to input—and the input that matters most to you comes from other humans. You are not a rock, you are not an island, and no amount of wishing will make it so!

If you're depressed, you're particularly vulnerable to negative interactions that trigger past trauma. The amygdala tends to get flooded with emotions, the hippocampus can't sort them out properly, and the frontal cortex can't turn them off appropriately. The resulting inability to think clearly and make decisions can lock you into a downward spiral. On top of that, you are probably unconsciously re-creating similar relationships to those that caused your problems as a child and will trigger them as an adult.

You must now create a safe and supportive relationship environment that counteracts the negative aspects of your childhood. You need to put strong boundaries in place to protect yourself. These will help create new neural connections that counter the old, negative beliefs about yourself. Marty, for instance, needed a respite from the neurochemistry of crisis set off by distressing interactions with her husband and others. Within these new, functional circumstances, Marty could begin to heal from the outside in.

BOUNDARIES VERSUS BARRIERS

How can you bring about such an environment? Like Marty, you can't control the people around you; no one has that much power over someone else. You *can* control the conditions under which you will agree to any relationship.

Everybody talks about boundaries, but most people are vague about what they are or how and when to put them in place. The lack of functional boundaries is the greatest roadblock to good relationships. Without clear, acknowledged limits and requirements of the other person, you can't feel safe or empowered. Relationships become traps.

In these situations, you tend to rely on dysfunctional childhood coping mechanisms. The only way Marty felt she could defend herself from the demands and emotional abuse of her husband and parents-in-law was to become ill. If she stayed in bed, no one could require her to do anything or criticize her for getting it wrong. Even her depression was in part a way of removing herself emotionally from an intolerable situation.

However, her physical and emotional illness prevented her from forming any relationship that might help her recover. If you don't have boundaries, you erect barriers, and these eventually bring about isolation, a major factor in depression. Boundaries make relationships possible; barriers shut everyone out. Needs provide boundaries that invite people into your life—on your terms.

Of course, a traditional hunter-gatherer wouldn't have had to worry about stating needs. Members of his band would automatically have met them. Boundaries, taboos, customs, roles, and ceremonies would have been built into the band's collective memory, a never-changing system that in itself offered security and held everyone together. The market for self-help books on relationships in a hunter-gatherer band would have been slim indeed!

In such a culture, one could talk about "unconditional" love, because the *conditions* for love were already being met by this invisible underlying system. However, in our dysfunctional culture, we have to re-create a workable system from scratch. And since (again, unlike the hunter-gatherer) we each came from a different childhood environment, every pairing or group will have to work out its own agreements.

Needy Is Good

Today, much is written about the "authentic self" and everyone wants to tell you how to find it, nurture it, base your decisions upon it, move from it, or create from it. But what is your authentic self? It is the you beyond your dysfunctional programming. The you based on your genetic inheritance as a human being, which is at present probably obscured by your conditioning. It is also the you built by taking charge of your environment.

How do you fashion this new, optimistic self? Through meditation and fasting on a desert or mountaintop? No. Through beating the competition? No. Ultimately, since you are a relationship-forming creature, the real you will emerge in the context of lasting, affirming relationships. A functional you will be born as the result of insisting on getting your functional needs met. They form the basis of that mysterious creature—your authentic self.

In Western cultures we are taught to be independent and self-motivating. If you're vulnerable or depressed, you "should pull yourself up by the bootstraps" (which is obviously anatomically impossible). In the end it "all boils down to you." You must not be "too dependent" (whatever that means), or people will turn away. Above all, you must never, ever be "needy" (an affliction women seem most prone to, according to men). We have heard this refrain so many times that we called one of our workshops "Needy Is Good!"

Marty was not ecstatic when first presented with the idea that she had to create boundaries and identify her needs, not just adapt herself to abusive relationships. However, during the Uplift, her view began to change. As she began to ask herself what she really needed others to do—and not to do—she came to see that she existed for something other than responding to the whims of others. She began to think of herself as an autonomous human being.

"I'd read almost every self-help book going, and this course seemed to contradict just about all of them!" she now says. "But I began to see that none of the old ways had worked. I had thought that I'd communicated my needs, but really I'd just expressed my *feelings*. No one seemed to hear me. So when people close to me ignored my requests, I thought there was something wrong with me. My husband and in-laws just kept telling me I was too needy and demanding, and I believed them."

During the Uplift, Marty discovered that rather than being too outspoken and loud, as she had feared, she had in fact let herself be cowed. "When I became really clear about my needs, gave them with conviction, and didn't back down, everyone got pretty upset at first," she chuckles. "I called Stan on it every time he criticized me or yelled. I simply refused to see his parents, because they always made me feel bad. If I started feeling guilty or like I should give in, I called a friend and talked about it or left the house and visited her. It was just as if I were an alcoholic determined not to take that first drink!"

Needs Go Against the Program

Marty's first, daring step was when, early one evening, Stan said, "Mom's cleaner is on vacation. I said we'd go over on Saturday and tidy the place." As usual there was no discussion, no bringing Marty into the decision-making process. No asking her if she might have other plans for the weekend.

Marty's reply was a revolution, a complete break with her program: "I need you to ask me before you make decisions on my behalf." Stan was dumbfounded. For a moment he just stared at her as if he couldn't quite understand.

"But they're my parents!" he countered.

"Yes. *Your* parents. I need you not to take me for granted. By that I mean I need you not to assume that I will help out every time your parents get into a problem."

Stan began to get angry and to gesticulate, punching the air as the words tumbled from his mouth. This led to the third need:

"When you get angry and act like that, I don't feel safe. I need you to leave the room."

By giving her needs to Stan clearly and firmly, Marty began to have a real relationship with him. At first, when he felt his control over his wife threatened, he reacted predictably: he called her selfish, yelled, sulked, and tried to manipulate her by complaining to mutual friends about his wife's "callous and inexplicable" behavior. But when she persevered with her needs, he began to meet them.

And when he'd behaved differently from her father for a while, her brain finally stopped perceiving him as such. Each time she asserted herself appropriately and he complied, her self-confidence rose. She began to make neural connections around self-empowerment rather than self-effacement and around safety versus powerlessness. She began to truly grow up and to finally leave home emotionally.

Under these circumstances, and with the use of RPMs and regular walking, Marty's original health and vigor have returned. She has occasional down or worried moods, but the depression and anxiety have not returned.

Marty joined a graduate program in psychology and achieved distinction during her first year as a student, getting high honors in spite of the voices from her past that said she was stupid. She is pleased and amused when her fellow students acknowledge her role as one who speaks up for her rights and tend to follow her lead.

CODEPENDENT VERSUS INTERDEPENDENT

When we talk about getting your needs met and relying on others, we are often met with the cry, "But isn't that being codependent?" The very opposite is true. Codependency means being at the mercy of someone's addictive or dysfunctional behavior and not challenging it. Basing a relationship around healthy needs prevents codependency and also allows interdependency.

Interdependency is your natural state. It is a state in which you can rely on others to meet your needs and you don't have to battle the world alone. You are supported in every aspect of your life to be the person you want to be and to accomplish what you want to accomplish. You are empowered because you draw on the power of others who, at the very least, care for you and respect you, and at the very best, share your hopes, dreams, concerns, and goals.

When you change the basis of your relationships, you break the cycle of codependency and offer other people the opportunity to heal. You invite them into a functional interdependence.

Both Marty's and Stan's dysfunctional behaviors had played into and exacerbated their unhealthy codependency. Marty's refusal to back down seemed to have a therapeutic effect on Stan as well. His brain had perceived Marty as his mother, whom his father heavily criticized and shouted at. He became his father when he acted similarly toward Marty. When Marty stopped accepting such behavior, she ceased to play the role of his mother. His brain was forced to create a different relationship template for this new woman in his life—his wife.

An even greater shake-up occurred when Marty asked Stan to tell her what he needed of her. This was much harder for him to do than even meeting her needs. He countered with many of the typical objections including: "But she should *know* what I want! If I have to ask, where's the romance, the spontaneity, what's the point?"

AVOID SECOND-GUESSING

When someone keeps you guessing about what he needs or wants, it's a form of control. Driven by an unconscious fear of abandonment, you may well try harder to please him, but he can simply move the goalposts and ensure that you always fall short. The ongoing sense of failure can cause your self-esteem to plummet, your program to take over, and the relationship to rapidly head south.

Have you ever asked someone—your spouse or your mother-in-law, for example—what she wanted for her birthday and been answered with, "Oh, nothing much"? If you did as she asked, perhaps an anguished "You should have *known* I didn't mean it!" or pained silence was the result. Wouldn't it have been better to receive a straightforward, specific request?

Having a clear map of what the other person needs and expects can be a great relief. Once you have honestly given each other your clear and functional needs and reached a satisfactory agreement regarding what each of you will and won't do, the relationship can't fail. (We use the term "to give" someone your needs because it is a gift—the basis for a functional, lasting relationship with you.)

You don't need to fear being left if you are meeting the other person's needs. You don't need to worry about doing the wrong thing or feeling guilty, as long as you are doing what you've agreed to do. You don't need to fight or argue, as long as you stick to the accord. Guilt, fear, or arguments may have been part of your childhood and helped form your program. Once these things are removed, your dysfunctional program will lose its power.

Even Stan came to see the benefits of the needs process. "When Stan started giving *me* needs, I realized I'd been critical in my own, rather underhanded ways," admits Marty.

"Now he tells me when he feels put down and we talk about it. What's even more amazing is that he's followed my lead and begun setting boundaries with his own family. It turned out *he* didn't want to be controlled by them either; he'd just gotten caught in his program!"

Marty's relationship and depression turnaround were due to a simple but revolutionary six-part process. We'll guide you through it over the next few chapters.

SIX ACTIONS FOR CREATING HEALING RELATIONSHIPS

1. Discover your functional relationship needs in all areas of your life.
2. Prioritize needs and define your bottom line.
3. Give your needs to others. Find out their needs of you.
4. Negotiate needs and set consequences.
5. Create the three Rs in relationships: rules, roles, rituals.
6. Expand your network of lasting, strong, and supportive friendships.

7

DISCOVER YOUR
REAL NEEDS

◉

What do you want or need in a relationship? Unconsciously—at that level we all search for Dad or Mom substitutes—most people have a pretty clear idea. At another level, they usually don't have a clue. Their first answers usually involve generalities or clichés. They want their lovers to "be good looking and kind, have a sense of humor, and respect me." They want their friends to "be there for me and share my interests." People tend to be even more vague about what they would want from bosses or work associates.

Why do so many of us have trouble formulating what we need from others?

Here's a clue. As a young child, were you ever asked your opinion about anything, particularly important family decisions? Did anyone ask you what you wanted in those situations? We often ask Uplift participants these questions and out of about a hundred people, we rarely see more than five raised hands.

At first, most of us have difficulty figuring out what we really need from others because no one in those crucial early years asked us what we wanted or required. Probably our parents themselves didn't know what they needed from each other. As a result, our brains never formed the neural connections around "What do *I* really need from the people around me?" But this is exactly what you need to do if you are to recover from depression.

One client of Alicia's had an even greater impediment to just thinking about his needs. "My mother used to ask me what I wanted and no matter what I answered I'd get something else," he said. "If I said I wanted potatoes for dinner, I got rice. If I asked for a skateboard for Christmas, I got school clothes. I learned *never* to let anyone know what I really wanted, and after a while I stopped asking the question even to myself."

Being unable to express our needs doesn't mean that some of us don't cajole, manipulate, or outright control others. It just may not occur to us that it's OK to simply ask for what we want.

Many unconsciously select relationships on the basis of dysfunctional needs because we learned to do so in childhood. For example, Marty's dysfunctional need to be controlled, criticized, and yelled at was set up in her original family and later met by her husband. Since as a child her only importance came from looking after others, she continued this pattern by caring for her patients and in-laws at the expense of her own health.

To help you clarify your functional needs (and stop being controlled by your dysfunctional ones), we've identified some very specific categories and criteria. Following these will make the process simple and foolproof.

FUNCTIONAL NEEDS

The needs that will change your life are those you have of *others, not yourself.* We are not talking about a to-do list or a set of New Year's resolutions: "I need to get more exercise," "I need to stop yelling at the kids," "I need to earn more money," and so forth.

In our view, all human needs (not drives, remember) fall under only four categories: physical safety, emotional security, attention, and importance. Thinking in relation to these categories can help identify them and ensure that they are functional. It can also be very revealing. For example, when Stan couldn't tell Marty which category his need for her to take care of his parents fell under, it was a clue that the need was dysfunctional. In reality, this need reflected his own dependency and ambivalence toward them.

FOUR CATEGORIES OF NEEDS

1. Physical safety
2. Emotional security
3. Attention
4. Importance

A functional need may fit under more than one category. Marty's need that her husband not yell at her came under every category: physical safety (yelling triggered memories of father), emotional security (so she could let down her guard), attention (that wasn't the kind she wanted), and importance (yelling is not a sign of respect). Placing needs under these categories can also help mutual understanding.

Physical Safety

At first, Stan couldn't understand why Marty objected to his criticism—it was just how people (i.e., his parents) spoke to each other. He began to listen when she explained that her need not to be criticized was crucial to her physical safety.

When a small child is constantly criticized, she may feel that her caretakers regard her as not good enough. And if she's not good enough, why would the adults keep her and not abandon her, like an unwanted puppy? Any young child fears abandonment even more than abuse—think of the certain death that awaited a hunter-gatherer toddler left by the band to fend for herself. If you come away with nothing else from this book, please understand that *no one has a right to criticize you.*

"But what about *constructive* criticism?" you might ask (someone always does). We believe that there's no such thing. *Criticism is always about control.* If you want someone to do or not do something, you tell her very specifically what you want. If you wish to express an opinion, you use an "I" statement and acknowledge that you are saying something about *yourself,* not about the other person. If you want to control someone by forcing her to try harder to please you, at the same time making it impossible to do so, you criticize.

Other examples of needs under physical safety include, "Don't hit me," "Drive at the speed limit and stop at red lights," "I need you as my boss to pay me $75,000 a year with full benefits and a month vacation," and "I need you to help me distribute pamphlets for my business."

For Marty's physical safety, she asked Stan to spend one day every weekend getting their house in better shape because it was an important financial asset. She also needed him to take care of her if she became sick, by driving her to the doctor, picking up prescriptions, and preparing food.

Men in particular often have trouble identifying their physical safety needs. "I don't need anything from my wife," Mike proclaimed to his Uplift group, sitting back with his arms crossed. "I just want her to be happy."

"OK," Bob replied. "It's all right with you then if she sleeps with other men, maybe men who have AIDS?"

Mike moved to the edge of his seat. "Absolutely not!"

"And if she spent thousands of dollars on remodeling the kitchen without asking you?"

"Don't be absurd!"

"Perhaps you have some needs of your wife under physical safety after all," Bob said softly.

"Yeah, I guess so," muttered Mike.

Emotional Security

Trust is the essence of emotional security. Needs under this category might include, "I need you to do what you say you're going to do," "I need you not to lie to me," "I need you [Daddy] to take me to the ball game Saturday like you promised," or "I need you to invite me along when you and the other junior executives in our department go out for a drink after work."

During a couples' session with her husband, Howard, Joni complained that she couldn't count on him to follow through on promises, even small ones. Howard had promised to be home by 10:00 P.M. after a drink with the guys at a local bar but hadn't come home until 11:30 P.M. Joni was furious.

"I didn't notice the time," groused Howard. "So what? It's not like I was out having an affair or spending lots of money."

Howard finally understood that his wife needed to be able to rely on his word, even in seemingly inconsequential things, to feel emotionally secure. He agreed he'd call her and let her know he was going to be late if the situation arose again.

One of your most important requirements under emotional security is probably that your companion tells you what she needs of you. People who don't let you know clearly what they need of you are—perhaps unconsciously—controlling you. Not knowing what the other person needs (or that she needs you for anything) will create uncertainty, low self-esteem, and fear of abandonment. After all, if the person has no needs of you, why would she stay?

Attention

The need for attention seems obvious on the face of it, but you will probably need to think about what you really want under this category. Many people's first attention need is to "be listened to." That's fine, but what does listening really mean to you?

When Alicia first started spending time with Bob, she discovered that he sometimes continued to read the paper when she spoke to him. "You're not listening!" she accused. "Yes I am," he replied. "I can do two things at once." That stopped Alicia for about thirty seconds. "But I don't *feel* like you are," she came back. Bob saw her point and from then on either stopped reading during a conversation or arranged for them to talk later, after he had finished.

So, what does an individual need to do to make you *feel* that he's listening? This might include not walking away, looking you in the eyes, not talking over you, making noises above the level of a grunt to indicate understanding, and showing an interest by asking questions.

Howard came up with a great need under attention, one that totally surprised his wife, Joni. "I need you to come after me when I leave the room during an argument," he admitted. "After all, there's nowhere I really want to go, but once I do, I'm embarrassed and feel I have to go out driving for hours or something." It was a need Joni, who herself hated to be left alone after a fight, was happy to meet.

Other examples of needs under attention might include, "I need you to take my arm or hold my hand in public," "I need you to smile and say hello when I enter the room," and "I need you to make eye contact and nod several times during a business meeting with clients to let me know I'm doing OK."

John Gottman, author of *Seven Secrets of Successful Relationships*, studied many couples in laboratory conditions to find out exactly what made marriages work. He believes that a sensitivity in making and receiving "bids" for the partner's attention is a major factor. These bids are unique to each person but are often ignored or simply unnoticed by the receiver. We suggest that you remove the guesswork by telling your partner exactly how and when you want attention or at least giving her the code for your subtle messages.

Importance

All of us need importance and we seek it with greater or lesser success. When do you feel important? What could those around you do to help you feel more so?

"Ben never introduces me to his friends," complains his girlfriend. "I feel like I'm some sort of pariah." Praise and acknowledgment, in public or private, are basic requirements for us to feel good about ourselves.

Another fairly ubiquitous need under importance is to have a say, indeed a veto, over all decisions that involve the person or the relationship. Allie remembers when her husband, Brad, drove up to the house and proudly showed her the new Mercedes convertible he'd just bought. "We're just scraping by as it is, and it won't fit both us and the kids," she protested in horror. "But I thought you'd like it," he replied, boyishly crestfallen.

It took a while for the relationship to recover from that incident, and both Allie and Brad now see it as a turning point. After they calmed down, they realized they would have to get clear about their needs if the relationship was to work. Allie insisted Brad consult with her before making any major purchase. They now discuss any expenditure of fifty dollars or over.

We know a fourteen-year-old whose need for importance is that his mother not kiss or hug him in public and a seventy-five-year-old who asks that her adult children not make decisions about her future without consulting her.

Another client, a dedicated FBI agent who was one of the few women to rise to her level in the bureau, felt she had hit the glass ceiling. She needed her bureau head to send a memo to his supervisor in Washington, D.C., outlining her successes and suggesting a promotion.

"Telling my boss what I needed was much scarier than going undercover in a drug ring," she admitted. "But I felt really good about myself when he did it."

CRITERIA FOR FUNCTIONAL NEEDS

Needs must meet certain standards for the other person to understand and be able to meet them.

FOUR NEEDS CRITERIA

1. Action-oriented
2. Concrete
3. Appropriate
4. Doable

Action-Oriented

Needs are about *doing* or *refraining from doing*. You have no control over what someone else *thinks* or *feels*—in fact, in the short term, neither does she. There's no point in asking her to "expect," "respect," "know," "mean it," "believe," "understand," "be sensitive to," "recognize," "be happy," "have a sense of humor," "love," "desire," and so forth. If she's motivated enough, however, she can change her behavior, even if it takes work and effort. You can't expect someone not to get angry, but you can insist that she not hit or yell at you.

Actions are also measurable. Someone may not be able to hide her disappointment, but she can agree not to accuse you of causing it.

Concrete

By concrete, we mean specific, not general. People use generalities as barriers against each other. By seeming to say something without really doing so, they harm or prevent good relationships. If your life partner says she wants "love," "space," or "respect," do you know what she means? Of course not; these terms mean different things to each of us (and they are not about behavior).

Gregory Bateson, a brilliant anthropologist, pioneer in the integration of systems theory into psychology, and an early mentor of Alicia's, used to call such terms "black boxes." We all think we agree about what's really inside them, but we have no way of telling. If you don't press for specifics, you will guarantee misunderstandings down the line. In fact, if you give a need only in general terms, you can be sure that it most likely won't get met, a failure that will probably suit your inner saboteur just fine.

"Surely," you might argue, "everyone knows what is meant by *respect*." Not so. How you want respect will depend entirely on your upbringing. A client of Bob's from rural North Carolina, for instance, said he showed his son respect by belting him.

"My boy can take anything I dish out, and he knows I know it!" he said proudly. His idea of respect is not ours or probably yours either.

The harm that using generalities can cause starts in childhood. Kids are very concrete thinkers. Even metaphors or slang can be confusing and upsetting. For example, as a child, Alicia can remember being very upset by the Harry Belafonte song lyrics, "My heart is down, my head is turning around, I had to leave a little girl in Kingston Town." She worried about this child abandoned in a busy city until the truth dawned years later.

Or, were you ever told by a parent or caretaker to "sit down and be good"? Did you have the vaguest idea what was meant? A small child, eager to please, might think, "How can I do that? A moment ago Mommy said to pick up my toys and that was being good. But they're all picked up now and anyway I can't pick them up if I'm sitting down!"

If Mother had said, "Sit down in your chair at the dining room table, pick up your fork in your right hand, and don't throw food at your little sister," the child could have done so and been praised. But in many cases she didn't and the child wasn't, which does not make her a bad mother, simply one who did not have sufficient job training. But if the child often can't please her parents because she can't understand what they want, she will be set up for failure, pessimism, and depression.

Appropriate

By *appropriate* we mean that the need is fitting and realistic for the relationship. For instance, your needs of your boss are different from those of your child or life partner. "I need you to set aside an hour each day to let me talk about my feelings and concerns," is an appropriate need for a partner or even perhaps for a close friend; it is not appropriate for your ten-year-old or probably your boss.

One Uplift student had a problem understanding what was suitable behavior around her former boyfriend, who was still a friend. She constantly quizzed him on who he was seeing and even clandestinely checked his cell phone to suss out who he'd contacted. Ultimately she lost the friendship as well as the romance because of her inappropriate behavior.

It is appropriate, however, for parents to check up on who their young teenager is dating, especially if they are concerned about that person's reliability. An employer has the right to set some standards of dress code. However, when a client's husband told her to dress up during all her waking hours as if they were entertaining, Bob advised her that it was an inappropriate need. Alicia told the same thing to a client of hers whose boyfriend insisted she never wear makeup. (Had these men explained what category their needs came under and what childhood trauma lay beneath them, some compromise or at least a deeper understanding might have been reached. But that wasn't the case in either situation.)

Doable

When we say your needs should be doable, we don't mean by any particular individual. Too often, people don't articulate needs even to themselves because they believe a specific person wouldn't meet them.

An Uplift participant said that she couldn't ask her husband to keep his own clothes tidy because he never had and it was probably too late for him to start. "Are you telling me a grown, able-bodied man can't pick up his own socks?" asked Bob. Rueful, sympathetic chuckles were heard from around the room. After a moment, the woman herself joined in.

"I think there are going to be some changes from now on," she said.

When you censor your needs, you diminish your self. Instead, think, "Would a person in the position of being a boss/wife/child and so forth be *able* to meet this need?" not *want to* or even *agree to*. Actually meeting the need might require a determined effort. It might involve self-examination, therapy, a shift of priorities, memory aids like rubber bands around the wrist, perhaps even a change in job or lifestyle.

But all you need to consider is would it be *possible* for such a person?

By acknowledging what you need—even just to yourself—you are affirming who you really are. Many of us try to squeeze ourselves into the shape others want us to be, and then we wonder why we have no sense of self!

Later we'll talk about the other person's right to say "no" and the negotiation process. But for now, as you think of your needs, think only of what you need from someone and whether it is doable by a person in his situation.

PRIORITIZE YOUR NEEDS

At some point during the Uplift Program, someone inevitably asks, "What's the difference between a want and a need?" It's a good question and has probably occurred to you too. Obviously, some needs are more important than others. Prioritizing your needs will form the basis for evaluating whether you want to stay in a relationship that may not meet them all. It will also provide parameters for negotiating your needs with others and setting functional consequences.

We've developed the "traffic-light" system to help you decide which needs are simply wants and don't matter that much, which needs are important but negotiable, and which are relationship breakers. The needs are graded by zone, in order of importance, from green through orange to red.

A green-zone need is basically a want or a wish. You definitely need this to happen to meet a category of need, but the other person can go about it in many ways. Everyone's needs and alternatives will differ. For example, "I need you to remind me not to buy any candy bars when we next go to the supermarket" might be a green-zone need for someone who's trying to watch her weight but isn't really all that concerned about it. But if someone is a diabetic, the need could be in the orange zone.

An orange-zone need is one step up from green. It has some flexibility, but not a whole lot. Tanya, who has two children in elementary school, needs her boss to allow her to leave early to pick them up from school two days a week (when her mother can't do it). But in special situations, she can stay later if her supervisor lets her know a few hours ahead of time.

A red-zone need is essential to your self-esteem, personal integrity, or safety. It is the bedrock on which your recovery stands, the ultimate boundary, and a condition of the relationship. It cannot be substituted and the only negotiation will involve when and how, not if. Everyone has red-zone needs, and it's important to know yours, even if they are already being met in your current relationships. Physical abuse or the threat of it is obviously covered under red-zone needs.

Marty's red-zone needs for Stan included that he not criticize her, yell, wave his arms during arguments, or insist she visit his parents. These needs define her bottom line. Others' examples include, "I need you not to threaten to leave the relationship unless you really mean it," "I need you not to charge me for services you didn't provide," "I need you not to reduce my health benefits," and "I need you to be honest with me."

If a red-zone need is not met (and you have no agreement to do so in a reasonable amount of time), you may have to choose between staying in the relationship and your emotional health.

GETTING TO CONCRETE

When Angie was asked to think of needs for someone during the Uplift Program, she decided to start with her teenage son, who was beginning to be emotionally distant, argumentative, and was slacking off on chores. As a single mother, she was feeling increasingly frustrated and powerless. Her first need, tentatively spoken to the group, was "I need you [her son] to stop driving me crazy and to be nice to me and helpful."

"OK, let's try to break that down a bit," said Alicia. "What would he have to do or not do to stop driving you crazy?"

"He'd have to be nice to me."

"What would it look like if he were nice to you? What would he do or say?"

"Well, he'd . . . I don't know. Speak to me more."

"OK, when do you want him to speak to you?"

"Oh, anytime."

"Anytime? What if you're on the phone or in the middle of your favorite TV program?"

"No, not then . . . in the morning, maybe."

"Good! What would you like him to say in the morning?"

"I can't tell my kid when to talk to me and certainly not what to say!"

"Why shouldn't you tell him what you want?"

"It would seem . . . silly, I don't know."

"How else is he going to know what you need from him?"

"Wouldn't he just know?"

"Evidently not. So what would you like him to say in the morning?"

"Well, 'Good morning, Mom,' would be a start." (Sympathetic chuckle from the other Uplift participants, head nods from the parents among them.)

"Excellent! Anything else?"

"Well, maybe he could say when he'd be home after school or what he was doing and not just when he needed a chauffeur." (More chuckles.)

"OK, good. Now put those two really fine needs into the needs format."

" 'I need you to say "Good morning," when you come down for breakfast and tell me when you'll be home.' But it's not going to work if he says it in a surly tone, and he's often in a bad mood when he gets up."

"OK, so form a need for his tone."

"You can't tell someone what tone to use!"

"But a different tone is what you need, isn't it?"

"OK. 'I need you to say it in a pleasant tone of voice and to smile at least once during the conversation, and say "thank you" for making breakfast.' How's that?"

"Perfect!" (Applause from group.) "That's really concrete. Now what's the category?"

"Attention and . . . importance. Also emotional security, so that I don't have to be tense all morning wondering what breakfast-time will be like."

"And what zone need is it?"

"Orange, because we could negotiate some, like about exactly what he says. But being pleasant is red zone."

IDENTIFYING YOUR NEEDS

Many people find working out what they really need from others difficult at first. The following process should help. Jodhi used our techniques to identify—in concrete terms—what she really meant when she said she needed her boyfriend Jarrod to "love her," and what he would have to do or not do to make her feel loved.

GENERAL	INTERMEDIATE	CONCRETE
I need you to love me.	I need you to say you love me.	I need you to say you love me twice a day.
	I need you to hug me.	I need you to hug me when you leave and when you come home.
	I need you to call me.	I need you to call me from work every lunchtime.
	I need you to be faithful.	I need you not to flirt at parties.
		I need you not to call your ex.
		I need you to introduce me to your friends.

Jodhi saw that in fact she had several needs of Jarrod. She could now say, "I need you to love me, and by that I mean I need you to say you love me twice a day." That way she could be assured there would be no misunderstanding.

Now it's your turn. The exercise Identify Your Needs leads you through the entire seven-stage process of identifying functional needs, which you'll go through whenever you identify a need for anyone. Perhaps you'll refer to this exercise at first; then later, you'll be able to do this automatically.

EXERCISE 8 IDENTIFY YOUR NEEDS

1. Write a need for a specific person or type of person. (General)
2. What sort of things would that person have to do or not to do to meet this need? Use the phrase "I need you to" or "I need you not to." (Intermediate)
3. Clarify these needs further by specifying requirements such as how, when, how often, and so forth. (Concrete)
4. Is each of these needs appropriate to the type of relationship?
5. Is each of these needs doable by a person in her position?
6. Which of the four categories do each of these needs fall under?
7. Which of the three zones do each fall under?

LISTING YOUR NEEDS

Now that you understand the basics of identifying your needs, it's time to start listing them systematically. You might want to work out your needs for the most significant person in your life first. Or you could choose someone who isn't so important to you so that the task won't seem as daunting. You'll want to write your needs for every significant person or type of relationship (spouse, colleague, friend, and so forth) in your life soon anyway.

Writing needs, rather than just thinking about them, is very important because it gives a strong message to your brain that you deserve to have them. Also, having a written record means no one can forget them (it's amazing how many people "lose" their needs lists because of unconscious resistance). Don't forget that you can always refine and add to your needs lists over time.

Keep your needs as short and to the point as possible, without explanations or excuses. Later you may choose to discuss them with the recipient in more depth, but not now.

EXERCISE 9 NEEDS LIST

Write ten needs under each of the following categories for someone in your life:

1. Physical safety
2. Emotional security

3. Attention

4. Importance

Make a note of the zone applicable to each need (green, orange, red).

GETTING FEEDBACK

If you have any doubts or confusion about your written needs, you might want to check them with someone. This could be a friend or therapist, but it should *not* be the potential recipient. Don't ask whether she thinks these are really your needs. That's up to you. Tell her what type of person the need is for and what category it falls under. Then ask these questions: Can she understand the need (is it concrete)? Is it appropriate to the relationship? Is it doable by someone in that type of relationship, not necessarily the specific person you plan to give it to?

Tell the person giving you feedback that you want to be sure you have asked for actions and not feelings. Ask her also to check that you haven't slipped in any "to-do" lists for yourself instead of focusing on what you require from the other person. Request that she point out any apologetic asides or lengthy explanations.

As you read on and clarify your needs, you are beginning to create new neural networks in your brain, stimulating it to come up with fresh and more functional options and solutions in other areas as well. You are doing well! On to the next step.

8

THE MUTUAL EXCHANGE OF NEEDS

◉

There is no perfect time, place, or way to tell someone what you need from him, yet most popular psychology books on relationships stress finding the right time and way to talk about issues. The truth, however, is that the *what* is usually more important than the *how* or *when*. Once you have a clear understanding of your needs, or at least some of them, you know the what. Then, it's important to just give them without worrying too much about the perfect opportunity that often never comes.

This was certainly true for Leah, whose husband, Tony, had erected such emotional barriers around himself that at times it seemed he was an absent husband and father even when he was in the house. When he wasn't working, he was watching TV sports or out drinking a few beers with the guys. When he was home, he tended to make derogatory comments to Leah and the kids. His lack of support for her or the family was a strong factor in her depression.

Tony was unusually resistant to change or even talking things over. Leah told her Uplift group, "I've tried using tact and 'I language' and waiting for the right time, just like the books said to do. But he just accuses me of complaining and says no wonder he doesn't want to spend much time together if I'm always on his case. He says I should just support him, and a couples' therapist we saw agreed. But I tried that and nothing changed."

We told Leah not to worry about the how just yet, but to get to the what first. After much hard work, she came up with a very functional set of needs for her husband. As instructed, she tried not to dwell as she did so on whether Tony would meet them. But now was crunch time. Her needs weren't doing her any good hidden away in a drawer.

One Saturday afternoon, she told her Uplift group, she came into the family room and switched off the TV set. "I'm putting our relationship on the line," she told her startled husband. "It's simply not working for me. I don't want to leave you, but I can't stay anymore under these conditions. I need you not to interrupt me or leave the room as I tell you what the conditions are under which I can stay. Just listen and tell me whether you will meet these needs. I'll make my decision about what I do next based on what you say."

Leah gave Tony her most pressing red-zone needs: spending at least two hours on weekdays with her and the kids, being on time for dinner, and not criticizing or snapping at the kids. On weekends, she wanted five hours a day, but he could choose the time so that he didn't have to miss his favorite sports.

As she read her needs, her voice trembled, but she didn't stop. There were no histrionics, no accusations. At one point a tear coursed down her face, but she wiped it off with her hand and went on. Finally, she looked up at her husband. Would he yell or threaten to leave? She was so emotionally exhausted she was almost numb.

"I didn't realize it was that bad," said Tony quietly.

"Well, it's not that there haven't been some good times, but yes, it is that bad."

"You really mean it, about leaving if I don't change, don't you?"

"Honey, I really do." She swiped at another tear but did not break eye contact.

"What if I can't stop saying things you think are critical? It's the way I talk."

"Well, I can't live with it, and it's bad for the kids."

"I'll try. But what if I mess up sometimes?"

The bombast was gone; the worry was real. Leah smiled, and her tears really started to flow. But they were tears of relief. "Then you have to have a consequence, just like the kids." A quiet chuckle. "You have to take me shopping for an hour and watch me try on at least ten outfits and give me your opinion of them with no criticism of me."

"TEN OUTFITS?" Mock outrage, perhaps relief. "You drive a hard bargain, woman!"

"Maybe I'm worth it."

"Maybe you are. Now, how about bringing me some potato chips while I catch up with the game. I'll . . . uh . . . be through about five, then maybe we can . . . uh . . . take a walk with the kids or something."

The relationship wasn't in the clear yet. But Leah and Tony had just had their first genuine conversation in years, perhaps ever. And as a result of Leah's giving her red-zone needs, the long-range forecast was looking a lot better, for both the relationship and her emotional health.

THE HOW-TO OF GIVING NEEDS

The method of presenting your needs, like the content of the needs themselves, will vary widely depending on what sort of relationship you have with the person they are for. For example, you can present them either verbally or in writing, separately or all together. However, a few overall guidelines—some of which we've already mentioned—deserve repeating:

1. Whenever possible, give the needs at a quiet, calm moment, preferably before a situation they refer to arises. However, if the person has crossed your boundaries, don't be afraid to state the need then and there, regardless of circumstances, as Marty did with Stan. For example, "That's not an appropriate way to speak to me. I need you not to criticize me again." Exceptions may include the children being in the room and your physical safety being compromised. In which case, give the need at the next appropriate opportunity.

2. State your needs clearly and to the point. Don't feel required to justify them. In a close relationship where you want the other person to understand you better, you can, however, choose to say why these are your needs and how they relate to your program.

3. Needs giving is a two-way process. For important relationships you will probably have to explain what functional needs are when you ask for theirs. Don't forget to mention that these needs will form the conditions of your relationship; they aren't simply whims.

4. The needs process often encounters a resistance minefield—both on your part and theirs. Give yourself and them a timetable for the exchange, and stick to it. Make sure you keep copies of needs you both agree to meet. These contracts have a strong tendency to get lost. You also need to keep these agreements up to date, as they may change. The important thing is to start the process soon.

Stating what you need from someone can be frightening if you're not used to doing so. If you're nervous about using the "N" word, here's a tip: use the word *need* whenever possible. Whenever you buy something, inform the clerk that you "need a receipt." Tell your grocer that you "need" him to tell you which vegetables are fresh today, your friend that you "need" to change the time you were going to pick him up for the movies, or your boss that you "need" him to tell you if the deadline for a certain project changes. Make a game of it and see how many times you can say "I need you to . . . " in a single day. Stop yourself every time you sense that your tone or words are apologetic when you ask for something.

Now let's look more closely at how to exchange more significant needs with specific people in your life. In the next chapter we'll explain how you negotiate your needs and come up with agreements, or contracts.

Lover and Life Partner

If your partner is receptive, you may want to start discussing the needs process right away, describing how you think it will help you and the relationship. You can give him some examples of your needs and encourage him to think about what he needs from you. However, at some point soon you will want to present them to your partner at a more structured needs meeting.

If you and your partner are having difficulty communicating, you may want to be fully prepared with a complete needs list before you try to explain the concept. But it's essential to keep up your momentum, so if possible don't let more than a week go by after you've prepared your initial needs list before presenting it or starting to.

It's also vital to get a commitment from your partner regarding exactly when he will give you his needs list. Remember that you both can adjust these needs as the relationship progresses. The real danger is that the process might get waterlogged and sink before you solve your problems.

Do not invite your partner to help you formulate your needs or offer to do the same for him. This is one of the few things you should do on your own. Otherwise, you risk being swayed by the other person's opinion and his program. If you feel confused, get feedback from a third party instead.

To ensure that the needs meeting won't be interrupted, take steps ahead of time such as organizing a baby-sitter or turning off the phones. Make sure you have your written needs on hand.

When it comes to exchanging needs, you can decide together how many to do at a time and whether to give all of one person's needs before the other starts, or to alternate. Most couples choose the latter. After reading each need, ask first if your partner understands what you mean, and then if he will meet it (here's where some negotiation may come in). We recommend meeting weekly or once every two weeks at first to exchange and review needs.

If your partner refuses to take your needs seriously or to communicate clearly what he needs from you, there is really nothing more you can do for the relationship. He is telling you either that he doesn't want a relationship with you or that he only wants it on his terms—which he won't discuss. And you have a right to reply, "I hear you!" and make decisions based on that information.

Family in the House

For any relationship to function well, it must act more like a tribe (or hunter-gatherer band) and less like a typical, highly stressed nuclear family. Once the parents agree about meeting each other's needs, it's time to begin to lay down the rules of the house (perhaps in conjunction with other adult relatives in residence). In this way they will be acting as the band's council of elders, in effect deciding what they need other household members to do or not do.

The next step is what we playfully call a family "pow-wow"—a term we borrow from American Indians. (By the time settlers began making records of real Native Americans, many of them lived in vast tribes, even cities, which were nothing like traditional hunter-gatherer bands. But the kids will get the idea.)

During the pow-wow all household members should have the opportunity to give their views regarding the rules. They can also state their needs concerning family decisions, ranging from what time dinner is to where to go on vacation and whether to move. All opinions should be invited and considered. The pow-wow can also be a forum for exchanging needs between all house members and resolving conflicts. The kids will be much more likely to observe guidelines and buy into decisions they helped make. In the end, however, it's the tribal elders who have the last say over those for whom they're legally responsible.

Adult children and relatives should be required to abide by the house rules as a condition of living there. We know of instances in which the parents feel obliged to care for these adults but unable to stipulate their conduct around the house or apartment. They become prisoners of their own hospitality.

Family as Friends

Where grown kids or your own parents are concerned, it can be hard sometimes to distinguish between obligation and real connection. Here's a simple question: "If this person weren't related to you, would you want him as your friend?"

In a hunter-gatherer band young people are treated as apprentice adults at puberty. By the time your children (if you have any) reach their early teens, you and they should be considering your needs of each other as friends. You can offer advice and set rules of the house, but the biggest influence you'll have on their emotional development from now on is as a role model and companion, not an authority figure. And if they have been involved in needs-based decision-making for a while, they will have the emotional maturity to handle appropriate responsibility.

When relationships between parents and adult children, or between siblings or any other relatives, aren't based on the mutual satisfaction of needs, the only connection is through obligation and guilt. These lead to resentment, and that's not good for the individuals or the relationship.

Twenty-one-year-old Rachael and her mother, Ruth, discovered this the hard way. When Rachael came to the Uplift, she was full of anger and guilt over her relationship with her mother. Ruth had leaned heavily on her daughter for support ever since she divorced Rachael's father when Rachael was ten. She constantly accused her daughter of abandoning her.

"I can't bear to hear that I don't love her anymore because I didn't call her last week or because I visited my father and his new girlfriend," said Rachael. "I devoted my life to pleasing her because she always seemed more emotionally frail than me. But nothing I do is ever enough."

Rachael was aghast at first at the idea of telling her mother what she needed from her and setting boundaries. "But she's my mother!" she exclaimed. "What about unconditional love? You're supposed to be there for your parents!"

Slowly, Rachael came to understand that the relationship with her mother had to be a two-way street. Moreover, she realized that by telling her mother what she needed from her she was not being demanding, as her mother had been to her, but setting clear and appropriate boundaries.

Rachael asked her mother to brunch one Sunday and explained that she wanted to put the relationship on a more equal footing. To that end she had a number of needs: that her mother not accuse Rachael of not loving her every time she felt slighted, that she not express anger if Rachael saw her father, and that she not call Rachael's cell phone at work. Finally, she required that Ruth tell her exactly what she needed from her daughter and to agree that that would be enough.

It took a few more brunches, and a few mutual tears, but Rachael and Ruth came to an arrangement. The accusations stopped. "It's a funny thing," Rachael told the Uplift group a few months later, "I'm actually seeing my mother as much or more than I did when it was just out of obligation. But now we have more fun."

Not all family relationships are so easily resolved, of course. One of the hardest decisions many of us have to make concerns whether and to what degree to maintain adult family connections when they are harmful to us. These can involve a violent or addicted adult child, an abusive parent, rancorous siblings—the list goes on.

These situations are the tragic by-products of a dysfunctional society that creates disharmony and often does not have the resources to heal it. But just because there is no hunter-gatherer band to do its job of caring for its members does not mean that you can or must.

Friends

If a friend is very close, or has the potential to be, you will probably want to exchange needs with him in the structured process for partners described earlier. With other friends or acquaintances you can do so more casually. Needs you might have of friends could include how much time you want to spend together or communicate by phone or E-mail and who initiates these contacts, praise and lack of criticism, keeping confidences, and not breaking agreements.

For women, personal confidences are an important currency of friendship, and many of their needs revolve around how this is done. Nico was concerned that most of her friends shared a common characteristic: they didn't talk much to her about their own lives. Three in particular were supportive—almost mothering—yet she knew very little about them beyond surface things. This kept her feeling like a little girl who had no important role in their lives. During the Uplift she recognized her dysfunctional need for dependency and decided she wanted to have relationships on a more equal basis.

After writing down her needs relating to friends, she scheduled separate get-togethers with each of the three women. Over lunch or coffee, she stated that as a condition of the relationship, she needed them to tell her about their worries, hopes, and emotions.

Two of the women agreed and said they were relieved she wanted to hear about them. They had simply been overwhelmed by Nico's emotional problems and figured that their role had been to support her, not talk about themselves. The needs discussion strengthened the relationships. The third woman refused to meet her need, and Nico simply stopped contacting her.

Nico also sent an E-mail to a few more friends and informed them of the healing process she was engaged in and how they could help by meeting her needs, some of which she listed. She included a description of how to make sure needs are functional and asked them to tell her what they needed from her accordingly.

Workplace Relationships

This category includes everyone involved in your work or charity activities including your boss, subordinate colleagues, employees, clients, customers, volunteers, and service providers. Your relationship with a very close colleague or business partner will benefit enormously from the same formal needs process as with a life partner. However, sometimes a quick comment is all that's required, such as "I need you to pass on to me any information relevant to what I'm doing on this project, OK?"

Telling your boss what you need can be a bit more intimidating but very productive. Stella, a twenty-four-year-old writer for a newsmagazine, was dedicated and a perfectionist, which helped her reach a position that few people her age did. However, because of her critical, highly controlling father, she was still timid and insecure.

Unfortunately, Stella's boss was an old-school male editor who liked to bark out commands, just as her father had. Increasingly intimidated, Stella agonized over every story and had trouble handing articles in on time. Her editor became more critical, using sarcasm and insults. A lifelong tendency toward low-level depression flared into a severe bout of depression.

We encouraged her to make a needs list for her editor. Stella did and made an appointment to see him just after the weekly publication had gone to press and they were less likely to be interrupted. She brought her written needs list with her and referred to it for exact wording. She stated that she needed him to give her a more detailed brief on each story, to make time for questions, to stop making personal remarks, and to praise her when her work was good.

The editor agreed to most of her requests and their relationship improved—along with Stella's ability to meet deadlines. If she felt a comment of his was insulting or inappropriate, she told him so, even while others were in the room. Her depression lifted.

If Stella had thought about what she needed from an editor before she joined the publication and said so during her job interview, she would probably have developed a better working relationship with him from the start.

Doing a needs list for a future employer can not only help you select the right environment to work in, but it can help you land the job. This happened to Adele.

A hospital social worker, Adele left the profession to have children. When her marriage fell apart, she needed income but was depressed and insecure about her abilities, especially after being out of the workforce for so long. After attending the Uplift and doing needs work with her friends, Adele started to feel better about herself and considered returning to social work. She applied for a scholarship program that would train her to become a supervisor.

She approached the interview with some trepidation but also with a complete needs list. "At first I was apprehensive when I saw I was to be questioned by a whole panel. Fear of being judged not good enough had contributed to my depression, and now I was being interrogated by four senior staff," she recounted.

"Then I remembered my own needs. I started asking them very specific questions about the training program; what would be expected of me, what would be offered? How much clinical supervision, autonomy, and support would I get? One man on the panel started asking me what I thought should be included and thanked me for my feedback. Before I left the room, they had offered me a place and thrown in extra scholarship benefits."

Casual and New Relationships

You have needs even of casual acquaintances, from your hairdresser to the members of your housing co-op or school board to your doctor. Letting these people know what you need from them is essential to your sense of autonomy.

A server where you regularly eat can play a significant role in your well-being and optimism, particularly if he greets you by name and remembers your needs, such as just how you like your hamburger cooked and to hold the french fries. Making sure your hairdresser is clear about how much you want him to cut and what extra services you are and aren't willing to pay for is vital to your self-esteem as well as your appearance.

When is the right time to let someone know what you need from him? Immediately, just as in a job interview. This will help you discover up front which relationships will be good for you and which will simply repeat old negative patterns.

Even on a first or second date, for example, you might want to set out some basic ground rules for the potential relationship. These could include that your companion agrees to do what he says he will, like calling within the week, and not canceling your next date at the last minute.

You can even be clear about how much physical contact you prefer early on in a relationship, such as when you like someone to hold your hand or put his arm around you. You may worry that being this clear will be seen as forward or blunt at first, but most people are very grateful for being told someone's boundaries and expectations. It certainly saves a lot of misunderstanding and embarrassment. And by the way, wouldn't you like to know what *he* wants? Why not ask?

You can share some of your green-zone needs (for example, "I need you to be willing to go on long walks with me") as well as orange ("If we're going out to dinner and it's my treat, I need you to agree to go to a restaurant where the bill won't be more than fifty dollars") or red ones ("I need the people I allow into my life not to criticize me"). This will be a lot more meaningful and interesting than the usual chitchat and generalities people often hide behind. Then, as the relationship looks as if it may become important to you, you can exchange a fuller set of needs.

Attracting New Relationships

"This is all well and fine," you may say, "but how do I find this hypothetical potential friend or mate?" Single women often bemoan the fact that "there are no available men" or no "nice men," while men tend to hole up with their computers or sound systems. Venturing out to meet people can be scary, especially if you believe you'll be rejected or wind up stuck in another hurtful relationship.

Chances are, however, that the right people for you are out there, but you don't see them because you've been programmed not to. Bob calls this the "McDonald's Law of selective blindness." If you were an alien traveling on an American highway, you would probably not notice the golden arches along the route; they'd just be part of the passing blur. But say you had an encounter with a Big Mac and either loved it or hated it. The next time you saw the golden arches you would notice them.

In the same way, "nice men" or "nice women" simply may not show up on your radar. But you can circumvent this problem by making a needs list for the person you *want* to meet. As you think of real needs you might have of him or her (and, of course, write these down), you begin to make new connections around who you'd like in your life. You also diminish the pull toward the type of person who's made you miserable. At the same time you ensure that if you do meet Mr. or Ms. Wrong again, you'll find out very quickly—based on your needs.

Of course, even if you've pinpointed your target you still need to place yourself in a position where such a person might be found. Peter, for example, made a research project out of finding groups and associations of people who shared his interests and found many on the Web.

We've found clients and students have almost uncanny success in finding friends once they've made the list. Yes, they can spot suitable people once they've done so and, yes, they aren't as frightened of getting burned. But it may even be something more. After all, the brain does receive and send out electrical signals. Perhaps we actually broadcast for the type of person we want, who picks up the signal and responds. Stranger things have happened. And it's all the more reason to make sure you're sending out the right signals.

WHEN TO SAY "NO"

In some situations there's no point in telling someone what you need from him. If you are being physically or sexually abused, for example, don't mess around with a needs list, *just get out of there*. Give your needs to the police, not the perpetrator. Stay away at least until the person has received *effective* therapeutic intervention and has proven over time that he has overcome the problem. Sadly, in most cases, this means staying away for good. Both of you are probably addicted to your roles as abuser and victim, and will only trigger each other, even with good intentions.

When exchanging needs or even thinking about it, remember that as an adult you never, ever have to do something just because someone says he needs you to. "No" is arguably the most important word in any language. Being able to say "no" when appropriate is vital to your empowerment and autonomy.

But many of us have difficulty saying "no" even to little things, like doing someone a favor when it's not convenient or agreeing to do something we don't really want to. You may in the past have given in to other people's needs because you felt they were more important than your own. But this is not good for you, nor will it create a functional relationship. To be a healing force for either participant, a relationship must be founded on mutuality rather than martyrdom.

One of the hardest things for some people to learn is that you must be the most important person in your life. This does not mean the most important person in the whole world, just in your own ambit, from your own point of view. This means that you think about what you need, not try to second-guess what others want from you or sacrifice your happiness for theirs.

Being the most important person in your life doesn't mean that you are selfish, either. Selfish people are actually terribly insecure and don't feel they are important or worthy. And because they feel they don't deserve things and won't be given them, they try to snatch what they want from others. Then they live in fear that they will lose what they have. It's a very lonely, unhappy way to live. Secure people can be open and generous within the relationships they choose and the boundaries they set.

Parents sometimes feel as if their children should be the most important people in their lives rather than themselves. But you can't give what you don't have. That's as true for self-respect and importance as for anything else. If you act as if you are unimportant, your children will learn to do the same thing.

"I get it!" one student told us. "It's like on an airplane, during the pretakeoff safety lecture. The cabin crew always tells you to place an oxygen mask over your own face before attending to others in an emergency. If you can't breathe, you can't help anyone else!"

Remember that other adults also have the right to say "no" to your needs, so you don't need to feel guilty about "imposing" your requirements on them.

How do you become comfortable with acting as if you were the most important person in your life? Probably the same way you learn any new skill, from playing tennis to typing. As a piano teacher of Bob's used to intone: "Practice, practice, practice!"

9

NEGOTIATION AND CONSEQUENCES

◉

How do you negotiate relationship needs in a way that fosters mutual understanding, empowers everyone, and helps heal depression? You've already begun to lay the groundwork for successful negotiation by examining your program and being very precise about your written needs and their relative importance to you. Here's where all your hard work in putting your needs under the four categories (physical safety, emotional security, attention, and importance) and the three zones (green, orange, and red) will really pay off.

Your green-zone needs are close to a want and highly negotiable, so you can be fairly flexible about compromise here. You might want your partner to bring you flowers once a week, but if money is tight, a loving note under your breakfast cup of coffee or a home-cooked dinner with candles might do. The mechanism in this case doesn't really matter as long as the underlying category of need—for example, attention and perhaps importance—is met.

Or perhaps a colleague tells you she's snowed under at the moment and needs you to spend some extra time on a project you're working on together. You might say OK on the condition that she take on some of your duties later. If she agrees, the physical safety (and perhaps importance) needs of both of you are taken care of.

Orange-zone needs can be a bit more difficult to negotiate. The trick is to thoroughly know your program and how it relates to your needs, particularly those that stem from traumas or relationship difficulties in childhood. That helps you understand where you can compromise without getting triggered and where you can't.

An orange-zone need Alicia had of Bob when they first started living together was that he not turn on the TV news during dinner. This need came under the category of physical safety as well as attention. Newscasts were a trigger for her, since the violence and loud voices brought back her family's arguments at mealtime.

Bob wanted to meet her need, but he had a conflict. Since his savings were in the stock market, he had to keep close track of the financial news when the market was in serious flux. It was agreed that during such times, he would ask Alicia's permission to either change the dinner hour or watch the news while dinner was eaten. Since his genuine request was both empowering and something that would have never happened in her original family, it mitigated the trigger. Also, since he more than amply met her other needs for physical safety and attention, she felt less threatened in general, and many things that had been issues stopped being so.

In our case, it helps that we can talk freely about our own patterns and where in our childhood they come from. We know that neither of us would ever take advantage of this information later in an argument, as happens in some couples. Nor would either of us try to argue the other out of a real need. Talking in this way deepens our awareness of ourselves and each other and allows us to work together to explore a wide range of options for meeting each other's needs. We are genuinely pleased when one of us comes up with a new need, because it will make the other person happier and thus improve the quality of our life together.

This mutual trust and support didn't just happen, by the way; it's the result of our doing the very process we're teaching you.

You may find that the needs process brings up underlying ideological differences. A need could be concrete, appropriate, and doable, but you or your companion still doesn't want to meet it. If this happens frequently, it may point to a basic incompatibility.

If you find that you often have trouble deciding whether to agree to green- or orange-zone needs or how much to compromise, here's a useful suggestion. By now you are probably learning to listen to the voices in your head that support the dysfunctional aspects of the program. If the voices sound something like, "Well, so-and-so is making a real effort to say 'yes' to most of my needs, and this is not a red one, so it's probably OK to compromise for now and see how it goes," you're on the right track. But if you hear, "Well, it really shouldn't matter to me," "If I don't say yes, she'll get angry and maybe leave," "But I'm all she has," or "This isn't the right time. I'll put my needs aside for a bit," then you're in the thrall of your program. Instead of putting down your needs list, it may be time to put your foot down and insist on getting your needs met.

Setting Consequences

For your important needs (orange and red zones) to be taken seriously, you may have to attach consequences. It's easy to see this with children. If Mom asks four-year-old Johnny not to run in the hall, little Johnny will almost certainly do just that. And he'll look back to make sure she sees him. Why? For Johnny, the rules and boundaries represent physical safety. He needs to know that they're there, and he will test them to make sure. And that means there must be consequences if he breaks them. A functional consequence is clear and consistent (as well as not involving physical punishment, threats of abandonment, or food in the case of children).

The same may be true of your life partner, boss, or clients. If someone has been going against your needs and getting away with it, what's the incentive for her to stop? That incentive may well be clear and appropriate consequences that she can count on your applying. Remember that every act has repercussions anyway. If your needs aren't met, the anger, resentment, and sense of helplessness will either turn inward against you in the form of depression or come out in ways destructive to the relationship. It's best to give needs.

Consequences were the key for Rita, who was married to a well-off dentist who constantly criticized her. Although she was a Cordon Bleu chef and prepared a three-course gourmet meal every evening, he complained about her cooking. She was a meticulous housekeeper, but when he came home from work he would run a finger over the hall table to check for dust. She felt increasingly resentful, powerless, and depressed.

When Rita first brought up her needs, her husband nodded absently and continued to behave exactly as before. Rita decided to apply consequences. She informed her husband that every time he criticized her she would refuse to have sex with him for a week. Since in spite of his behavior their marriage was a passionate one, this was a real deprivation. She also decreed that for every time he denigrated her cooking or housecleaning he would have to get his own dinner.

A few weeks later, Rita joined her Uplift group looking like the prototypical post-canary cat. "My husband is tripping over himself to pay attention to me," she reported. "When I sit down, he asks me if I want a cushion for my back. Instead of criticizing me, he actually says how great the food is. Oh, and our sex life . . . well, it's never been better." Rita had demonstrated that she was important. As a result, her husband stopped taking her for granted and began to treat her as such.

Ideally, consequences should be part of the negotiating process and agreed to by both parties. They can function as humorous or even enjoyable reminders of green or orange needs that the receiver is willing to meet but sometimes slips up on.

Leonard, who was somewhat of a workaholic, forgot his wife's birthday because of a work deadline. Chagrined, he agreed to arrange an extra week's vacation for the two of them within the next two months. They both enjoyed and benefited from the time away.

Leonard also had a tendency to come home later than he said he would. Since his wife had told him she needed him to be home for dinner at 7:00 or call to let her know, he had made an effort to change, for the most part successfully. For those times when he relapsed, however, the agreed-upon consequence was that he take her out to dinner soon. His wife would stand gleefully by the door, checking her watch, when it looked as though he might be late. Laughter and a dinner out replaced recriminations and, in truth, both came to enjoy the ritual.

IF THEY "CAN'T" MEET YOUR NEEDS

What happens if someone says she can't meet your orange- or red-zone needs because she doesn't believe the behavior is changeable? If she expresses willingness but worries about not getting it perfect—as Tony did when Leah put their relationship on the line—you can give her consequences to help maintain motivation, as Leah did. But if she says she can't meet a need that is concrete, appropriate, and doable, then she may have a problem. (If she says the problem is your neediness, she's trying to control you.) Her inner saboteur may be in charge, but that doesn't mean you have to accept the result. It does mean she may have to put in some hard work to change, just as you've been doing.

When Ned's long-term gambling addiction nearly wiped out the last of the family savings, his wife, Natalie, threatened to leave unless he took immediate steps to get the problem under control. They worked out a plan in which he put total power over all of the family finances into her hands, including checkbooks and credit cards, starting immediately. He would then enter a three-month daytime treatment program for gambling addicts and agree to do whatever he was told there, including attending meetings of Gamblers Anonymous on an ongoing basis. If he stayed away from gambling for a year, she would recommit to the relationship, but if he "slipped" before that, she would start divorce proceedings and take custody of the children.

Although the inability to control behaviors such as criticism or yelling may seem less dramatic than Ned's gambling addiction, the results can be just as devastating emotionally. If someone claims that she can't either meet your functional needs or give you hers, you have a right to insist that she does whatever is required so that she can. Her willingness to do what it takes to change must be just as great as Ned's and the recovery plan just as concrete. This may involve seeking professional assistance or joining a self-help group, doing the exercises in this book and reexamining her priorities, reorganizing her life in accordance with new goals, or all of the preceding.

An agreement must be reached that includes three factors: (1) a set of behaviors that will lead to change, such as therapy or quitting a job that simply requires too much of the family; (2) a precise timetable for execution and completion; and (3) a process of monitoring and review to make sure the person keeps her word.

DEFINING THE BOTTOM LINE

"Should I stay in this relationship?" is a common question from people who come to us. No one can make that decision for you. But the needs process can help you reach your own conclusion.

Ultimately, if someone won't meet your red-zone needs or a significant number of orange ones or draw up a plan you can agree to for doing so and stick to it, you don't have the basis for a functional relationship. Continuing to interact will most probably prevent you from healing and getting the relationships and life you really want.

We sometimes get asked, what's the difference between a consequence and an ultimatum? Usually the assumption behind this question is that an ultimatum is a bad thing. This is true only if the person hasn't thought through the reasons for the ultimatum and isn't ready to live with the result. These sorts of ultimatums are often no more than threats that aren't carried out. Crying wolf often in this way can harm you. It traps you further in a dysfunctional relationship because the other person will, of course, take less and less notice of your needs, safe in the assumption that she has nothing to lose anyway.

The ultimate consequence, of course, is leaving the relationship. If you feel that this is not a possibility for you because of guilt, the children, a childhood fear of abandonment, or concern about financial loss, you are not in a functional relationship. You are in jail and the other person is your jailor.

After fruitlessly broaching the subject of her needs to her husband of thirty-five years, Patricia became convinced that he simply wasn't willing to make the necessary effort to meet even the smallest of them. He refused, for example, to praise her, to give her a say in decisions regarding their finances, or even to cook nonspicy food that did not hurt her stomach. The last straw came when he sold off the memory-laden vacation house that had been in her family for generations without consulting her. At sixty-four years old, Patricia was terrified of leaving the relationship with her outgoing, prominent, and financially astute husband. But she was even more afraid, as she put it, of "being so controlled that I never really have a life."

To the surprise of her married friends, Patricia found her postdivorce life satisfying and exhilarating, if sometimes challenging. She had to move from their large waterfront home to an apartment and learn to deal with all the administrative issues he'd handled, from car, home, and health insurance to taxes. On the plus side, however, she could spend more time on her real passion—music—and both her voice teaching and composing thrived.

STAYING ON TRACK

You now have all the information you need to begin to do the needs process with everyone in your life. Don't forget to keep working on new needs lists for different people.

You might like to keep a Needs Log of your experiences as you begin to give needs to others and ask them to give you theirs. Here is an excerpt from the Needs Log that Leah, who was married to the recalcitrant Tony, wrote:

Wednesday: Needs meeting with Tony. Very productive. I gave him five more needs, including that he praise me once a day, and he agreed. Told me he needed half an hour to himself with no demands when he gets home. I said fine. Since the two of us started talking about our relationship and spending more time together I feel so much better.

Thursday: Told Tony I needed him to clean out the garage. He said yes. I then asked him to do it this weekend. He said he felt nagged but would do it anyway.

Monday: Tony didn't clean garage. My feeling was betrayed; felt he had lied to me. I said he'd made a relationship statement to the effect that I wasn't important to him. He said I was important, and that he'd get around to it next Saturday. I said that'd be great but if he doesn't do it, he has to take me for a romantic weekend away instead of going on a fishing trip with the guys next month. He reluctantly agreed.

Monday: He cleaned the garage. And told me he'd made a booking for us at a nice bed-and-breakfast (on a different weekend from his trip with the guys). I felt wonderful!

Another person's log might include:

Thursday: I used the phrase "I need you to" for the first time when asking the convenience store clerk for a receipt. Felt nervous using the phrase, but empowered when he agreed.

Friday: My boss said he needed me to finish the reports before next Monday P.M. I said no because that would involve working over the weekend. Felt afraid he would get angry like my father would have. Felt much better when my boss wasn't. He even asked me how long I needed to finish the reports.

To keep track of the needs process with important people in your life, you'll need a record of the following for each one: your needs list for them, the needs you both finally agree to, consequences, problems that come up which involve adding or renegotiating needs, and instances in which needs aren't met.

EXERCISE 10 NEEDS LOG

Describe when and how you give your needs and other people give you theirs; what it feels like, and how your program participates in the process or tries to prevent it.

You might want to do this for at least a week, but feel free to do so longer.

10

RULES, ROLES, AND RITUALS

◉

All relationships are based on what we call the "three Rs," each of which are vital to preventing or healing depression. The three Rs are not the old "reading, 'riting, and 'rithmetic"; they are *rules*, *roles*, and *rituals*. Every relationship must be governed by rules, which provide emotional security and physical safety. Each person must have a role to belong and not fear abandonment. And a group (be it two or fifty) must have rituals to bind it together and give it identity.

Hunter-gatherer bands required all three of these elements to stay together and function cohesively. And so do modern groups, from the family to the corporation to a country. In the animal kingdom, a hunting pack of dogs establishes clear rules with each other, bees have well-defined roles between the queen and the drones, and no one who has ever seen the intricate mating dance of the male whooping crane could fail to be awed by the ritual.

Having or not having the three Rs can make the difference between a happy, healthy couple or community, and a group plagued by problems; between a thriving, harmonious company and a bankrupt one. Although the need for the three Rs is encoded in our genes, the details of the rules, roles, and rituals themselves are learned.

A FAMILY IN CHAOS

In our experience, relationships that lack concretely defined rules, clear and agreed-on roles, or maintained rituals are at risk. The people within them tend to be controlling, fearful, pessimistic, depressed, anxious, or some combination of these.

How are functional rules, roles, and rituals introduced into an existing but troubled family? It's really not that difficult.

Maryann and Rod had been married for seven years, most of them stormy and difficult. She was a successful commercial artist and the main breadwinner of the family. He had had a number of careers and was presently working as sales manager for a local furniture manufacturer. Rod also suffered from acute depression and a deep sense of pessimism. The household included two children, five-year-old Amy and Brett, now a nineteen-year-old college freshman, from Maryann's prior marriage.

The couple had undergone a number of trial separations but always came back together "for the sake of the children." Amy, a highly verbal and intelligent but troubled child, had developed a number of dysfunctional behavioral traits to try to divert her parents' focus away from each other and minimize the fighting. These included tantrums, incessant talking, and an absolute refusal to eat anything except hot dogs for lunch and dinner.

Brett was falling behind at college and thinking of quitting. He stayed away from the house for days at a time without letting anyone know where he was, and when he was home, he shut himself up in his room.

Maryann and Rod both agreed that Amy was spoiled and Brett was in trouble, though they each accused the other of causing the problems or making them worse.

"It's you who lets Amy watch TV until midnight," he threw at her.

"It's you who lets her talk over both of us," she retorted.

"She got that from Brett who was doing it well before I came along!" And so on through each of the initial sessions the couple had with Bob.

Clearly this household had no rules and no boundaries.

RULES OF THE HOUSE

Both Rod and Maryann had come from highly abusive homes that had—as is usually the case in such families—no consistent and agreed-upon rules or boundaries. As with many couples, they reacted badly to the thought of having a fixed set of rules. Each saw rules as being too constraining, too formal. Each professed worry that the spontaneity would go out of their relationship. Often these expressed fears are code for "I don't want to give up control," or "I don't want to be controlled."

Maryann was afraid that Rod would be the one to lay down the law; he was afraid of losing his freedom. But they agreed to try.

"How do we know what the rules should be?" asked Maryann. Bob introduced them to the concepts of the council of elders, the needs meeting, and the family pow-wow.

"As the council of elders you must first agree on needs of each other you can meet," explained Bob. "Then you can think about what you need the kids to do or not do. Many of these needs will become the basis of the house rules. The house rules have to be obeyed by everyone."

Bob guided the couple through their first few needs meetings, in which a number of grievances were aired. "You've been seeing altogether too much of Kathy," Maryann accused her husband.

"She's my assistant, for heaven's sake!"

"But all those business trips with her! You don't tell me how long you're going away for. And you never called me, not even once! What am I supposed to think?"

"You are so suspicious! No wonder I don't want to tell you things!" Rod retorted.

Bob made the T-sign to signal a time-out. He suggested that in any discussion, when things got heated, one of the participants should signal a time-out. During this time there would be a count to thirty while tempers cooled.

"What are your needs around business trips?" Bob asked Maryann when the meeting resumed.

"I need him not to go anywhere with Kathy," she said.

"Then I might as well walk out of the job right away," Rod replied. Another time-out.

The couple finally agreed that Maryann's need came from a fear of abandonment, which would be allayed if Rod gave her the phone number of where they would be staying and the length of their stay. He also promised to call in daily while he was away.

Bob asked the couple whether this need was one that would apply to all members of the household. They agreed that it was. Bob designated the need as a rule of the house and asked them to write it down and initial it, which they did. Over the rest of the session the couple came up with a number of needs for each other that could apply as house rules.

At the next needs meeting with Bob, the couple worked on rules for the kids. "What should be Amy's bedtime? What are your needs around that?" Bob asked.

Rod and Maryann both needed her to be in bed by eight, and that rule was written down. And so it went until their house rules looked something like this:

1. Children under seven shall be in bed by 8:00 P.M.

2. Criticism of any member of the family is not allowed.

3. Everyone in the house will eat dinner together. The TV will be off. Snacks may be eaten in the kitchen but nowhere else.

4. No outsiders will be invited into the house without the advance agreement of both Rod and Maryann. (Rod and Brett had been guilty of last-minute announcements that "I've asked so-and-so to dinner, I hope you don't mind.")

5. Each family member over eighteen will have the right of veto over any decisions that affect them or the family generally.

6. Any member of the family going away for more than a day must say where they can be reached and call in twice a day.

7. Each family member shall have the right to a daily time to themselves of one hour.

8. No swearing.

9. These rules will be reviewed every six months.

Maryann said she'd type up the list and stick it on the refrigerator. "What happens if someone breaks the rules?" asked Rod.

That, Bob explained, gets decided in the pow-wow.

THE FAMILY POW-WOW

The pow-wow happens when the other members of the tribe get invited to join the elders' needs meeting. The house rules are discussed and altered if necessary. Consequences for rule breaking are agreed on, as are the roles of various family members.

Again, Bob facilitated during a few family sessions. At first Rod and Maryann were worried that Amy couldn't sit through the meeting.

"I'm sure she won't," Bob agreed. "But at this stage the important thing is for her to know she has the right to sit in on these family meetings and to be asked her opinion, especially about consequences. That way she'll begin to learn how to participate in decision making and the needs process. You don't have to do what she says, although she might have some good ideas. Just listen to her. Afterward, she can go off and play."

First the family discussed the rules that Rod and Maryann had come up with so far. After some negotiating (Brett agreed to call home once a day, but not twice, and that was acceptable to his parents), they discussed consequences for different family members for breaking each of the rules.

Since Amy would probably tire of the process soon, Bob began with her.

"What do you think should happen to you if you refuse to go to bed on time?" Bob asked her.

She thought for a minute before saying, "I should be punished!"

"OK," Bob replied. "Tell me how."

She giggled and then looked at Bob with great seriousness and made a series of gestures that indicated that she should be hung until dead.

"I don't think so, dear," said Maryann. "We'd miss you. What about no cartoons on Saturday morning?"

Amy looked horrified. She could tolerate hanging since she had no real idea of death, but no cartoons?!

"No bedtime story then!" she proffered and immediately left to play.

It was decided that if Rod, Maryann, or Brett criticized any family member, they had to put ten dollars into a jar. The money would go toward a weekend at the beach or skiing. And so on through the list.

The rules having been established, the next job of the pow-wow was to work out the roles that members of the household should have.

GENDER ROLES

Our choice of roles both at home and at work are influenced, to some extent, by our genetically based legacy from all those millennia as hunter-gatherers. In those days the major roles of men and women were fairly clear-cut: men hunted and women gathered and did most of the child raising. Who washed the dishes or vacuumed the carpet wasn't an issue (no dishes, no carpet). This seems to have worked fairly well, probably because the roles were regarded as equally important and economically valuable.

Of course, it's true that gender roles have never been absolute and that even among our cousins the chimpanzees there are females who hunt, but they are exceptions and hunting is overwhelmingly a male activity. (According to University of Southern California anthropology professor Craig Stanford, hunting among chimps is not primarily about food gathering, though animal protein plays an important role in their diets, but rather about gaining mates and socializing. That hunting is primarily about socializing Bob can attest to from his own observations of modern hunter-gatherers.)

For modern humans as well, genetics and environment play an intricate dance. They can produce men who adore the business of diaper-changing and women who are happy in the corporate "hunting" environment.

The problem is that, since we ceased to be hunter-gatherers, we have come to denigrate one set of roles and elevate others. Physical power (vital for territorial protection, farming, and animal husbandry) and single-minded dedication to objectives, which are male characteristics of the hunter in our species, have been elevated. The warmth, empathy, and understanding that are essential for child rearing and intimate emotional relationships have been belittled.

Yet the biological rational for gender-based roles still exists. All this makes it difficult to sort out fulfilling, well-acknowledged roles for all members of the family.

HOUSE ROLES

In any relationship, it's important for each person to have a clearly defined role or set of roles he is comfortable with, whether these are traditional gender roles or not. Each person must also receive acknowledgment and praise for performing that role.

Rod's depression was heightened by the fact that he felt ashamed of not being the major breadwinner. This was made worse by the fact that his wife's home-based business was thriving, with constant phone calls and customers coming to the house even on weekends. He resented that often he was pressed into answering the phone or helping out as an unpaid assistant. He also felt he was being asked to do too much of the housework and child minding.

Maryann felt that Rod was trying to force her to give up or scale back her business so that she would become a dependent housewife as her mother had been (while her father had affairs and then divorced her). Her fears of abandonment and lack of importance were triggered. She responded by working longer hours and insisting that Rod do even more of the housework.

Brett complained that he was always being asked to do things, which was one reason he often stayed away.

Bob suggested that the family members each make a list of what they thought their roles were. Often people's ideas of what they do and others' observations are different, and this was the case. Rod, Brett, and Maryann were each convinced that they did most of the housework. "You can't all be doing all the vacuuming!" Bob commented.

The roles they each thought they carried out were:

MARYANN	ROD	BRETT
Co-breadwinner	Secondary breadwinner	Baby-sitter
Household management	Household management	Household cleaning
Chief child-rearer	Co-child-rearer	
Household cleaning	Household cleaning	
Meal preparer	Meal preparer	
Child chauffeur	Maryann's unpaid secretary	
	Maryann's client-entertaining manager	

Amy didn't know what her jobs were. But she quickly got the idea (sort of) when asked what she'd like to do. The discussion turned to roles that each actually wanted. The lists became:

MARYANN	ROD	AMY
Co-breadwinner	Co-breadwinner	Licking the frosting bowl
Household finances	House repairs	Petting the dog
Chief child-rearer	Secondary child-rearer	Picking raspberries
Co–meal preparer	Co–meal preparer	Greeting Dad at the door
	Client-entertaining manager	

The interesting thing is that these revised lists are closer to the roles of early hunter-gatherers. As far as Brett was concerned, what emerged was that he didn't want any role in the household at all. For the first time, he admitted that he wanted to stop going to college full-time and perhaps take only evening classes. He planned to find a job and move into a shared house with some of his friends (the equivalent of joining the other young men in a hunter-gatherer band).

NEGOTIATING TASKS

Bob asked Maryann and Rod (not Brett, because he was no longer a member of the household, and not Amy since she was already watching cartoons in another room) to concretize their desired roles by writing down exactly what actions they thought each role entailed and which of these they would be willing to do. For example, to Maryann, being the co–meal preparer meant planning, shopping for, and cooking meals two nights a week. Rod was willing to cook three nights a week but hated to shop. She agreed to buy the groceries. The other two nights they decided to go out to eat or do take-out.

Neither wanted to do the laundry or clean house. However, they accepted the necessity of doing so, given their modern lifestyle. The household chores were divided between each of them, including Amy. She was given the jobs (in addition to those on her list) of making her bed, picking up after herself, choosing her clothes for school the evening before, and setting the table.

They also discussed the issues underlying how they felt about their roles. Rod said that he needed praise and recognition for his work. Maryann agreed to give him these so long as he didn't belittle her. She also said that she really appreciated his help with her work. He said he was happy to continue as long as she took him into the decision-making process of the business. Shortly after, he joined her company as a partner in charge of marketing.

Amy said she wanted Mom to bake more cakes so she could lick more frosting. Both of her parents agreed instantly that cake once every two weeks was enough. Bob pointed out that this was one of the few opportunities for Amy to do things with her mother. Maryann decided not to work on weekends and suggested she and her daughter go out every Saturday together to look for raspberries or firewood, depending on the season.

The pow-wows had already begun to work. Brett had declared his independence, and the adults had agreed on the rules and roles of the tribe. Since their disputes were far fewer and less acrimonious, Amy was able to let go of most of her attention-seeking antics. She jealously guarded her own newly minted roles.

Role Choice

Roles aren't just important in families; they are the basis of *all* relationships. Knowing that you have a clear role in any group will help prevent or eliminate feelings of rejection and abandonment. Among a group of women friends, for example, the roles may be the organizer, listener, empathizer, or caterer. Often you find that a role has been assigned to you almost by default and it may not be one you would have chosen.

In some groups, these roles are fluid, with different people taking them on at different times. In other groups, the roles become fixed. To be an effective antidepressant, a role must elicit praise and be acknowledged as important.

What are your roles within each relationship or group? The exercise Choosing Your Roles will help you decide what you want them to be.

EXERCISE 11 CHOOSING YOUR ROLES

1. List your current roles within various groups such as colleagues, family, friends, church congregations, clubs, and associations.
2. List the actions you think each role entails.
3. Mark those you feel comfortable with. Mark those in which you get praise and acknowledgment.
4. List the roles you would prefer to have within each group.
5. Describe the steps you could take to achieve the roles you would like.

The Bonding Power of Ritual

The last of the Rs is ritual—also an essential component of our relationships and our lives. People often think of rituals in terms of spirituality and religious ceremonies.

The famous French thinker Arnold Van Gennep in his seminal 1908 work, *Rites of Passage*, said that rituals are basically and universally cultural. Rituals only get mixed up with religion when a religion permeates a culture for a historical period. In other words we need a ritual for marriage, for example, but the form it takes will be swayed by the religious beliefs and customs of the time. Thus marriage ceremonies will be different in Roman times or in thirteenth-century Catholic Europe or even modern China. But the bonding mechanism that ritual provides will be constant.

In our society, some of the most obvious secular rituals include sending Christmas cards, singing the national anthem at school assemblies, toasting success with champagne, gathering in Times Square on New Year's Eve, giving birthday presents, graduation ceremonies, and synchronized cheers at football games. Unfortunately, many of these, particularly around holidays and gift giving, have become largely commercialized. Certainly their power as a bonding mechanism is greatly diminished.

Rituals permeate our own daily lives, often without our classifying them as such. We are marvelously inventive in making them up. We each create rituals about going to bed, waking up, eating, exercise, and sex. We use them to invest the ordinary with significance. For example, the two of us go for a walk every lunchtime, no matter where we are in the world, and use the time to discuss not only what is going on in our professional lives, but also to muse about nature, spirituality, and personal problems.

When they thought about it, Maryann and Rod came up with a number of existing family rituals—saying grace before the evening meal was one—and they invented others as their relationship strengthened. If they had had a disagreement and one wanted to reestablish closeness, he would tap his chest over his heart and then his partner's, twice. This was the silent code for "I love you." When one wanted to be rescued from a dull conversation at a gathering with neighbors, he made sure no one else was looking and crossed his eyes. Good news was celebrated in pleasant weather with a picnic that always included deviled eggs (the recipe came from Maryann's grandmother) and a jug of local cider.

Even Amy got in on the act, inventing the "Ig and Wort" game, which she insisted on playing with Rod every evening before bedtime. She would chase him around the house pretending to be a terrible creature called a Wort. A Wort is very bad. Rod would insist that she was an Ig, which is very good and can't chase people. Amy would catalogue all the terrible things she'd done during the day that prove that she was a Wort, and Rod would list all the good things she did, indicating her essential iggishness. An Ig can't chase people, but Worts can. In the end the ritual dictated that he always lost and was chased.

As a bonding ritual, the Ig and Wort game is perfect.

AWARENESS, CONSENT, AND REPETITION

The essential difference between ritual and habit or custom is summed up by David E. Cortesi in his book *Secular Wholeness: A Skeptic's Path to a Richer Life.* He says, "I think the difference between a ritual act and a habitual one lies in awareness and assent. An act becomes a ritual for you when you perform it with conscious awareness of its symbolic and emotional meaning, and with willing assent to those meanings. Unless you act with both awareness and assent, your act is merely a habit (if it is unique to you) or a custom (if you share it with others)."

Habits can be helpful, neutral, or actually damaging. However, they are always unconscious and unquestioned, and thus can reinforce the program. When habits become compulsions, they can interfere with one's life and relationships. Henry was an obsessive-compulsive disorder (OCD) sufferer who could not bear to have anything out of place. He even made sure that all the labels on the jars in the cupboard faced out and was irritated with his wife if they didn't. With Henry, this routine was about safety and about controlling his own anger. Until his anger had been dealt with, the routines that he had developed around keeping order were a matter of compulsion not choice. These were not relationship-enhancing rituals!

However, rituals that are undertaken and repeated regularly with mutual consent strongly reinforce feelings of safety. In doing the ritualized acts together, the members of the band, group, business, community, or family reaffirm their shared oneness, sense of belonging, continuity, and stasis.

In the Uplift Program we begin each day or meeting with a chant, in spite of a few groans and good-natured mutterings of "not the chant again!" However, we receive far more complaints if we ever forget it.

The chant—collected by an anthropologist friend of ours—comes from a small band of hunter-gatherers in the Kalahari. It goes as follows (with a rough translation):

Bonekeke falabaa
With the members of my tribe
(Click) tokemetaan izeeta
I am never alone
Yo tefawa eh!
We together are the all
Yo tefawa eh, hey!
We together are the all, yes!

The chant begins slowly and then gets faster and faster and louder and louder and ends with loud banging on whatever instruments we have at hand.

In the exercise Create Your Own Rituals you can evaluate your existing rituals and formulate new ones.

EXERCISE 12 CREATE YOUR OWN RITUALS

1. List some of the rituals that are already carried out within your relationships or groups. State how often these occur and how often you participate. Remember that a functional ritual involves awareness, repetition, and assent.

2. Do these rituals function well for you? Describe the changes you would like to see, including frequency, to add most fully to your sense of connection, belonging, and safety.

3. Create some new rituals and write down the activities in detail so that others can understand and follow them.

4. Discuss these ideas with your friends and invite them to share theirs. Bring these agreed-upon changes or new rituals into your lives on a regular basis.

BUILDING A
SUPPORTIVE TRIBE

◉

Imagine what it might feel like to be surrounded in everything you do and everywhere you go by people you could count on to be supportive, share your goals, and let you know how important you are in their lives. Men and women who survive crises or battle together sometimes describe that sort of absolute mutual confidence and camaraderie, but it all too soon disappears when the situation changes. Our hunter-gatherer ancestors, as we've seen, thrived in and relied totally upon this mutually sustaining environment. And we believe that, for economic and safety reasons if nothing else, society will eventually move back in this direction.

So far, we've been nudging you in the direction of making all your relationships—whether they be as a couple, family, friends, colleagues, or even casual acquaintances—more like hunter-gatherer bands. Now we're going to invite you to explore new ways of expanding your nexus of relationships to bring them even more in line with this ideal.

Our definition of a functional modern-day band (or "community," "tribe," or whatever you wish to call it) is a group of people who share a common purpose or outlook on life and who agree to abide by a set of rules based on their real needs.

BEYOND THE NUCLEAR FAMILY

To allow yourself the many advantages of such a nexus of supportive relationships, you may need to re-examine some of your beliefs around the nuclear family. If you're part of a couple or family with children, do you feel duty bound to put all your relationship energies into your partner or kids? If you're single, do you neglect your friends once a romantic partner enters the picture?

We don't mean to downplay the beauty and wonder of marriage or romantic partnerships. We ourselves have been exceptionally happily married for nearly two decades and have worked together closely for much of that time. Our friends tease us gently when we express considerable hesitation at spending any time apart, whether it be for lunch or professional engagements. We make no secret of our ongoing love and physical affection for each other.

In spite of our inter-reliance, we understand that the *isolated* couple, with or without children, cannot fulfill all the needs of both parties. Even rewarding work, unless it is the source of strong attachments, can't solve the problem.

In hunter-gatherer tribes, women carried out most of their activities in the company of other women, and men did the same with other men. Today as well, many women particularly enjoy doing some things together such as shopping or window-shopping and sharing personal experiences, gossip, and emotions. Men commonly participate in or watch sports together or discuss stocks or electronic gadgets.

A man or woman can be trained to take on the role of a same-gender friend, and for many modern couples this process is essential, if somewhat awkward at first. Bob, for instance, knows how to give Alicia the empathy she needs. However (like many men with the women in their lives), he still agonizes if she has a problem he can't solve. With practice, over time he has even learned to shop with her and appraise her outfits. And she listens closely to his daily account of the stock bargains he's bagged. But this does not preclude needing same-gender friends.

Your children will also benefit greatly from spending time with functional adults other than the immediate or even extended family. This is most beneficial when there are no more than one or two children per adult. It does not refer to the usual school or day-care situation in which a few adults care for a large number of children. Being around a variety of grown-ups provides more attention and also a range of role models.

If you're depressed, which probably also means you're often tired and apathetic, you may feel that the last thing you want to do is venture out into the world and meet new people. However, now that you've learned our foolproof techniques, you don't have the excuse that you can't make new friends! You can start gradually; even just smiling at people on your daily walk will help break through the resistance.

But in the end, you will have to at least poke windows through the walls you have built around you and then doors to let people in. You cannot afford to stay isolated. The way out of suffering—the only way—is through connection. So how do you begin to bring more supportive people into your life and perhaps that of your family, given the many restrictions of time and distance most of us face?

Joining with Others

You can start this process with a very simple question. What can I do with others, be it tasks or for relaxation, that I usually do alone or just with family? Human beings create community by doing things together. (Think of how people even congregate to meditate!) Walking, child minding, grocery shopping, or running errands with a friend are all opportunities to chat while you both accomplish necessary projects. So is commuting together to work, whether you share a ride or catch the same train or bus; taking classes jointly; or even starting a business together.

You might think that entertaining requires a lot of preparation or expense, but you can get together for a meal without either. The next time you're going out for a quick bite or bringing home take-out, why not call a friend or two and ask if they're up for joining you? Or throw together a quick supper and let your guests know you need an early night. A friend of ours designates Monday evenings as "potluck" night, and friends drop by with food to share.

In addition to bringing people together, buying as a group can save time and money and, in some cases, be environmentally sound. It's not unusual for people to jointly buy food in bulk, purchase investment properties, or share the expenses of boats and vacation homes.

Neighbors can also share tools, lawn mowers, and gardening equipment; clothes washers and dryers; storage freezers; and sporting gear. People who work at home can jointly purchase expensive office equipment, such as high-resolution printers, copiers, digital cameras, and laminating machines. The exercise Shared Activities can help you think of opportunities to spend more time with others.

EXERCISE 13 SHARED ACTIVITIES

1. List some activities that could be enhanced if you did them with others.
2. List the people you might want to invite to join you.
3. If you can't think of a particular person, write down steps you might take to find someone who would share these interests. For example, if you want to start a walking group, why not put up a notice in a health-food or sports store? If a reading group, talk to your local bookstore.
4. Discuss the activities with candidates and carry them out.

GROUP RULES AND BOUNDARIES

While selectively adding more people to your life offers greater opportunities to get your needs met, it also increases the potential for misunderstandings and conflict. Many people are anxious about relationships in general and relationships with more than one person at a time in particular. This is probably because group situations—from the dinner table to the classroom—weren't comfortable for them as children. You will need to be especially clear about your needs when interacting with larger numbers of people, as they will be your boundaries.

Groups that engage in certain activities will have specific needs, rules, and roles regarding those pursuits. A wilderness camping club, for example, should work out safety guidelines and a roster concerning who cooks, puts up the tents, gathers firewood, and so forth. A food co-op requires clear agreements around the responsibilities and rights of members; neighbors sharing a lawn mower and leaf-blower need to agree up front about who uses what when, maintenance guidelines, and who is responsible for equipment upkeep.

Although engaging in activities together is vital to building community, what you do is less important than who you choose to do it with. When deciding who among current or potential friends you want to spend more time with or bring into your inner circle, let your needs guide you. (If you haven't made a needs list for friends or members of certain groups, now is the time!) Choose only those who already meet a majority of your needs or agree to do so.

Of course, even if someone agrees to meet your needs, you may still not like her or want her in your life. And you probably don't want to jump into a committed relationship on the basis of one or two conversations, even if they're about needs. Just as romantic relationships take time to develop, so do deep friendships. You'll probably find yourself being very selective about who you wish to engage in the needs process with. Just as you will want to be selective about the groups you join. After all, if a group isn't meeting your needs, why stay?

LIVING TOGETHER

Student co-ops and other shared-housing arrangements are increasing, according to Laird Schaub, executive secretary of the Fellowship for Intentional Communities, an organization that has compiled a database of three thousand groups around the world and publishes a directory.

A friend of ours, Nadia, wanted to turn her share-house into a real community when she discovered that most of her current friends—including the woman she sublet a room in her house to—did not meet her needs. This situation had contributed to her depression.

Nadia asked her housemate, who was unpleasant and refused to even discuss their difficulties, to move out. She then advertised for two people to share her living space, but in a very different way than she had ever done before. She stipulated that applicants demonstrate a commitment to collective living by engaging in group activities and abiding by house rules. She wrote a needs list for potential housemates and worked out house rules based on them. She then handed the written rules of the house to people who came for interviews and explained that they were the conditions for joining the house.

Nadia's needs included some fairly standard group-house rules, such as no drugs on the premises, prompt rent payment, and sharing of expenses and chores. She included less standard requirements, such as attending monthly needs meetings and a weekly house dinner, addressing issues directly when they arose, and letting at least one housemate know if they were going to spend the night out.

Nadia's first "catch" was Simone, a woman she met who already had a place to stay but was so delighted by Nadia's idea of a needs-based community that she agreed to join. Together, they interviewed the rest of the applicants and soon invited a young man who was a musician into the fold.

Somewhat to their surprise, no one rejected their vision. Those who decided not to join the household did so for reasons having nothing to do with their concept, and one of those asked for copies of Nadia's rules of the house to apply to other situations. One woman, who didn't join because she decided she had to live closer to work, became a friend of the group and unofficial "tribe member" anyway. Other friends and later partners began to attend the house dinners. Many became involved in the house garden and reaped their reward with enough vegetables to reduce their food bills. Inspired, they started an informal food co-op and even took overseas vacations together.

Although not bound by all the original rules of the house (such as chores and reporting in regularly), the larger, nonresidential band also used the needs process to resolve disputes and guide their decisions as a group. They agreed on a set of collective goals: to have fun, seek out new and innovative ways to save money and live more ecologically, and to meet each other's needs under the four categories.

Nadia's solution may well not be yours. But you have lots of options for living more closely with others. Besides creating your own live-in community, you can, of course, join an existing one.

HEALTHY COMMUNITY

"Intentional" communities are on the rise, particularly in the United States but also in Canada, Great Britain, Germany, and Australia. Students seem to be most enthusiastic about collective living (perhaps because it's cheap). Other groups range from cohousing communities (numbering about 60 in the United States as we write this but with another 150 in various stages of development) that share land but not necessarily a common vision or other possessions, to income-sharing groups (far fewer in number) whose commitment is more inclusive. Many are spiritually based, and almost all espouse ecological values.

"Of all the aspiring intentional communities that started in the 1990s, it's my impression that about 10 percent survived," says Diana Christian, author of *Creating a Life Together: Practical Tools to Grow Ecovillages and Intentional Communities*. "Sometimes this happened because of logistical problems, such as the very real difficulty of gathering enough capital and getting local planning approval. But most people disband because of internal conflict. All those dreams and good intentions too often wind up as heartbreak and lawsuits."

Although this saddens us, we're not surprised. Very few people understand how to resolve conflicts and arrive at consensus in any situation, much less the intense conditions of living together. Most of the problem arrives from people thinking that one joint idea, such as "wouldn't it be great to share land and common areas," can be the basis of real unity.

But a really cohesive entity evolves over time because of joint visions and goals. We encountered one group who had spent three years trying to purchase land together in Connecticut for cohousing but found, somewhat late in the game, that they really shared little common ground in terms of values or commitment.

The organizers invited us to attend one of their regular planning meetings in which the members discussed the status of the project and tried to reach agreement on how they would actually live. That evening's topic was meal preparation and dining together. In accordance with their tradition so far, the group agreed not to prepare anything that would offend anyone. However, many had stringent and non-negotiable dietary restrictions, including low calorie, low cholesterol, vegetarian, macrobiotic, and kosher. It seemed to us that the only thing members would actually achieve together would be weight loss.

What these well-meaning people certainly wouldn't achieve, without a powerful vision to unify the group, was a community that added to the pleasure and personal growth of all.

It seems to us that three main criteria exist for a successful and healing community. Not surprisingly, these would have been met in any hunter-gatherer band.

1. The community is about *doing*, rather than just *being* a community. Traditional activities would have included rites, dancing, storytelling, and other pursuits as well as what we think of as work. Modern examples of joint activities could include exploring ecological living alternatives and agriculture, cultivating members' creativity, or being a clearinghouse for information on human rights.

2. Members hold similar interests, beliefs, values, and customs, including shared goals, rituals, and codes of conduct. (Of course, ideally all decisions and relationships would be based on an ongoing needs process.)

3. The community evolves naturally, from the ground up. A vital, supportive band emerges as the result of people wanting to be together, because they enjoy each other's company and feel they can achieve their goals better together than alone.

BUILDING A GROUP VISION

You don't have to sell the family home and join a collective to heal from depression or find happiness. You do need to reassess your current relationships, including those within groups or associations you belong to, to ensure they meet your needs and provide functional rules, roles, and rituals. At the same time, you can use these elements to widen your circle of supportive friends.

In the exercise Create a Vision for Your Tribe, you can begin to build the foundation for a really functional nexus of people. Your vision can be centered on an activity or range of pursuits you all enjoy, a cause, or a set of beliefs.

The creation of a harmonious group based on a shared vision and the functional needs of those within it is a step toward not only healing your own depression, but establishing a saner world. It is within these sorts of bands that people can rediscover their humanity. And being fully human means living in interdependence with others, not violence or war, altruism not selfishness, and generosity not greed.

EXERCISE 14 CREATE A VISION FOR YOUR TRIBE

Write a vision for your tribe. How would its members meet your needs? What could you do together that would add to your enjoyment or purpose or bring you closer to your goals? Write in as much detail as you can. Don't forget to include functional rules, roles, and rituals.

When you have finished, read it to some of your friends. Find out what ideas and desires they have for a more cohesive association.

MEDITATION: TRIBE

Sit comfortably in a chair, this meditation is not for lying down. Close your eyes and let your mind picture the painted desert of Arizona.

Imagine you are a Hopi Indian hunter squatting at the edge of your mesa, gazing out over the treeless plain at sunset. You watch as the gullies at the bottom of the hill fill with dark and become the doorways to the world below.

Behind you in the village you can hear the cries of children at play and you can picture the women making meals and the men exchanging ideas in the smokehouse.

Before you the rocks and sky dance together exchanging hues and in the distance a lone coyote howls his greeting to the moon.

As evening gently falls you can see the lightning of dry storms too distant for the sound to reach you.

While you watch the world go grey and silver, children's voices die down and only the crickets can be heard.

It is as if the land were going to sleep under your gaze. As if the Spirit had closed her eyes and given the role of watching Her creation to you.

You wonder, then, what it is to be human. What it is to be a member of your species, of your tribe, of your family. When you hunt, you and the other hunters are of one mind and that mind encompasses your dogs or your falcon.

When you dance, you and the dancers are of one mind.

When you love, you and your lover are of one mind.

When you sing the praises of the Spirit, you and the Spirit are of one mind.

When you sing and you hunt and you dance and you love, it is good to be of one mind.

The moon gives you a shadow, and that shadow is part of you and yet also of the moon. You and the moon are one.

You remain there on the edge of the mesa lost in wonderings, between this world and the Spirit. Feeling Her sleeping presence over all.

Behind you men have come to be with you, to sit with you, murmuring a chant. Your mind expands. Community.

The Spirit softly replies to the chant.

I am the Earth.

I am the Sky.
I am All There Is.
Community.
You leave the mesa and return to your own body, to your own room. You open your eyes.

PART III

Value
Happiness

STEP 4:
ELEVATE YOUR
SELF-ESTEEM

◉

Contrary to what the advertising industry would have you believe, self-esteem, like value happiness, can't be bought. Like much else that we have discussed, your sense of self can fall prey to the false dictates of your childhood program.

Take Janet, for example, a stockbroker who works for a small regional brokerage house. She has a number of loyal investors and is well respected within her firm. However, all her life she has suffered from a very low sense of self-worth and recurrent bouts of depression. When she first came to Bob, she was on high doses of antidepressants.

"No matter what I have or achieve, it's never really good enough. The problem is me," she said during her first session. For example, her house was too small and in the wrong location (she'd moved quite a few times because the house was always wrong). None of the holiday destinations that her boyfriend suggested was ever right. The clothes she could afford were rarely suitable. Her job wasn't prestigious enough. Her income—which exceeded $150,000 a year—was too little.

Janet's parents had been intensely critical of her. Her father (who was the CEO of a major corporation) saw worth as based solely on the trappings of wealth and influence. In his view, success came only from having an important position in a major corporation and the income that went with it. He was caught in the modern tendency to define himself in terms of "I am what I earn," "I am my job," and "I am what I own."

Janet had taken on many of her father's attitudes but never had her father's financial resources. Yet, to her internalized parental voice, self-worth equaled a level of financial success and power unachievable by her or almost anyone else. The early criticism she received had certainly driven out any idea that she could be worthwhile for herself.

FALSE VALUES

Our society, through the media and especially advertising, teaches a false idea of self-esteem. Our social status depends largely on having possessions, particularly money. This idea has no basis within our evolutionary heritage and is highly dysfunctional.

According to University of Rochester psychology professor Richard Ryan, self-worth that relies on possessions or power is transient and requires constant reinforcement. Yet the erroneous idea that you are what you own is the hallmark of our consumerist society, and in a way the whole edifice of our economic system is based upon this lie. So you are fighting a lot of vested interests in trying to counter this lie within yourself.

Another problem with the "I am what I own" scenario is that it's ultimately deeply pessimistic. It's based on the shifting sands of what others will admire us for having. This admiration, most of us subconsciously believe, will make us feel safer and more acceptable to our peers. Yet no amount of possessions will really create that safety, love, or sense of worth. The euphoria of acquisition rapidly dissipates into pessimism as we realize that what we have just acquired isn't enough. It'll never be enough.

The same is true of power over others and achievements; they will simply never be enough. Nor, as poets, mystics, and philosophers down the ages have tried to tell us, can you count on them. Life is too complex and subject to interdependent variables for that.

SELF-WORTH IS SUBJECTIVE

The classical view of self-esteem was formulated in the nineteenth century by the psychologist William James. He proposed that a person's self-esteem is a function of the gap between his level of aspiration and his level of performance. James expressed this idea as an equation: self-esteem equals success divided by ambitions.

(Don't worry too much about the math on this one.) In other words, you feel good about yourself if you're very successful at what you do and have correspondingly low aspirations. Conversely, you feel bad when your success level is low in relation to your aspirations.

To have a lasting sense of self-esteem, therefore, your goals, at least your short- to medium-term goals, must be realistically achievable. The problem is that we acquire our ideas of what we can or ought to achieve, like everything else, from the outside, usually from our parents.

More recently, psychologists have seen self-esteem in terms of an individual's perception of her rank among her peers or social attention holding power (SAHP). Yet as we've seen, SAHP is extremely subjective; it relies on what we think other people think of us. This makes us very vulnerable because first, we may be wrong (our programs would see to that) and second, these people's values may not be ones we really want to be judged by.

ESTEEM FROM THE OUTSIDE IN

Unfortunately, a number of self-help authors take an opposite view, saying essentially that you have to find self-worth from within and not rely on what others think of you. That if you just alter the way you think, the external reality will be less important.

Many cognitive behavioral therapists state that depression, anxiety, and anger do not actually result from bad things that happen to you but from the way you perceive those events. They call changing the way that you think about what happens to you "reframing."

Putting a positive spin on things is great, but the way you perceive situations is the result of childhood experiences embedded in your subconscious that cannot be changed simply by conscious reframing. Nor can you control the effect an event will have on your brain and central nervous system by a mere application of logic.

Because of this, guilt is often the result of attempting to reframe unpleasant events in this way. "I ought to be able to just let it go," clients say, "But I just can't. There must be something really wrong with me!"

Most people's goals and aspirations are the result of other people's values and expectations in their childhood. For example, little Johnny's father thinks his son ought to be on the tennis A team, as he himself was in his youth. Little Johnny will try his best to live up to his father's aspiration. But if he fails, his sense of self will plummet because he has adopted his father's goal for him as his own and believes his worth depends upon it.

Johnny's self-esteem will only be revived if his father, or a father surrogate, can convince him that he is worthwhile even if he's not on the A team. He must come to see that the original goal of being on the A team was not his at all. It might even have been impossible for him to compete at that level, because either his physique or temperament just wasn't right for champion-quality tennis. Recent research has hinted that temperament itself may be genetically based. Johnny may not have inherited his father's temperament, which was obviously suited to the game, but his mother's, which may not have been. This would make it even more absurd for him to try to emulate his father's tennis prowess.

Johnny needs to externalize the negative belief ("I'm only good if I get on the A team") by seeing it as his father's and not his. Only then can he distance himself from it and stop feeling a failure for not fulfilling his father's aspirations.

Self-esteem comes from achieving goals you have set for yourself after you've learned to step back from the program-generated "oughts" and "shoulds." You will need other people who you can really trust to help you question your perceptual framework and build a new one.

Lasting self-esteem comes from harmonious interactions with others. It comes from surrounding yourself with people who, by their actions and particularly by their praise, demonstrate that they value you and appreciate being with you. It comes through being with people who are prepared to meet your needs.

ELEVATE YOUR SELF-ESTEEM

We've outlined six simple actions that, if you follow them, are guaranteed to significantly bolster your self-esteem.

Action 1: Search Out Negative Beliefs

Your unconscious negative assumptions are powerful blocks to self-worth. You've already probably identified a good many of them in Chapter 4, in which we introduced you to your inner saboteur. You might want to review what you wrote in the exercise Behavioral Patterns and Beliefs where you were asked to identify your self-

SIX ACTIONS TO ELEVATE YOUR SELF-ESTEEM
1. Search out negative self-beliefs.
2. Give the negative voices a name.
3. Stop self-deprecating remarks.
4. Ask others to "call" self-deprecating comments.
5. Don't accept put-downs.
6. Elicit praise.

defeating behaviors and beliefs. (If you didn't do the exercise, now would be a good time!)

Perhaps a few additional misconceptions about yourself occur to you. These may be ones that were so deep-seated that they were invisible to you. They may also involve societal assumptions you haven't yet questioned. Do you feel, for instance, that your self-worth relies only on your accomplishments or what you can buy? Do you believe or feel something like: "No one would marry someone with an income like mine," "I'm only worthwhile if I hold an important position in a prestigious firm," "I can't invite people to the house because the furniture is shabby," or "I can't leave the house without makeup"?

Action 2: Give the Negative Voices a Name

To successfully combat a belief that reinforces your low self-esteem, it's not enough to simply label it false. You can recognize the faulty logic inherent in an idea such as "I'm not lovable unless I'm perfect," but that doesn't make it go away. Assigning a name or face to the belief can help you externalize it and empower you to resist its influence.

In the exercise Identify the Sabotaging Voice in Chapter 4, you looked at the origins of some of your negative beliefs. Now do the same for any others that occur to you. For every negative self-belief, ask yourself "Whose voice is that?" and "Which significant adult in my childhood might have held such a belief or said such a thing about me or acted in such a way as to make me feel it?"

It's important to remember that just because you hold a belief doesn't mean it's yours. Your negative ideas about yourself may have been reinforced by subsequent experiences. But these situations were largely created by your program to perpetuate your negative beliefs.

If you can't work out whose voice is behind a negative belief, you can make up a person and ascribe it to that fictitious identity. For example, "I can't remember who said I was a bad person, but I realize I wasn't born with this belief. It must have been Archibald or Esmeralda" (or any other name you can think of).

Action 3: Stop Self-Deprecating Remarks

We all do it. We make little asides that put ourselves down, such as "Oh, silly me!" "This may sound off the wall but . . . ," or "There I go again!" They seem so innocuous, so harmless, so reeking of modesty as to be almost endearing, and in some people they may be. Those are the lucky ones who have a high level of self-esteem, are not depressed, and whose overall outlook is optimistic. They can perhaps afford this kind of modesty. You can't.

These types of remarks reinforce your own negative beliefs—your brain believes you. And if you tell others enough times how dumb, clumsy, incompetent, and so forth you are, they also will probably come to take you at your word.

Such remarks can also be a request for reassurance. "I'm too fat" is really a plea to be told you're not. You are calling out for someone to deny the belief or the fear, to help you rid yourself of it because you can't defeat it on your own.

Bob remembers a client who made more than twenty self-deprecating remarks during the first fifteen minutes of his session. Clearly, the man had a severe self-esteem problem. These remarks not only flagged his low self-esteem but reinforced and perpetuated his depression.

In the next session, Bob gently pulled the man up each time he made a negative comment about himself. Bob asked questions like "Who in your childhood made you feel like that?" or "Who said you were stupid?" After a while the client learned to stop himself before making such a comment or at least laugh and say ruefully, "There I go again! That's Mother and it's not true!"

You must realize that you cannot be optimistic or have a positive sense of self-worth when you are constantly putting yourself down. It's important to break this self-destructive habit and maintain vigilance in your battle against the flood of early negativity.

Your efforts are similar to that of the U.S. Army Corps of Engineers in its battle to contain the great Mississippi River. The Corps builds levees and diversions to make sure that the river doesn't overflow its banks and swamp vast acres of farm-land and even urban centers. Usually they do the job. But when rain or a spring thaw is particularly heavy in the Black Hills of South Dakota, water surges into the Missouri and then the Mississippi River, causing local or even widespread flooding in the Mississippi basin. Levees have to be repaired, diversionary canals redug, and the river, once more, tamed.

In the same way, you may be able to keep the negative aspects of your program at bay during normal times but become overwhelmed when you are subjected to powerful triggers. The number of self-deprecating remarks you make can be an indicator that your defenses against the program need shoring up.

A Log of Self-Deprecating Remarks will help you keep track of these types of comments. Note the remark, the context, your feeling, and the significant adult whose voice is behind the belief. Here's an example:

Remark: "You may think this is stupid but . . . "

Context: I was making a comment about the company's marketing plan at a staff meeting.

Feeling: I was unsure of how what I was going to say would be received. I was nervous since the company brass was present. I didn't want to look foolish. I was waiting for the put-down.

Voice: Sam, my older brother who always scoffed at my ideas.

You will need to keep up this log for a week or so or until noticing these comments becomes second nature and you are well on the way to stopping them altogether.

EXERCISE 15 LOG OF SELF-DEPRECATING REMARKS

Keep a record of all the self-deprecating remarks you make. Note self-derogatory thoughts as well, since they can be as damaging as the words actually uttered.

Write down also the context and feelings you had at the time and whose voice the comment reflected. Remember that the remarks will originate from significant adults in childhood and refer to something they said, believed, or implied by their actions.

Action 4: Ask Others to "Call" Self-Deprecating Comments

No matter how alert you try to be regarding such comments, some may still slip by unnoticed because you are so used to saying them. They have become part of your speech pattern, part of your "modest personality" perhaps, so you will need to enlist friends, family, and even coworkers in the cause of your self-worth. Their job will be to remind you every time you put yourself down. You'll probably be surprised how many times you get "called" in this way. At first it might even be annoying to find that your conversations with these designated watchdogs are interrupted every time you put yourself down. But after a while you will stop, and it will be worth it. This request is not an excuse for them to criticize you or play therapist. All you're asking them to do is to respectfully draw attention to your self-deprecating comments.

Oddly, most of those who suffer from low self-esteem seem to think that people will reject them if they ask for help. In fact, the reverse is probably the case. We'd bet that your real friends will be perfectly willing to assist you as they get to feel altruistic at very little cost to themselves. And it helps to cement the bond between you.

Ideally, you should engage those who could use some help with their own self-esteem. Make a joint pact with them to catch each other's self-critical remarks. You may both find yourselves laughing at how frequently and with what inventiveness you put yourselves down. Catching each other's slips can often be done in a loving manner. "That's no way to talk about my wife!" chides one woman's husband gently when she says something self-derogatory.

We encourage Uplift participants to help each other in this way, and the process becomes one of the binding rituals of the groups. Recently Dave was sharing some of his problems around giving needs to his wife in a follow-up Uplift group. "It's always the way with me," he said. "I chicken out. I guess that just shows how cowardly I am." An instantaneous and affirming response was heard from the rest of the group.

"I don't believe you're a coward!" said the person sitting next to him.

"Who called you a coward?" someone else caroled out from the other side of the room.

"My father!" replied Dave. "There he is again! Get out of my head, Dad!"

When Dave first did the Uplift, he was deeply depressed and with a self-esteem rating near zero. He felt incapable of getting a job (he had been unemployed for several years) and his marriage was on the point of breakup. By the time this incident happened, he was pretty well depression-free, he had a job, and he was working on straightening out his relationships. He puts his progress down largely to the group constantly pulling him up in this way.

"It made me realize how deeply entrenched my lack of self-esteem really was and I got very determined to make it better," he says. "I still slip up sometimes, but it's rare." Dave is by no means unusual in finding mutual support around this step to be essential.

At this point it's a good idea to write a list of all the people you can engage as fellow guardians of your recovery and for whom you may be able to do the same in the exercise Self-Criticism Feedback. You might even ask them to read this section of the book so that you're all on the same track.

Remember to be very clear about how you want your collaborators to give you feedback. It can be with a respectful comment of their own, a signal, or even a cough; it *can't* be in a form that strikes you as critical or controlling.

EXERCISE 16 SELF-CRITICISM FEEDBACK

1. Write a list of all the people you can enlist to catch your self-deprecating comments.
2. Write down how you would like each person to let you know that you've just put yourself down.
3. Ask the people on your list to assist you in this way. Ask those for whom you feel it would be appropriate if they would like you to do the same for them.

Action 5: Don't Accept Put-Downs

Some people delight in aiming put-downs at others and some seem to attract this sort of behavior. It's as if some of us with low self-esteem wear a large target just waiting for the arrows of negative remarks.

Sometimes these put-downs are dressed up as jest and are accompanied by phrases such as "I was just teasing," "I wasn't really serious," "Hey, can't you take a joke?" or "You're pretty thin-skinned, aren't you?" The intention is always the same—to try to bolster their own self-esteem at your expense. The trouble is that, like self-criticism, these remarks reaffirm your lack of self-esteem and your pessimism about your abilities and your future.

Remember, just as there is no such thing as constructive criticism, there is never a negative remark that is only a joke. Just as criticism has to be countered, so do negative "jokes" and demeaning teasing, none of which you should accept.

In most cases, a simple "that's not funny" or "I need you not to make those kinds of remarks" ought to be sufficient. If the person won't stop, he is making a relationship statement. He is saying that the only terms under which he will have a relationship with you is as a controller and that he reserves the right to use you as the foil for his own lack of self-esteem. That is not a situation you want to remain in.

Andrew's colleague Gavin constantly baited and criticized him. Gavin made snide comments about Andrew's age (he'd just turned forty), his divorce, and his work. Andrew told Gavin that he needed him to stop making these comments and that if Gavin didn't, he would make a complaint to their supervisor. Gavin reluctantly agreed but was slow to stop. Andrew called Gavin on it every time he made a critical comment. The baiting finally ceased.

Action 6: Elicit Praise

The final step to self-esteem is perhaps the most difficult, especially if you come from a household where criticism was rife and praise thin on the ground. But praise is one of the most potent tools for jacking up your self-esteem.

Especially if you're not used to receiving praise, you have to learn to ask for it, indeed, to expect it. Many people tell us they feel awkward asking others to say nice things about them and they wind up making all sorts of excuses for why this shouldn't happen. "Praise should come naturally," they say, "It should come from the heart." Or "If I ask for praise, how do I know that it's genuine?"

These are all valid concerns and you have no way of knowing for sure whether someone means it or not. You could, of course, hook him up to an fMRI machine and do a quick brain scan to ascertain the truth, but that would expensive, cumbersome, and essentially unproductive. In the end, simply the fact that he's willing to praise you consistently shows that he cares and thinks you're worth having in his life.

And yes, praise should come naturally. But often it doesn't. Many people are stingy with compliments merely because these were so rare in their original families or even at school. Some people tell us that they actually don't know how to phrase praise, either to give it to others or to suggest ways that others could praise them, because they haven't heard it much! You *shouldn't* have to ask for praise, but in this society you *must*.

There are two kinds of praise: praise for what you do and praise for being you. Both are necessary for self-esteem. A child who is only praised for what he does will grow up trying to do more and more and nothing will ever be enough. He will probably see himself as a failure, even if he becomes world famous.

Kristina, originally from Finland, had had a very critical workaholic engineer father and an emotionally absent mother. The only praise she ever got was for her academic prowess. While still at school, she won a number of science prizes and even had an experiment she devised carried on one of the shuttle missions. She went on to get a Ph.D. in physics and at twenty-five was one of the stars in a scientific think-tank with numerous specialist articles to her credit.

But it was never enough. She saw herself as a fraud and a failure. Her relationships were a mess. She believed that no one could possibly like her.

Cheryl, an Australian client of Bob's, had the opposite problem. Growing up, Cheryl had been exclusively praised for her pretty face, slim figure, and fashion sense. She was her father's "shining jewel." No one lauded her for anything she did, including schoolwork, sports, or hobbies. As a result, she focused on nothing except her appearance. She married a wealthy man considerably older than herself who regarded her solely as a social adornment. Cheryl felt dissatisfied and useless yet unable to achieve anything.

Both Cheryl and Kristina were praised but only given one kind of praise. This lopsidedness led to their misery and lack of self-esteem. They both did eventually escape their doldrums by seeking out and finding people who gave them praise for both aspects of themselves—what they did and who they were.

People tend to be slightly freer with the "what you do" praise than they are with the "who you are" variety, and the former is somewhat easier to ask for. At work "I need you to tell me when you think I'm doing a good job" is really not an inappropriate or difficult request. If you're not getting recognition for doing something well, ask for it.

Praising a person for who he is isn't so difficult once someone gets the idea. "What a wonderful woman I have!" Bob exclaims to Alicia on a regular basis, alternating with "How did I get so lucky to have such a fantastic wife?" At first Alicia found she was uncomfortable with such compliments. After all, she hadn't *done* anything to deserve them! (Praise for anything was very scarce in her family of origin.) However, she came first to tolerate, then enjoy, and finally to expect and rely upon this warm and steady stream of approval. And her self-esteem went from zero to good because of it.

You can ask for praise by telling your spouse, "I need you to compliment me every day," or "I need you to tell me why you like being with me." Need for this kind of praise is every bit as valid as for the "doing" variety.

If someone says, "But you should *know* I find you beautiful" (or the equivalent), stick to your guns. A person with low self-esteem doesn't know anything of the sort. In fact, he assumes the opposite.

You may discover that as you receive praise on a regular basis, you find yourself habitually looking for opportunities to compliment others. They in turn catch the habit. A culture of praise can grow up to replace a climate of indifference or even criticism within a group, whether it be a family or a corporation.

"But I don't *know* anyone I could ask to praise me," objected one client, a divorced and reclusive software developer who worked at home. Finally, he came up with the New York waitress whose table he always sat at for lunch. Outgoing and sympathetic, she was happy to respond to his request that she say something nice about him every day. This broke the ice and soon he was seeking out other opportunities to talk to people.

The exercise Eliciting Praise will help you understand the role of praise (or the lack of it) in your childhood and how it may correspond to areas of confidence and competence or the lack of it today. It will also help you plan how to go about getting the praise you need and deserve.

EXERCISE 17 ELICITING PRAISE

1. Write down what you were praised for in your early years and who did so. Note which things you were praised for related to what you did and which concerned who you were. Were you predominantly praised for doing or being? If you can't remember any praise, note that too.

2. Write down what you're praised for now and by whom. What things are you praised for now that you were also praised for as a child?

3. Describe accomplishments or aspects of yourself you would like to be praised for now.

4. Write down who you would like to praise you for these things now and how.

13

Step 5:
Uncover Your
Competence

◉

Sit for a moment and think of your job, friendships, and family. Think of the things you do in each of those realms.

Which actions are the most satisfying—which give you a deep-down sense of pleasure? Not transient feel-good sensations, but a sense that you are really good at these things, and because of that, you are more worthwhile for having done them. For some people, and you may be one of them, the answer is none or very few.

One of the main components of satisfaction in life is what is called a "sense of competence." It's difficult to feel any lasting self-esteem without it. Indeed, when researchers at the University of Missouri set out to identify the satisfying elements of satisfying events, a sense of competence turned out to be high on the list.

What is a sense of competence, this important component of value happiness? How can you get it? It is the inner knowledge that you do some things really well, such as raising your children to be happy and healthy people, painting exquisite watercolors of local scenes, making things that other people find beautiful or useful, or even perhaps heading a large corporation.

How do you know that you do these things well? Simple: other people tell you that you do. There is probably no universally agreed objective test of competence in most areas of life. "Doing well" shifts with time: job requirements, standards of performance, and aesthetic criteria are all social constructs and subject to revision. Lucky the hunter-gatherer whose life and what was required of her remained the same for more than two million years.

We are relationship-forming animals, as we have said often before, which means that your sense of self relies upon others. If they say you are good at something, the chances are that you will feel competent at it. Of course, you will want to study and hone your skills to acquire a certain expertise and to some extent you can rely on the internalized standards you've learned. But only people with personality disorders like schizoid personalities believe they alone know the absolute truth and don't need to check in with others. Even the people who are most prominent in their fields consult their peers and rely on feedback. We all rely on others to get a feeling for how well we're doing. But not just any other people—they have to be people who matter to you.

You live not in "society" at large, but rather in a number of smaller "societies"— call them bands or subgroups within the overall. First and foremost, you have your family of origin—your parents, siblings (particularly the older ones), and other adults who live with you. Then you move on to other bands within which are other significant individuals—teachers and dominant playmates.

It is in early childhood that praise and attention matter most. According to Marianne Miserandino's research, children come to believe in their competence or otherwise at a very young age, certainly by the third grade, and it has little or nothing to do with their actual achievements. Rather, it has to do with what is going on in their home life.

Finally, there are the groupings of people in your adult family, the organizations you belong to, and your workplace. At each stage, you look to people in these groups for reassurance as to your capabilities. What they say about you is the standard by which you judge your competence. If you do what we suggest, you will uncover your innate excellence, your unique genius, within these settings.

RECOGNITION FROM OTHERS

You don't have to be the world's greatest mother, watercolorist, or manager to achieve a sense of competence; you just have to *feel* that you're good at what you do. Obviously, if you feel competent at something, you're more likely to stick to it and perhaps even excel at it. You may then get more praise and feel even better about your abilities. *But from the point of view of healing your depression and getting to optimism*, any "objective" scale of excellence is irrelevant. Happiness depends on being able to do things that make you feel competent.

Helena, a friend of ours in Sydney, was proud of the children's stories she wrote and illustrated and which delighted her friends and their children. None had ever been published; she said she didn't want the "hassle" of sending them to agents and publishers. The greatest source of her pride lay in a writer's group to which she belonged, where she would read her stories and receive enthusiastic praise for her inventiveness, lyrical language, and engaging drawings. She was told that she had the ability to "really get into the mind of a child."

Would her books have been lauded by professional publishers and critics? Who knows; the question is irrelevant. More important, she knew her work was good because she received praise from friends and members of a social circle that was important to her. She went to the writer's group happily expecting plaudits for her work. The meetings were the highlight of her week.

UNDERESTIMATING YOUR ABILITIES

People might lack a sense of competence in many ways, and some of them may not be obvious at first. For instance, some people feel they can't do anything well and have difficulty accepting praise even when they get it. Some people rarely get the chance to exercise their competence or feel that what they do well doesn't matter. Finally, some feel competent in one or two very narrow academic or intellectual areas but are terrified that a challenge will come along outside their expertise and wipe out their very fragile sense of self.

Issues of competence can show up slightly differently in men and women because each sex, for societal and evolutionary reasons, tends to place more importance on different aspects of their lives. Jacquelynne Eccles, a professor of psychology at the University of Michigan, has noted that almost universally researchers have found that girls generally underestimate their abilities in math, science, and sports, areas where boys will often overestimate their abilities. On the other hand, the reverse happens with reading and social skills. That this has little to do with real ability is seen from the fact that in math tests, for example, girls score just as well as boys. According to Eccles, the magnitude of these gender-based differences in their sense of competence increases as children get older. So your lack of competence probably has little to do with your real ability.

Another cause of a poor or lacking sense of competence is depression itself. Research carried out by University of Illinois associate professor Eva Pomerantz and others shows that a child's depression is a strong predictor of both low self-esteem and a low sense of competence, both academically and socially.

"The negative views of the self and the world that result from emotional distress may color how people interpret evaluative feedback, interfere with how they defend themselves when they are critiqued and cause them to refrain from pursuing challenging tasks," Pomerantz says. "Each of these consequences may then result in the underestimation of competence."

No Praise, No Competence

If you received a lot of criticism or not much praise (which amounts to the same thing) in your early years, your view of yourself will be distorted. You will probably feel that nothing you do will ever be right or good enough. If you succeed in anything, it will be "through luck" rather than your ability. Doing almost anything will be stressful, and your fear of failure will be very high. You will avoid anything—promotion, challenging tasks—that will place you in this anxiety-provoking situation. If people do praise you, it will be because they can't see the "real you." If you do succeed, you may experience a constant fear of being found out.

If your parents or teachers didn't seem to take any interest in the things that mattered to you, then it's likely that you won't see these as important either. Yet, they may be activities that you are potentially very good at and that you have natural abilities for. It's our firm belief that we are all geniuses at something; that's the beauty of human beings. Our experience with clients shows that each person, whatever the childhood circumstances or handicap, is born with the capacity to excel. That excellence can be our ability to use our hands or our minds, our voices or our bodies. Dustin Hoffman's character, the severely autistic man who was a mathematical genius in the film *Rain Man*, illustrates the point.

A cheetah can only excel at running fast; an albatross at flying vast distances without landing; an ant at carrying, comparatively speaking, huge weights. But humans are capable of a wide range of talents as Daniel Goleman discusses in his book *Primal Leadership*. In business leadership alone, he lists three types of competence: technical skills, such as accounting and business planning; cognitive abilities, such as analytic reasoning; and traits showing emotional intelligence, such as self-awareness and relationship skills. And within each of those categories of competence a wide range of specific talents is found.

In our ancestors' hunting band, this diversity was a key to survival. All the men may have been good at hunting in general, but within that category would be the strategist, the tracker, the fast runner, the talented spear-thrower or archer, the one who could read the wind and weather, and so forth. Each could feel competence in his talent and have the chance to practice it.

But what if you had a great natural talent that was dismissed as irrelevant by the adults whom you regarded as gods in your early youth? Initially you will follow their lead and, perhaps, keep that talent under wraps. On the other hand, you may be lucky.

Jay, a client of Bob's in New York, was a champion downhill skier. He and Bob were discussing the issue of competence during a session and Jay mentioned that in his youth he never thought that he would be any good at skiing. His parents weren't interested in sport of any kind; indeed, they ridiculed his interests and criticized him for "wasting his time" skiing. (He'd become hooked on the activity ever since he'd gone to a nearby ski run with a young friend and his parents.)

When Jay was thirteen, he was noticed by an instructor who was interested enough to time Jay's downhill runs. He praised Jay for his speed on the slopes and it was only then that he began to feel *competent* at it. This sense of competence increased as he joined a weekend ski team and gained recognition from other team members and the coach. He gradually became optimistic about his chances of becoming a world-class skier. At the awards ceremony for his first win in a major competition, Jay didn't mention his parents, who weren't there anyway. He saluted his original mentor.

BUT NOT ALL PRAISE IS GOOD

Getting no praise is bad and—to a somewhat lesser extent—getting the wrong kind of praise is not good either. Research by Columbia University psychologists Claudia M. Mueller and Carol S. Dweck illustrates that complimenting children just for their intelligence and academic performance may lead them to believe that good test scores and high grades are more important than learning and mastering something new. While lauding a child's scholastic aptitude is intended to boost her academic performance, it can leave her ill-prepared to cope with setbacks.

According to Dweck, ''Praising children's intelligence, far from boosting their self-esteem, encourages them to embrace self-defeating behaviors, such as worrying about failure and avoiding risks. However, when children are taught the value of concentrating, strategizing, and working hard when dealing with academic challenges, this encourages them to sustain their motivation, performance, and self-esteem."

The ineptly praised child's sense of competence collapses when faced with a challenge that takes more than just cognitive ability to solve or is outside her narrow realm of specialty. Label a child "gifted" and she is put on a perch from which it is all too easy to fall. She has a fragile sense of competence, and it requires constant bolstering by purely intellectual challenges. When they grow up, such people often claim to be "above average."

This may be why, according to Cornell psychologist David Dunning, a statistically impossible 94 percent of college professors claim their work to be above average for their profession. These highly functioning yet fragile "walking wounded" often become depressed, and we see them frequently in our practices and in the Uplift. Of course, no one in our society feels really good enough unless they are "special." This phenomenon is gently parodied in Garrison Keillor's Public Radio program "The Prairie Home Companion." Every week, he broadcasts his regards from the fictional town of Lake Woebegone where "all the women are strong, all the men are good-looking, and the children are all above average."

Reclaim Your Competence

So how do you reclaim the sense of competence you were designed to have, that which every hunter-gatherer had (or indeed has) in one way or another? How do you free yourself from the depression and pessimism that come with a lack of this sense or a competence that is so fragile that it may be lost at any time?

You can take four actions to regain your sense of competence.

Four Actions to Reclaim Your Competence

1. Identify the voices that undermine your competence.
2. Find out what you really *like* doing.
3. Search out others who acknowledge your efforts.
4. Inform others of your limitations and enlist their support.

Action 1: Identify the Voices That Undermine Your Competence

Two kinds of voices from the past conspire to reduce your sense of competence. One is the voice that says that no matter what you do, you are never going to be good enough. The second voice directs you into particular occupations, often ones that don't suit your temperament. Sometimes the voices combine, sometimes not.

Many people are trapped into doing things—in the workplace or in the home—that they feel they ought to because people in their childhood told them that they were the right things to do. In the Uplift, we have met hundreds of such people, including a doctor who would rather be a horticulturalist, a housewife who dreamed of being a psychotherapist, a software expert who wanted to be a yoga instructor, and a lawyer who wanted to own a ski shop in Colorado.

When we probed them as to why they chose their original occupations, their answers almost always related to what they thought some significant person in their past had expected of them. The physician's father, for example, had pressured his daughter to follow in his footsteps. The lawyer's working-class parents deprived themselves to send him to law school. Both carried the burden of this expectation and "succeeded" at the cost of their own emotional health.

The voices that undermined you as a child may have been openly critical (though often you can't remember exactly what they said) or they may simply be critical by default—through lack of praise or interest.

The negative voices are trying to prevent you from leaving the emotional prison of your upbringing, to prevent you from being your own person, and to prevent you from following your dream. Perhaps even to prevent you from having a dream. In essence, they try to preclude you having autonomy, one of the other essential ingredients of happiness.

It's a point that Edward Deci makes in his book *Why We Do What We Do*. In the opening chapter he says, "To be autonomous means to act in accord with one's self—it means being free and volitional in one's actions. When autonomous, people are fully willing to do what they are doing, and they embrace the activity with a sense of interest and commitment."

On the other hand, when people are controlled by the critical voices of the past, their program, or by controlling individuals in the present, "people act without a sense of personal endorsement. Their behavior is not an expression of the self, for the self has been subjugated to the controls. In this condition people can reasonably be described as alienated."

Recapturing the possibility of a sense of autonomy and competence means nailing these internalized lies, discovering the voices behind them, and working out your needs around praise and appreciation. Once your brain hears genuinely positive comments from the outside, it will begin to rewire itself. The more approval you receive, the more the negative voices will lose their power over you and your future.

You have the tools to unmask and expunge these insidious influences in the "Six Actions to Elevate Your Self-Esteem" in the previous chapter.

Now ask yourself, if these voices didn't exist, if I weren't driven to do work that I'm not comfortable with, if I weren't so afraid of failure, what would I really like to do?

Action 2: Find Out What You Really *Like* Doing

How do you know what you really like doing? This may seem an odd question, but we meet so many people who don't know the answer. They are too used to doing things not because they enjoy the process but because of what they think the results will be. Many of us get stuck in occupations for some longer-term reason, either ours or someone else's—to have enough money to retire on, so the kids can go to college, because it's a safe job, because it's what my father wanted me to become— and we lose the enjoyment of the now. But a sense of competence is, essentially, the ability to enjoy the process of what you're doing.

This is not to say that longer-term goals and aspirations are a bad idea. Of course they're not. But unless you feel competent in your ability to achieve the goal, or at least reach the way stations along the route, you are bound to fail.

In his book *Flow: The Psychology of Optimal Experience*, Mihaly Csikszentmihalyi described a state of peak performance as being "in the flow." Flow, as he defines it, is the ability to harness positive emotions in the service of whatever you're doing. It is a state of self-forgetfulness, of freedom from depression and anxiety. It is often perceived as an ecstasy of experience akin to great lovemaking. It is being in and at one with the process. And all human beings can, in whatever work they do willingly, get in the flow.

Hunters stalking a woolly mammoth were in the flow—the single-minded concentration on the task at hand. On a conscious level they were oblivious to the dangers around them, relying totally on their emotions and experience. Within this activity there is a deep, deep, ultimate satisfaction.

In this state the brain cools down. There is, paradoxically, even in complicated tasks, less thought, less activity in the central cortex. There are fewer emotional surges in the limbic system to overwhelm the rest of the brain. The chatter of the program is silent.

It was this sense of rightness, of being competent, that kept hunters going out hunting. And in this state you can be truly happy. The flow is concentration without effort. If you have to force yourself to concentrate, then you are not in the flow, you are using more cortical power to do whatever it is, and you are not being efficient with the use of your brain.

Of course, not every moment of every day can be spent in this state. But just as our remote ancestors could experience this flow each day as part of their work, so should you be able to. If doing what you do doesn't do it for you, then it's time to stop and ask yourself a couple of really serious questions.

First, "What could others do to help me get into the flow when I'm working?"

Madeline, a freelance graphic designer, became anxious and frustrated when working on her own. "I just couldn't keep my inner voices quiet that said everything I did had to be perfect and that I would fail." She invited a good friend and former work colleague, Kelly, now also freelance, to share office space. She and Kelly agreed to bounce ideas off each other and to break regularly for tea or lunch. "Just having someone with me who I knew I could count on for support made all the difference," says Madeline. "I found I became lost in the creative process and discovered a new freedom and joy in my work."

If you can't find a way to love what you do, then the next question is: "What steps can I take to find an occupation that will provide me with supportive people and the curiosity necessary for me to get into the flow?"

Of course, the activity that you have a passion for may have nothing to do with "work." It may be building model airplanes, raising a family, or gardening. Our hunter-gatherer ancestors didn't divide the world into work and other the way we tend to do. To them the separation didn't exist; each activity was simply part of an overall pattern of life.

It's important to give yourself the time and opportunity to be able to increase your skills in your area of passion. Above all, don't keep your skill and passion a secret. Depression thrives on isolation, and sharing your pride and excitement in what you do is an indomitable weapon against it.

Action 3: Search Out Others Who Acknowledge Your Efforts

Self-esteem and a sense of competence both require praise to grow, but in terms of competence, you are looking for praise around a particular activity, whether it's social or work related. Your best source of understanding and encouragement may be others who are also engaged in your field of competence or interest.

It's often said that being a writer, for example, is a solitary occupation, and to some extent it is. Bob's parents were both novelists though they wrote radically different types of novels. (Bob's father was the crime writer Max Murray and his mother the romantic novelist Maysie Greig.) For hours a day they would cloister themselves away in their respective dens and pound out their words. However, when not writing they would seek out the company of other writers, either in formal organizations such as International P.E.N. Club (an international organization of poets, playwrights, editors, essayists, and novelists) or through individual contacts.

Not only did this mingling enable them to survive the pressure of publication deadlines and book reviews, but it also kept them up to date with their craft and, through the mutual praise and support that they got, increased their sense of competence.

We are not saying, by the way, that you should never accept or ask other people for their opinions and advice unless it involves praise! Honest feedback is essential in honing any ability. But choosing carefully who you are willing to receive it from and letting them know your needs around this sensitive issue will ensure that your sense of competence thrives rather than diminishes.

Action 4: Inform Others of Your Limitations and Enlist Support

If you're suffering from depression, one of the most difficult things to do is to reach out and seek help. In this state, you probably feel pessimistic about how people will react to you. You are also in all likelihood certain that the last thing anyone would want to do is help you or listen to your problems. But having to battle with a difficulty on your own will exacerbate, if not create, the loss of a sense of competence. Human nature isn't about struggling on your own, and keeping your pain a secret ensures that nobody can help you.

Twenty-five-year-old Miguel struggled all his life with dyslexia, although he had never been diagnosed or even tested for it. Being labeled a "slow learner" in school and "stupid" by his parents had made him depressed and left him feeling incompetent in almost every area of his life. Because of his disability, he found reading, remembering numbers, and even comprehending directions difficult. As an adult, he went from job to job, none lasting more than a few months. He felt that, at any moment, he was going to be asked to do something impossible for him, which kept him in a constant state of anxiety.

Miguel felt that he had to hide being slow, and the effort to do this added to his anxiety. He also felt he had to keep his depression a secret from the world. The combination left him cut off and isolated, without friends or support.

When Miguel explained his situation to Bob, he was given a standard test for dyslexia. The young man was surprised to learn that he had a disability and at the same time relieved to know that the problem had nothing to do with his intelligence, and many issues from his school days and later life fell into place. "But I still can't hold down a job," he said.

"You've got to tell people about your problem so that they can make allowances for it," Bob told him.

With great reluctance Miguel began to do so. He found that people were willing to help. He would say things like: "Could you repeat that number and let me read it back to you, I'm a bit dyslexic," "Don't tell me to turn right or left, say 'turn my way or yours,'" or "Excuse me if I take a bit of time reading this, it's my dyslexia." Eventually these explanations became second nature to him, part of his coping mechanism. Miguel's sense of competence increased, he became less depressed, and his anxiety disappeared.

Admitting the problem, whether it's physical such as dyslexia or emotional such as depression or anxiety, and seeking assistance from others around you are the keys to overcoming low self-worth. You are not making excuses for yourself; you are just refusing to carry around a disabling secret.

Again, it's the social context. If you are in a situation in which it's impossible to share your problem because of ridicule or lack of understanding, and your needs around these issues are ignored, you're running with the wrong tribe and it's time to move on.

Finding or creating the right supportive environment of people is in the end, of course, the secret to feeling competent. It's their praise for your endeavors that allows you to realize, in all senses of the word, what you do best. Focusing on that activity can provide a haven from the chaotic thoughts and feelings generated by the program, by the lies of the past.

At the same time, fully engaging in an activity with other people keeps you anchored in the present and allows your brain a time-out from depression and a chance to heal. It also enables you to enter the pleasurable realm of the flow. And engaging with others in an activity that's meaningful to you is at the heart of a sense of life-giving purpose, as you'll find in the next chapter.

14

STEP 6:
ACCESS THE POWER
OF SHARED PURPOSE

◉

Each of us needs a sense of purpose to be depression free and optimistic and, according to the latest research by Julienne E. Bower of UCLA, for our immune system to function properly. We need to believe that we have a reason for being here and that our existence matters. But in the jumble of life, and with the pressures of career and family, advertising, and social obligations, we are in danger of losing that belief.

Yet we are genetically wired to have a sense of purpose, and so we will be happier when we acknowledge and follow it. Each one of us will conceive of our purpose in a slightly different way, but a functional purpose will meet certain criteria.

The purpose must be *altruistic*. We are, as the noted biologist Matt Ridley has stated, an altruistic species, which is also backed up by recent research by psychology and anthropology professor Barbara Smuts and others. We get satisfaction from doing things for the benefit of others. Of course, the closer those people are to us, the more intense the satisfaction we get.

The purpose must be *communal* in nature. Because we're a social animal and our mental and physical health depend on our being able to interact with others in a satisfactory way, a functional purpose is one we share.

A functional purpose also *survives* us. Though achievable goals may be met along the way within the overall purpose, it must be ongoing. In modern society, our lives tend to be marked by points of loss, such as loss of early childhood freedom, structure from the ending of school or during times of unemployment, meaning when our children move away or when we retire, loved ones, or a place to which we are attached. Each of these can be traumatic and can lead to or exacerbate depression, anxiety, and pessimism. An overall purpose can help us deal with loss by putting it in the context of a greater something that gives us meaning and which we can rely upon to always be there.

As Prof. Stephen Reiss says, "Value-based happiness is a sense that our lives have meaning and fulfill some larger purpose. It represents a spiritual source of satisfaction, stemming from our deeper purpose and values."

A LESSON IN LIFE FROM THE PULKIDS

Pulkids are a group of students (ranging in age from eight to twelve years) and teachers from the Preparatory School at Pulteney Grammar in South Australia. They meet regularly to learn about information technology and how to put it to good use. Their purpose is to advance the cause of peace, and their intentions are to promote purposeful and positive Internet connection between educational communities and peacemakers throughout the world. Their main focus is to share the good news happening within these communities. In so doing, they believe they are making the world a better place for themselves and others to share.

The Pulkids' project has all the elements of a functional purpose. It has a socially altruistic goal and is pursued in the company of others. It is also not achievable within one lifetime yet its numerous subgoals are.

Later in life, the individuals in this class may move on to adopt other life goals, but in all probability their sense of purpose will remain. Of course, the Pulkids are lucky; they have adults who can guide them to develop a functional purpose. Most people do not.

Rather, we are taught in school and by the media to aspire to things that *can't* bring us the value happiness Reiss talks about: career advancement; acquisition of wealth and goods; sexual gratification; thin, muscular bodies; and so on. Society is based not on purpose but on the pleasure principle: the good life is one in which there is more pleasure than pain, more good feeling than bad. If you can structure your life so that you maximize your immediate pleasure, then all will be well.

And yet most of us know this is a lie. If it were true, our lives would be pointless. We would just be so much protein running around waiting for some predator—be it a tiger or a virus—to feed on. And all of the pleasure would just be a way of passing the time until the inevitable happened.

We—and we suspect you as well—cannot accept this view of life. We search for something deeper, the something that the Pulkids have. a reason to be. We have not come across one depressed person yet who fully believed that his life had meaning, and we have not met anyone who felt his life had meaning who was depressed.

You Are Here to Do Good

Because humans are an altruistic species, we get pleasure from doing good. It's a more deep-seated pleasure than we get from the materialistic chase-the-buck or chase-the-sex-object kind. Yet altruism infuses even our desire to find a life partner. Research has shown consistently that women prefer altruistic men—men who do good for the community—over other possible mates, ensuring that altruistic genes will be passed on.

Ridley and others have surmised that we humans are more altruistic than other animals and more able to cooperate because of our larger brain and cognitive ability. Cooperation is vital for our survival. As a species, we have no other physical mechanisms for defense: no claws, fangs, horns, speed, or camouflage. All we have is the ability to cooperate with each other. In a cooperative society, altruism must be widespread, since a large number of freeloaders would doom it.

This is in contrast to the earlier more pessimistic ideas of Richard Dawkins. In his book *The Selfish Gene*, Dawkins states that our altruism extends no further than our immediate blood relatives. On the contrary, says Prof. Smuts, "There's a general trend in evolutionary biology toward recognizing that very often the best way to compete is to cooperate."

Altruism involves the ability to empathize with the fate of others, which, according to many researchers, is rare in the animal kingdom. Given our natural tendency to altruism, only an altruistic purpose will trigger our natural biochemical reward system and make us feel really happy, at least in the long run. As a bulwark against depression, altruism is a powerful tool.

But single acts of kindness, though good in themselves, will not help to break the hold of a persistent mood disorder. The altruism has to be part of a pattern and have a consistent theme. Depression can easily defeat a one-off instance of helpfulness, just as addiction can defeat a one-off day of sobriety.

Researcher J. R. Peteet of Harvard Medical School wrote in the *Journal of Substance Abuse Treatment* that there has to be a conversion from the self-obsessed guilt of depression or addiction to altruism. Only then can you regain a sense of integrity. But how do you convert? Peteet gives as an example the twelve-step programs such as Alcoholics Anonymous. The members' first step is to admit that they are powerless over the forces that compel them to seek pleasure or solace in transient ways that are ultimately self-defeating.

THE POWER OF PURPOSE

Admitting that you on your own are powerless over an addiction (or depression or negative programming) can be an opening that enables you to allow help in, whether it is the help of other people in a group such as a twelve-step meeting, a supporting voice against the negative ones from your past, or perhaps a spiritual experience that reveals your life purpose.

Our friend Mark came to his life purpose after his own realization of powerlessness. When the Vietnam War began, he was in his early twenties and working as a salesman. He came from a particularly abusive household. His father was a brutal alcoholic and his mother made no effort to protect her son. In fact, she set him up for the beatings and heavily criticized him. Despite his background, he managed to gain a master's degree at a small Midwestern university.

Mark felt his life was empty, and he drifted from job to job and relationship to relationship without any clear sense of direction. Though he wasn't violent, he had certainly inherited his father's alcoholism. To him, the purpose of life was to exist from one drink to the next and, when he was sober, from one woman's bed to the next.

He slowly realized that he was profoundly unhappy (awareness of depression as such was limited at that time), and that the alcohol and sex were merely ways to cover up his agony. He admitted to himself his own powerlessness against the pain and self-destructive behavior.

One day he overheard a group of people discussing the Vietnam War and realized quite suddenly that the rest of his life had to be devoted to the cause of peace. He became a conscientious objector and when he was drafted, refused to be spirited away to Canada. He chose instead to stay and make a point. He was jailed and put in a maximum-security institution (which was standard practice in some states for conscientious objectors) where he was brutalized by the guards and by his fellow inmates.

"Before that moment when I realized there was a purpose for me, I had nothing to live for," he told us. "After it, there was everything. They couldn't beat that feeling out of me—nothing they did was as bad as what my father had done, anyway. In fact, my childhood helped me to survive in that place. Most of the other conscientious objectors didn't; they either enlisted to get out or were taken out on stretchers."

The knowledge that you are doing good (as you see it) and that you are dedicated to doing good is overwhelmingly powerful. Once aligned with your evolutionary altruistic heritage, your commitment helps blow away the program. You have something to live for rather than just something to fight against.

A COMMON CAUSE

Along with altruism, a common cause also helps give meaning to our lives. To get the highest emotional and mood benefit from your sense of purpose, you must pursue it in the company of others.

People are at their best when they work together for some shared purpose. Examples abound, but some of the most moving include the group courage and dedication of New York firefighters in the immediate aftermath of September 11, the day-to-day bravery of ordinary Londoners who helped each other withstand the blitz of World War II, and the collective determination of villagers involved in the rescue and cleanup after Hurricane Mitch hit Nicaragua in 1998.

The experience of the Nicaraguans who survived Hurricane Mitch also illustrates the importance of communal purpose for mental health. The rural Nicaraguans were mentally and emotionally better able to cope with the effects of the 1998 disaster than the residents of Dade County in South Florida who were hit by Hurricane Andrew in 1992. Comparison research by a team headed by Michael Rank of the University of South Florida found that the essential difference lay in the fact that the Central Americans had a greater sense of community and shared purpose than the Floridians. The Americans lacked that strong, interdependent sense of community and group purpose and waited for someone from outside the community to come and "do something." They were more dependent on U.S. government handouts, and as a result, the South Floridians largely experienced their pain in loneliness and isolation and suffered more depression and PTSD than their Nicaraguan counterparts.

The researchers speculated that what kept the Central Americans going was "being a part of something," which blitz survivors and New York firefighters also reported. But just as a single example of altruistic behavior or shared purpose doesn't have much of a lasting beneficial effect, a transient instance of social cohesion following a disaster won't have an enduring effect on the residents. For that to happen, the mutual interdependence that occurred during the crisis has to evolve into an ongoing communal purpose.

In the Company of Others

A doctor from the international humanitarian organization Médecins Sans Frontièrs can go from one emergency to another and not suffer the breakdown that so many New York firefighters did once the immediate crisis was over. He is part of a community with a purpose that survives the event and can draw strength and support from it. When Bob was a TV producer, he visited a number of war fronts in Asia and Africa and came across many examples of these tight and dedicated communities of aid workers. What struck him was the satisfaction and happiness they found in their vocation.

One individual who sticks in Bob's mind is a French nurse named Colleen DuBois. He met DuBois in the late 1970s while covering a particularly nasty civil war in the North African nation of Chad, where she was working for the U.K. charity Christian Aid. He learned that she had volunteered as a relief worker on numerous war fronts starting in the late 1940s. Bob found her upbeat mood and her personal air of optimism in the midst of such suffering amazing.

"It's the people I work with," she told him in her thick French accent. "And the dream we share: a world without war. I want a world in which people are not forgetful of the real problem. Aid comes in too late and when newspapers have moved on to new headlines the aid stops. Forget for a moment the starving babies; they're just a symptom. The world must see that it's morally wrong to arm dictators, that war never solves anything, that most borders themselves are a cause of war. Do you know, I really believe it will happen." As she put it, her strength came from the people who shared her dream and who accompanied her from war front to war front.

You don't have to be an aid worker, of course, to have a cooperative sense of purpose. It can come from keeping your neighborhood safe, feeding the hungry in your city, or rescuing stray and unwanted dogs. All of these are usually done in the company of others and that gives them their power.

Yolanda, a New York client of ours, joined her local PTA as a way of reaching out to make friends. Soon she came to realize that the district schools were in very poor shape. Some lacked basic amenities and others were badly in need of repair. She galvanized the other PTA members, who up to that time had been rather quiescent, to campaign for staff changes and increased funding. The local PTA became a force to be reckoned with.

Yolanda herself found that the combination of a sense of purpose and the camaraderie of the other members lifted her out of her depression, and their achievements gave her a real sense of optimism.

By working with others for an ongoing purpose, you are creating a community around you and you are in the flow of your evolutionary and genetic heritage. You cannot achieve this by working for prestige and money, no matter how dedicated you are. To our ancestors work was a small, if important, aspect of their lives. What mattered most were socializing and the ongoing overall welfare of the band. Altruism and community are, of course, bound up together.

A PURPOSE FOR LIFE

Given our education and upbringing, it's hard for modern humans to come to grips with the notion that our priorities—principally work and family—are transitory. The goals we strive for within them, and the community involved in related activities, come to an end. We experience multiple endings during our lives because of events such as divorce, unemployment, and the kids growing up and leaving home. Each time we lose our jobs, for example, we lose our tribe (something that would never happen to a hunter-gatherer) and we are in danger of losing our identity.

This was true for Marina, a very successful and busy teacher in her early sixties. When she took the Uplift in Raleigh, North Carolina, she was suffering from depression and a sense of increasing emptiness in her life. She spoke to the group about her career, her recent divorce, her grown-up children living in Europe, and her planned retirement in a year or two.

"What then?" asked Bob.

"Oh, I don't know," she said. "I've always had a problem with planning for the future." From her eyes it was clear that after retirement there was a vacuum. "The closer I get to retiring, the more depressed I get."

It was as if she were the cartoon character Wile E. Coyote charging toward the edge of a cliff. In a short while, she would be over the edge with her legs still churning and nothing underneath her, no career to give her a sense of meaning or identity.

"I've never thought of purpose outside of teaching and my family," she confessed.

This is one of the ways in which we are startlingly different from our hunter-gatherer forebears and their modern equivalents. Their society was not geared toward thinking or planning for the future. They knew they would never lose their role or purpose within the tribe. Since children were raised communally, and the band as a whole was more important than the nuclear groupings within it, when children did leave—because of marriage outside the clan or for some other reason—the loss was not that great.

Encoded in their genes and their society was one overriding purpose to which they all contributed: the preservation and continuation of the band as a whole on a day-to-day or season-to-season basis. Everything was geared toward that: their religion, customs, rituals—everything. It was a purpose that was never ending.

A REASON TO LIVE

It is best to find your life purpose when you are young, although, as with the painter Grandma Moses, it can come at any age.

At whatever age you discover your mission, a sense of purpose becomes increasingly necessary as you grow older. It gives you a reason to live; prevents you from feeling useless; and, as recent studies have shown, helps save you from falling into the trap of depression.

Developing a life purpose is rather like saving for retirement. A prudent person will begin the saving process early, slowly building up his nest-egg account over the years until the time comes when he will have to depend on the investments to survive. The same is true of purpose. As you grow older, you devote more and more time and thought to it until there comes a point when you are free of the minipurposes of career and family and your overriding mission becomes the focus of your life. Your mission then becomes the basis for how you define yourself.

Aligning yourself with an ongoing mission is more functional than getting your identity from your career. A hunter-gatherer would never define himself by the work he did. Yet ask anyone of working age in an "advanced" society about himself, and the first thing he will say is "I'm a carpenter" or "I'm a lawyer," as if that were the most important thing. Our sense of self and our occupation are usually closely entwined. Even retired people will say, "I'm a retired carpenter" or whatever their ex-occupation was. We spend so much time working or with our nuclear families that we define our sense of self very narrowly and by transient things. Yet, when Bob asked the same question of the hunter-gatherers in southern Africa, the answer was "I am a !Kung." Their identity was linked to the band, to the group, to something solid and ongoing.

Hunter-gatherers don't retire. When they reach a certain age, they become members of the council of elders. The earlier concerns of hunting and child raising are put aside and new, equally important duties are taken on. In a sense, they have been in training for this time throughout their whole life. They experience no loss of status or identity, rather a recognition of knowledge and skills.

Many studies have shown that the most dangerous time in a modern person's life is directly after retirement. This is especially true for a man, though a recent study by Prof. Christine Price of Ohio State University has shown it to be increasingly true for professional women as well. After retirement, the goals and the values of work are no longer available. Most people's friendships are related to their jobs, and when they leave they are isolated. Often death follows hard on the heels of the cessation of work.

It seems that on retirement, unless you have an ongoing purpose in your life, the brain sends signals to your immune system and to the various organs of your body saying, in effect, that your useful life is over. These signals appear to be sent regardless of whether the job loss happens to a fit, young person or to a sixty- or seventy-year-old.

A study headed by Joan K. Morris of St. George's Hospital Medical School in London found that men younger than fifty-nine who had lost employment either through retirement or layoffs were twice as likely to die within five years as those continuously employed. The main killers were cancer and heart disease. Other studies have also shown that the risk of suicide is much higher among the recently retired or unemployed.

What will you do when you retire or when your children leave home? What reason can you give your brain to keep you alive? There is no council of elders for you to naturally move into. The good news is that getting a sense of purpose in your life is not all that difficult.

Planning for Purpose

We all have within us ideas of how our neighborhood, city, nation, or world should be. These convictions or moral outrage are the seeds of your sense of purpose. But just expounding on them isn't enough.

By definition, a purpose is about doing something. Yet if you're depressed, the "doing" is the hardest part. The voices are clear: "You are worthless." "Your contribution would be useless." "No one would want you on his team." "Nothing you do would make any difference and, anyway, it's all too difficult."

Before you go on, you may want to revisit the exercise Identify Your Program in Chapter 4 and work on your issues relating to effectiveness. As in every other aspect of your life, the lies need to be stripped away.

Life purpose involves thinking both over the short and long term. However, for many of us, long-term planning is difficult. Humans aren't designed to think in this way. So it's only natural for you to want to see the results of your actions immediately. What's more, studies have shown that people's grasp of reality lessens the further they look into the future. As Yaacov Trobe of New York University put it, "In the distant future we think about how much the outcome is attractive to us. In the near future we think 'is it feasible?'" We tend to make abstract goals for ourselves with little regard to the practical steps needed to get there.

For example, if you plan for a holiday in the south of France a year from now, you are filled with happy pictures of yourself lying on the beach at St. Trop gazing at beautiful people with waiters bringing you exotic drinks. In your vision you are slim, fit, and attractive enough for the beautiful people to class you as one of their own. Only when the trip comes closer do you begin to focus on the downside: you really need to lose some weight, the passport has expired, you're not looking forward to the long hours in the cramped economy section of a bankrupt or near-bankrupt airline (can it afford maintenance?), and the unfavorable exchange rate means you can't afford the drinks (or even the beach).

In other words, we are good at *conceptualizing* the long term but not good at *planning* for it. This is one of the reasons why we need to work out some near-term doable goals to mark our way points, to give us something to achieve so we don't quit and fall into the "it's all too much" trap.

At first, your overall life purpose is bound to be an abstraction, perhaps in the "abolition of war," "saving the redwoods," "ridding the world of poverty," "freeing the neighborhood from crime," or "spreading my faith" category. That is the way of long-term goals. You can envision peace on earth in some far-off future. You can vaguely picture what it would look like. However, in the short term you see wars or the threat of them, riots in the Middle East, famine, belligerent dictatorships, and a whole range of other problems. The temptation may be to give up, to put the whole purpose in what the British and Australians vividly call the "too-hard basket."

The key lies in *chunking down* the problem. Chunking down involves breaking the large picture into doable bits, "doing goals" as we call them. With doing goals, you can develop timelines and achievable way points.

For example, from the general to the specific: helping people affected by disasters → rebuilding Nicaragua → rebuilding the most devastated county → selecting the first village to be rebuilt → building the first house → laying the first stone. The first general goal is daunting; the particulars are not.

We've segmented the exercise Finding and Advancing Your Purpose into the following actions.

SIX ACTIONS FOR FINDING AND ADVANCING YOUR PURPOSE

1. Work out your overall purpose.
2. Define your mission in concrete terms.
3. Set short-term goals.
4. Give tasks a timeline.
5. Stick to your targets.
6. Find people to pursue your purpose with.

EXERCISE 18 FINDING AND ADVANCING YOUR PURPOSE

Action 1: Work Out Your Overall Purpose

Write down a list of all the problems you see around you that you care passionately about. Give it some thought and select one. This may not be your final choice for a mission, and indeed, you may change it many times as you go along. For now, it's important to choose one, if only for this exercise.

Doing something about the issue that concerns you will probably, at first glance, seem too difficult. So let's make it doable for you.

Action 2: Define Your Mission in Concrete Terms

For a moment, let's assume that the life purpose you wrote down just now was to bring harmony to the world. Now write down what you mean by this. What would it look like if this goal were to be achieved? Here you might put something like, "People would relate to each other on the basis of their functional needs. There would be no war and conflicts would be resolved peacefully. People would treat animals humanely, and nature with respect."

Good so far. At least you've got a grip on what the world would look like if the goal were reached.

Action 3: Set Short-Term Goals

Next, work out what you could do *in the short term* to help achieve your overall goal. This is the first pass at working out what your doing goals are going to be; don't worry if the actions are not very specific. "I will work out my needs of everybody in my life and encourage friends to do the same thing. I will not be drawn into dysfunctional relationships. I will strive to avoid conflict; I will walk from any situation that can't be resolved peacefully, and I'll encourage others to do the same. I will support the work of my local animal shelter and environmental group."

You're getting there. These are good generalized doing goals.

Action 4: Give Tasks a Timeline

The next step is to concretize these a bit more and give these specific tasks a time frame.

GOAL	TIME
Work out a needs list for my wife and children	Begin today
Ask them to do the same for me	Begin tomorrow
Contact animal shelter to ask about volunteering	Next Tuesday

And so forth. These specific doing goals will change as some get met and others come to mind.

Action 5: Stick to Your Targets

Keep a log and try to stick to your targets. Make a note of why you missed some, and list any emotional or program blocks that prevented you. You may want to go back to the exercises in Chapter 4 and work out which voices from childhood were getting in your way and what you can do to counter the relevant aspects of your program.

Action 6: Find People to Pursue Your Purpose With

The next step is to find other people who share your life purpose, or at least significant parts of it. Don't forget that the functional way of striving for a social end is socially. Be sure to join groups that involve you in joint actions that you would enjoy, such as meetings, marches, fund-raising activities, and other volunteer work. Groups that just ask you to give them money may help the world, but their value to you is limited. If you can, involve your friends and present family (not necessarily your family of origin). The more you share your purpose with them, the more solid your relationships will be.

If you construct your mission in this way, several things are absolutely certain. You will never lack friends. You will never have to say, "I have nothing to live for." You will be physically and emotionally healthier and you will probably add years to your life.

STEP 7:
DEEPEN YOUR
RELATIONSHIP
TO THE DIVINE

◉

Spirituality, along with functional relationships, is the ultimate antidepressant. We are hardwired for spirituality just as we are genetically programmed to be social animals. Our spirituality is part of our essential humanity. This does not mean that you have to believe in a religious creed or undergo rigorous spiritual practices to be happy and emotionally well. It does mean that freedom from depression and the leap to optimism can involve a spiritual renewal.

Many of the great spiritual thinkers have counseled people to "just be." Just be for the moment and soak up the wonder of the universe and the gifts that have been bestowed on you. This is a very difficult ask for twenty-first-century humans. Humans are "doing" creatures. We want to "do" something about our spirituality. We want to go somewhere where it gets "done," like going to the gym to get our body in shape. "Just be" seems foreign to us.

We believe that our "doing" nature and the "just be" of the mystics can be reconciled if one word is added so that it reads: "Just be *human*." Looked at in this light the doers, the spiritual thinkers, and even the evolutionary psychologists come together. Unfortunately, humankind has lost its way, and increasingly we are turning aside from the very elements that make us human.

In a sense, we are all captive to a society that is both controlling and out of control. Even many religions use faith to disempower or devalue us. Yet to fully access the empowering spiritual potential within each of us, we must reclaim our humanity. Of course, this is what you have been doing all through the book as you slough off the aspects of yourself that are not congruent with your real nature and build a relationship environment that will nurture and sustain the real you. But there are additional ways you can enhance your spiritual experience.

THE GOD SPOT

A wave of recent research has shown spirituality—including belief and spiritual practices that don't involve adherence to a specific creed—is tied in with healthy brain function. It is also closely allied to freedom from depression.

In the pioneering study, scientists at UC San Diego under the leadership of Prof. Vilayanur Ramachandran discovered a small part of the brain within the temporal lobe that they called the "God Module." Their discovery was promptly seized upon by the press and nicknamed the "God Spot." This series of neural circuits reacted strongly to words such as *God* or *worship*. It seemed that this region was specialized in belief (see Figure 15.1).

The announcement of the "God Spot" was made in October 1997 and was widely reported. The finding caused a great deal of controversy, with one side saying that this is proof that God had created our brain and the other side saying that this is proof that our brain had created God. The scientists who made the finding claimed that it proved neither contention.

However, it is not really surprising that there is such a part of the brain or that we are, literally, wired for belief of some kind. Psychologists have long assumed that there must be some genetic foundation to religion, because no society in the world is without it. What's more, it seems to play a prominent role in our sense of optimism and hope and therefore our survival as a species.

Imagine for a moment two bands of hunter-gatherers; call them Tribe A and Tribe B. Tribe A has a belief system that includes a rain god and an antelope god. Tribe B has no such belief. They are rationalists, unbelievers to the core. Now imagine that a ferocious drought comes. The plants and even roots they depend on wither and die and the antelope no longer come to graze.

Tribe A does their rain dances and their ceremonies to propitiate the antelope god. They are sure that the gods will provide. The members of Tribe B look at the sky, scratch their heads, and don't know what to do. Which tribe will last longer: A or B? Probably A, because it has hope based on its beliefs and this hope will sustain its members until the drought breaks and the rains come. Tribe B will most likely develop severe depressive symptoms, give up, and die out.

FIGURE 15.1 MAJOR BRAIN REGIONS INVOLVED IN SPIRITUALITY

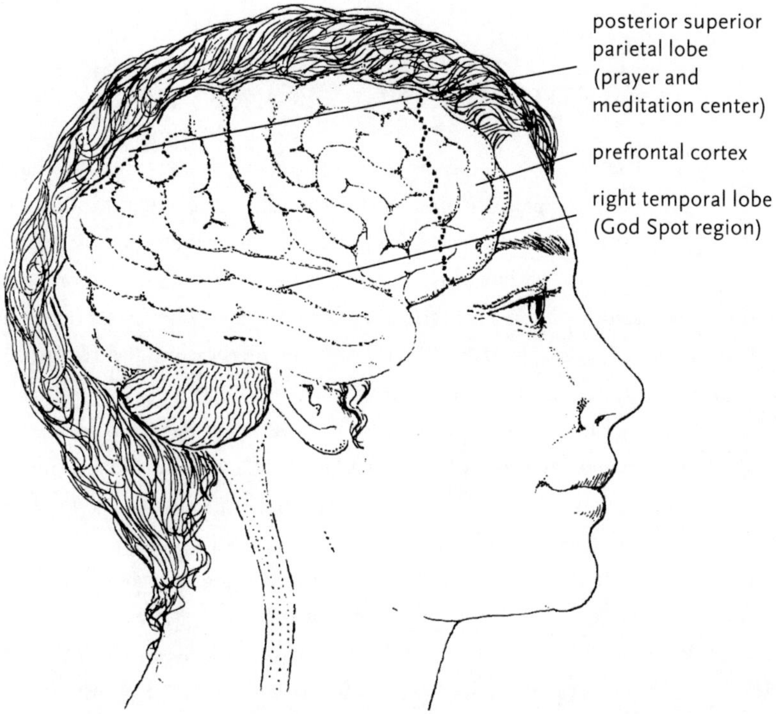

posterior superior
parietal lobe
(prayer and
meditation center)

prefrontal cortex

right temporal lobe
(God Spot region)

A personified god may not be fashionable in some circles these days, but as human beings, historically, we tend to develop beliefs that have one thing in common: a sense of a power greater than ourselves that protects us. In the words of Gershwin, we long for "Someone to Watch over Me."

Modern people also seem to withstand tough times better if buoyed up by faith. A detailed 2002 study by Prof. Peter Coleman of the University of Southampton for the U.K. Economic and Social Research Council showed a statistical link between the strength of religious conviction and the absence of depression. The study looked at older people who had lost a spouse, since the elderly are among the most at risk for the disorder. Those who had strong religious beliefs became far less depressed after their loss than those who had weak or moderate beliefs. It is no wonder that the incidence of depression has increased throughout the developed world, especially among the elderly, as faith in traditional religions has declined.

MEDITATION AND PRAYER

Scientists have observed the closely linked functioning of two areas of the brain that may be related to the gains people report from prayer and meditation (see Figure 15.1). One is a small region near the back of the brain, called the posterior superior parietal lobe (PSPL), which constantly calculates a person's spatial orientation, the sense of where one's body ends and the world begins. This area is normally a hive of activity. However, during intense prayer or meditation and for unknown reasons, this region becomes a quiet oasis of inactivity.

It's as if sensory information coming into the PSPL has been blocked. According to Prof. Andrew Newburg of Pennsylvania University, who discovered this attribute, "It creates a blurring of the self-other relationship. If meditators go far enough, they have a complete dissolving of the self, a sense of union, a sense of infinite spacelessness." In his book *Why God Won't Go Away*, Newburg says that when this happens "the brain has no choice but to perceive that the self is endless and intimately interwoven with everyone and everything that the brain senses. And this perception feels utterly and unquestionably real." This is then the main prayer and meditation center of the brain, the area that makes deep apart-from-self states possible.

During meditation, activity increases in the prefrontal cortex, the area that is activated when anyone focuses attention on a particular task. A complex interaction between this thinking part of the brain and the PSPL occurs during spiritual or mystical experiences.

In meditative states, people seem to turn off what Gregg Jacobs, professor of psychiatry at Harvard Medical School, calls "the internal chatter" of the conscious brain.

Through its links to the central brain and the central nervous system, this concentration of cells in the PSPL is able to moderate the anxiety-provoking sympathetic nervous system and to bring a deep sense of calm both to the body and the brain. It also provides a much clearer picture of reality without the chatter—in other words, without the voices from the past.

Over thousands of years, humans have developed numerous ways to use this spiritual capacity of the brain to divert the mind from the triggers that perpetuate depressive episodes, to calm the sympathetic nervous system and thus reduce stress, and as the common expression says, to "take you out of yourself."

If you want to look into some traditional methods of attaining this or a similar state, including meditation, lots of information is available on the Web and in your local library, and many groups teach spiritual methods.

THE POWER OF PRAYER

Prayer also appears to be a universal human activity. Evidence from burial sites and cave paintings suggests that humans have been engaged in some form of prayer since the earliest days of our species. As soon as humans developed a consciousness of their relative powerlessness before the forces of nature, the precariousness of their existence, and their own mortality, they no doubt began giving expression to intense feelings of petition, praise, or thanksgiving.

Belief in a deity or anything beyond the here and now is not necessary to get the benefits of prayer. Buddhism, which is literally a non- (or a-) theistic religion, still sanctions prayer.

For example, Daisaku Ikeda, president of the Japanese Buddhist sect Soka Gakkai, has written that Buddhist prayer may be thought of as a focused expression of the sentiments of yearning, commitment, and appreciation. It is, however, distinguished by the fact that Buddhism locates the divine within the life of the individual practitioner. The purpose of Buddhist prayer is to awaken our innate capacities of strength, courage, and wisdom rather than to petition external forces.

In our view prayer has five benefits:

1. Prayer enhances a sense of connection to someone or some being who we believe watches over us. Ever since humans learned to speak, we have used talking to create relationships and let ourselves know we are not alone. Prayer, then, is a bonding dialogue with the divine. Even silent prayer can enhance this sense of relatedness and comfort.

2. Prayer organizes the subconscious to prioritize and match our desires to our values. We often think by means of internalized conversation. What better partner for this process of cognition than a representation of our most cherished ideals?

3. Prayer organizes the subconscious to mobilize resources and make the event happen. Repeated or frequent prayer keeps our goals alive within us.

4. Praying with others can enormously strengthen the bond between you and reinforce shared beliefs. Churches, synagogues, mosques, and even whole countries often urge their faithful to pray at the same place or, if that's not possible, at least at the same time.

5. Once the deity has been asked to provide something or do something, then the subconscious will organize the believer's perception of events to convince her that the prayer has been answered. This in itself will lift her mood and inspire optimism. Psychologists might laud this as unconscious "reframing"!

YOUR BELIEFS AND THE PROGRAM

But what if the entity you pray to is harsh, judgmental, or even threatening?

Susan, who came from a devout Christian family, told Alicia that as a little girl she went to bed in terror every night that God would finally get around to punishing her for her "sins." As an adult, this underlying guilt pushed her into abusive jobs and relationships, and, of course, depression.

When Alicia asked her about her beliefs, hoping to unearth some spiritual foundation for a sense of safety and comfort, Susan burst into tears. "How could God love me or want to help me? I'm so bad!" she sobbed.

Slowly Susan came to see that the face her God wore was that of her father, who would beat her with branches around the legs whenever she did something "evil," such as speak out of turn or not do her chores right. Slowly, Susan came to accept that if God existed, "He" probably didn't fit the exact profile of her father. After further thought, she came to the conclusion that the amount of "evil" a little girl could get up to was limited, and that it would be a very unfair God to punish her for it.

"But I'd hate to lose the idea that there was nothing outside of myself to comfort or protect me," she told Alicia.

"Then imagine what that comforter would look and sound like," Alicia suggested.

Susan finally imagined a tall woman with long blond hair who smiled at her and spoke lovingly. "It really works," she reported. "Whenever I feel frightened or in anguish, I picture her and I feel cared for and safe!"

All of our beliefs originally spring from our program. If your beliefs are empowering and bring comfort, all the better. If they don't, you might want to re-examine them. Of course, doubt is frightening; we want to cling to the scant certainty left to us in a changing world. But if spirituality is intrinsic to our nature, then it can probably withstand a little probing.

CONNECTEDNESS

Even if you have no religious inclinations or beliefs, don't want to pray, or find meditation difficult, you can still make use of the spiritual antidepressant you were born with.

Each one of us is capable of remembering or imagining a time and place or set of circumstances in which we were at one with ourselves, with other people, with nature, with the universe, or with our own representation of the divine. Some people call this "at one with the Way." We like to think of this as being present in the moment or a state of heightened consciousness of the things around you. In that sense, it is quite different from the "flow" we discussed in Chapter 13 or the temporary sensory deprivation that occurs when the prayer and meditation center takes over. Like these other states, however, being in the moment is a powerful spiritual experience. It is a deep connection to nature, to the divine, or to your fellow humans, and is at the very essence of spirituality.

If you are one of the lucky ones who does not suffer from depression or chronic anxiety, then you may be in this state on a regular basis. If you are not, then the cultivation of these experiences can give your mood a powerful boost. As with everything you do to make yourself feel better, you may have to consciously go against the whispers of the dysfunctional program.

Each of us will find different ways of becoming present in the moment. Bob uses listening to classical music, having a meal with friends, walking on a mountain forest trail with Alicia, or, late at night, taking in the silence and the stillness. Alicia finds herself present when, for example, she walks on a beach with Bob while watching the dogs and children play exuberantly, or even shops for clothes with women friends. During these times of being in the moment, people find that they can sidestep the control of the dysfunctional program, allowing their mood to elevate.

You'd think that once someone had felt this sense of bliss they'd do anything to get it back. Yet, we find that most of our Uplift students have never really asked themselves what kinds of experiences put them into this connected state, much less sought to replicate it. To perpetuate itself, depression tricks its sufferers into losing sight of the high experiences they've had and leaves them focusing on the low ones.

ALLOW YOURSELF TO
BE IN THE MOMENT

Linda, who came to the Uplift in Sydney, told the group how a friend, Glenn, had persuaded her to go bush-walking over the weekend before the workshop. She went very reluctantly, fearing that her depressed mood would not only make the experience painful for her, but would upset her companion as well. At first, she walked slowly, her footsteps leaden. She had trouble keeping up with Glenn and she felt that she was destroying the pleasure of the walk for him.

An hour into the walk, Linda began to feel a deep sense of calm and then, for the first time in many years, buoyancy. Her pace quickened. As she later wrote:

> I became acutely aware of the trees I was passing; the smooth-skinned red eucalypts, which I wanted to run my hands over; and the impossibly shiny green leaves of the palms. I strained to see the noisy green and red lorikeets and the magpies, whose singsong calls always sound to me like Chinese. I caught the rustling of lizards and the sounds of wallabies hopping through the undergrowth. I found myself really enjoying just being with Glenn and sharing what I was seeing and hearing. I also remembered, for the first time in many years, instances in my childhood when I had been really happy. These were when my brother and his friends would take me walking in the woods or when I sat happily dangling my feet in the water while they fished in the creek.

Later in the week, when the depression returned, she found it difficult to accept the fact that she'd been happy. The memory of the first part of the walk came readily to her—the fatigue, the struggle to keep up, the feeling of uselessness. But the memory of the joy and the connectedness to nature and to her friend was less easy to recall. It was as if the earlier, blacker experiences were more real.

Linda's inner saboteur was blocking out the good times, particularly those that would stimulate her inner resources for healing and renewal, and trying to prevent any more. In fact, when Glenn, her companion, suggested that they go again, she turned him down. Her program-driven fear was that the happiness would never return and he would see her for the depressive she was.

During the Uplift, Linda was able to recall the good parts of her bush walk with Glenn and wrote the paragraph earlier. We call this an "in the moment piece," a short description of a situation that allows participants to feel in the moment and experience what that state feels like. By forcing her mind to recollect details of the walk, Linda found the joy of it returning. She kept what she had written as a reminder that she could be happy. Going very much against the program, Linda summoned up the courage to suggest to Glenn that they go bush-walking again. He was happy to accept.

EXERCISE 19 IN THE MOMENT

1. List the circumstances or activities that allow you to be present in the moment.
2. Write a paragraph or so—longer if you wish—about each.
3. Participate in these activities or ones like them as often as you can.

To defeat the saboteur who may try to dissuade you from seeking out these positive experiences, encourage others to remind you to participate in those activities and invite friends to join you.

A PORTAL TO SPIRITUALITY

Our ancient ancestors developed belief systems that reflected and consolidated their sense of oneness with the land, sky, and plants and animals around them. The natural world is a portal into your own spirituality.

If you lose your connection with the natural world, you lose contact with your own spiritual nature. You become prone to depression. If you live in a city surrounded by concrete and without frequent access to trees, grass, and wild animals, you are shut off from a vital source of strength as well as inspiration. If you cannot lose yourself in the wonder and majesty of nature without, you lose your sense of the majesty within.

You don't have to climb rugged mountains, explore unspoiled forests, and brave wild storms at sea to feel connected to nature. Your interdependence with nature is much broader than that, and at the same time far more intimate. It comes from watching your cat sleeping in a patch of sun, the sparrow feeding on your windowsill, the dandelions in your yard, the squirrels and pigeons in a nearby park. It comes from feeling mist on your cheek or standing in your shower enjoying life-giving water that over the eons has sojourned as rain in the Amazon or the thick brine of the Dead Sea.

Anything that sparks a connection, however fragile, to nature seems to awaken our deepest healing capacity. We would view this innate healing mechanism as deeply spiritual. The many reports that aromatherapy makes people feel better may be because it stimulates the sense of being in the natural world.

A well-planned garden can have a strong healing effect, according to Chris Rowlands, the charge nurse who runs Bredon House, a home for dementia sufferers in Worcestershire in England. At a minimal cost, Bredon designed a garden that made a big difference in the mood of his charges. Created to stimulate all five senses, the area contains scented flowers such as mock orange, lilac, honeysuckle, and jasmine. Wind chimes and water features produce soothing sounds. Thyme is planted into cracks in the patio so that it crackles when residents walk on it, releasing the scent of the herb.

Living with pets harkens back to our hunter-gatherer days, when we moved among the animals as one of them, not as a dysfunctional conqueror. We are almost surely genetically predisposed to be in close proximity to other animals. Humans and dogs, for instance, have a shared history going back hundreds of thousands, maybe millions of years. A 2002 study by Dr. Bruce Headey at the Melbourne (Australia) Institute of Applied Economic and Social Research found that people who had pets visited the doctor 10 percent less frequently than non–pet owners, saving the health system $3.86 billion annually. Studies carried out in Germany came to similar conclusions. This shows that a connection that close cannot be severed without dire consequences to our physical, psychological, and spiritual health.

Nurturing the Divine in Each Other

Spirituality is often portrayed as an intensely solitary experience: the monk in his craggy domicile on a storm-drenched Irish island or a lone searcher trudging across the desert sands praying for a vision. In reality, however, spirituality is not exempt from our communal nature. In fact, it relies largely upon it.

It's perfectly possible to experience a powerful and life-altering spiritual state or insight on your own. But your ability to stay connected to this aspect of yourself will depend largely on support from others.

A number of years ago Bob, at the time a confirmed atheist, had a peak experience of interconnectedness that sent ongoing ripples through his life and profoundly changed his view of himself and the world. Bob's program tried to reassert itself, creating vulnerability and confusion for a while. Without Alicia's enthusiastic encouragement to talk about his feelings and emerging new ideas, he is sure he would not have developed the increased tolerance and compassion that blossomed from that moment.

Unfortunately most people don't have that sort of support.

Daniel was a client of Bob's in Florida who also had a profound spiritual experience that did not fit into any particular religious context. He saw a vision of multiple concurrent universes in which everything was not only possible, but certain, and not reliant on the will of any god. It gave him a profound sense of being timeless and at one with everything that was happening, had happened, and would ever happen.

His wife and most of their joint friends belonged to a small and very fundamentalist Baptist church who felt that what had happened to Daniel was contrary to their own beliefs and morally wrong to espouse. Every time he tried to talk about his experience to his wife, she flew into a rage, accusing him of being in league with Satan. She spoke about her fears to her pastor and he advised her to leave Daniel, which she did.

Daniel was devastated and sank into a clinically depressed state, which lasted for the next five years. He felt that the vision that he experienced was the cause of the failure of his marriage and he resolved not to talk about it again to anyone.

This only made matters worse. The denial of your own spiritual feelings and experience is one of the greatest triggers for depression, as a recent WHO study has shown. The researchers concluded that the suppression of religion in the old Soviet Union was the prime reason for that country, together with the Soviet bloc nations of eastern Europe, having nearly the highest rate of suicide and depression in the world.

Daniel began to heal from his illness when he allowed himself to speak to someone, in his case Bob, who regarded him as neither mad nor bad. Whatever your spiritual beliefs, it is important to seek out people who share them. This reaching out for spiritual support is a natural part of our humanity.

SHARED BELIEFS

It's not just that relationships are good for spirituality; shared beliefs (or even talking openly about your beliefs to each other) are good for relationships. Researchers such as Tim Heaton of Bingham University have shown that sharing spiritual beliefs makes relationships more satisfactory and long-lasting. Although political or any other strongly held attitudes help bond us together, shared spiritual or metaphysical beliefs are particularly powerful since people tend to see these as being more fundamental or important.

The absence of shared belief, or even worse the presence of contradictory ones, can be a high hurdle for a relationship. We know of some couples who couldn't reconcile their different beliefs and whose relationships suffered or ended. Even among hunter-gatherers, fundamental differences about beliefs arose that caused some members to leave. As Anthony Stevens and John Price point out in their book *Evolutionary Psychiatry*, this often happened when the band was over the maximum optimal number of people.

But if you both want to make the relationship work, the first step is to agree not to disparage each other's beliefs. Use needs to set boundaries around actions that you feel are harmful to you or the relationships. Talk to each other and seek out areas of philosophical and theological commonality.

The exercise Shared Beliefs will help you clarify your own convictions and explore areas of compatibility with others in your life. You may also find it an uplifting, if at times challenging, experience.

EXERCISE 20 SHARED BELIEFS

1. List the theological and philosophical opinions that you share with your partner and/or close friends. This will involve talking to them about their beliefs as well as your own.
2. Work out a shared set of beliefs, or creed, for your tribe. Ask yourselves what rituals would be appropriate for this creed.

FINDING YOUR OWN PATH

Whatever your path to spirituality—through connection to nature, meditation, belief, or deeply supportive relationships with other human beings—you can connect with your true humanity. You are, in the end, a spiritual creature, and optimism and freedom from depression arise from going with the flow of your evolutionary inheritance.

In his book *Darwin's Cathedral: Evolution, Religion, and the Nature of Society*, David Sloan Wilson argues that religion and spirituality provide "the bio-cultural cohesive force that binds individual humans into coherent groups that function as a single organism." It is within that organism—the band in hunter-gatherer terms, the different groups to which we belong in ours—that we find our self-esteem, our sense of competence, our safety—and our spirituality.

As you may have discovered on your voyage with us, the process of emerging from depression into optimism deepens over time. At first, in the depths of your despair, you look up at the sky and see a thick bank of clouds with no possibility of light and no sense of optimism. Occasionally, however, the mood will lift and you may notice a small break in those clouds, maybe a long way off, illuminating a part of the landscape, enlightening other people, bringing them warmth and happiness. You see that not everyone shares the gloom. But, of course, at this stage you believe that the light will never reach you.

Gradually, as you heal, as you come to terms with your real self, the sky opens more and it becomes possible that you, too, may be taken into the sunshine. At this stage you're almost afraid to hope. And then, at last, the warm rays envelop you and you wonder how you could ever have been depressed.

Our humanness is that chink in the clouds—something almost obliterated by the society we have created over the last few millennia. Awakening to our spiritual nature opens the clouds and gives us the hope to get to, and the courage to welcome, the light. And the techniques we have shared with you will provide the way.

MEDITATION: ALL THERE IS

Relax and close your eyes. Clear your mind of thought. Good.

I invite you to look through your closed eyes as if they were not yours. As if they were those of someone you trusted to love you. Maybe a friend, or a lover, or a family member, or even a smiling spiritual presence.

Imagine you as that being sees you—through the eyes of love. Imagine your perfection. It is perfection beyond the details of your body, beyond the transience of your mood. It is love and it sees the soul.

Imagine that that person, or entity, takes your hand and pulls you gently to your feet, and without a sound bids you walk, hand in hand.

Outside there is a garden. Sweet scents flow up to you, flowers eager for your sight present their colors. Trees turn their leaves in the breeze, bidding you come closer.

Your feet can sense the carpet of grass beneath them. You can feel the stability of the earth. You take off your shoes. You are one with the grass, with the soil that gives this garden life. The one who holds your hand says, softly, "I am the Earth."

From the end of the garden you hear the call of a small bird, insistent for your attention, which you give. You let go of the hand and raise up your arms as if they were wings. You are a child. You run around the lawn flapping your arms, making birdsong, imagining that you could soar on your pinions and ride the thermals.

With your wings you fly on your imagination through gaps in drifting clouds. You surf down their slopes, you dive into their storms, you cleanse yourself in their moisture.

You cry, "I am the Sky!"

Now you land back in the garden and the friend, or the lover, or the family member or loving presence is waiting. You take the outstretched hand.

Suddenly there is no barrier between you and the inhabitants of the garden, or the earth, or the birds that visit. Or the being beside you.

Love is a smile, and love is a hand, and love is eyes that see you as perfection.

Safe within the smile you allow yourself to grow to you, keeping the connection. There is no you beginning nor you ending. You are infinity and infinity is you.

"I am all there is," you whisper.

I am the Earth.
I am the Sky.
I am All There Is.
Stay within the eyes of one who loves you, and let that one be you.

APPENDIX

To Friends and Family

◉

In this book, we've spoken mostly to people who want to free themselves from depression and pessimism. However, we haven't directly addressed those whose lives are entwined with people suffering from these conditions. According to government statistics, even if you are one of the lucky ones who escape depression, your life is likely to be affected by those who haven't.

This appendix is for you. (If you yourself are the sufferer, you may want to share these pages with those who are important to you and hope that they will be inspired to read the book.) It is also a message of hope. The process of helping a loved one or colleague through the illness using our techniques can not only contribute immeasurably to their healing, but enhance as well your own emotional development, optimism, and happiness.

This appendix is also different because I, Bob, am writing it, not we (Bob and Alicia). For the first time in the book I can use the "I" word.

Living with depression is not easy, either for the sufferer or for his friend, colleague, or life partner. Clinical depression is a black hole into which come only brief flashes of light, quick glimpses of what the relationship might be like "if only . . ." Even if the depressed person's friend is not depressed, the friend can suffer almost as much as his companion who is.

Nearly all of the research in this area—and there's a lot of it—deals with the plight of the person who "has" depression, not those who suffer along with him. Support groups for carers do exist, and these can be very useful, if only to see that you are not alone and it's not your fault.

Even with all that has been written about it, depression is still largely a secret disease. People don't admit to it readily and certainly don't reveal that someone they love has it. I have known people who've kept a secret of their dark moods for many years, even from those closest to them. Yet to seek help, that acknowledgment has to be made.

Depression is a sneaky disorder, and it's often difficult for the nonsufferer to spot. When you do find out, you may feel helpless because there is seemingly nothing you can do to ameliorate the situation. However, this is not true. Allow me to briefly share my story and insights with you.

My Personal Experience with Others' Depression

For twenty years I have seen clients in therapy who were depressed themselves or who were in a relationship with someone else who was (or both). I myself have also had very close relationships of different kinds with three sufferers.

These three people were my mother, a good friend and work colleague, and Alicia (when she was depressed). Most of us who are drawn to depressed people as adults come from a home in which someone was depressed. I was no exception. We who've had depressed parents have unfinished business. Our program, from very early childhood, is to try to rescue the parent, or later on, the parent surrogate. This is true even if we don't, as children, recognize depression as such. Obviously, though, we can't make a sad parent happy. We try all our lives to make up for our perceived failure.

So it was with me and my mother, who was an alcoholic and who, after my father's death, manifested the symptoms of depression. I felt deeply guilty for leaving her in England after my father's death when I was fifteen and returning to Australia to finish high school and college.

Before I began to earn my living as a psychologist, I found it difficult to recognize the illness in people around me. But looking back now, I can clearly see the signs in some of them. One of my most engaging and brilliant colleagues was a TV scriptwriter I'll call Brian, with whom I worked closely as a producer. He and I created a number of children's series for British television, two of which won awards. Brian was married and had three children but he rarely, if ever, spoke of his home life. His main interest was sailing and, given the chance, he would talk about that endlessly.

The first inkling I had that something was wrong was one day when we were working under a particularly tight deadline, and he didn't show up. I called his home and got his wife on the phone. "Brian's in bed," she said. "He hasn't really been up for several days."

I asked her what was wrong and she hedged. "He gets like this," she finally admitted.

In the end, I wrote the script myself. It worked, but it didn't have his flair. Carrying Brian became something I, and the rest of the television crew, became used to doing. Brian never admitted his illness and never went into treatment. I wish I could say that there was a happy ending, but there wasn't. Eventually we gave up on him and he drifted out of my life.

When I met and fell in love with Alicia, it was at a time when she was in remission from the illness. Depression, we now know, is cyclical in nature and there can be long symptom-free periods. Also an event—falling in love, an outstanding career success, even a severe crisis that calls for immediate action—can jolt the brain out of a depressive period.

Unfortunately that is the way with depression; the light flooding the black hole may be temporary but the victim, and his companions, wants to believe that it is permanent. Of course, Alicia's blackness returned and I watched her sink into profound pessimism, illness, and hopelessness. Unlike Brian, Alicia did not respond to the illness with lethargy. She would throw herself into work, seeing far too many clients. She would berate herself if she had a free hour in a week. Her mood would lift temporarily when she was very focused on either writing or seeing clients, so she was trying to work her way through the illness. And then she would break down.

As with many people in my position, I tried at first to make it right for her, to be the rescuer. I tried to appease the dysfunctional demands her program made. It was never enough, but sometimes, by extraordinary effort, I was able to satisfy some element of the program and the depression would wondrously lift. I got hooked into a pattern of trying to rescue by giving in to the dysfunctional needs of her angry and abused inner child.

I knew that what I was doing was, in the end, futile, but depression uses love to create the circumstances of its own survival. The illness teaches partners, colleagues, and friends how they should behave by the rewarding respites, the flashes of light. For a while their loved one, the creative worker, the supportive friend, returns and any sacrifice to that end is worthwhile.

Sometimes the victim's mood is so irrational! He is down when everything is going well and you want him to share your joy; he declares everything is hopeless when there is only a small problem; he's unable to appreciate it when you have gone out of your way to do something or get him something you thought he liked. And in spite of yourself, you get angry, you want him to "just snap out of it." But he can't.

The general trajectory of the relationship between a depressed person and those close to him follows a pattern. The disorder is publicly denied, is slavishly catered to, and in the end becomes more important than you or the relationship. You slip into codependence. Since Alicia and I developed a deep awareness of our patterns and a commitment to honesty with each other, we were able, fortunately, to quickly extricate ourselves from this pattern. Most people are not so lucky.

Alicia and I began to work out the basis of a healing relationship. We looked outside of the narrow framework of our original studies and developed ways in which both of us could be healed. Just as it's important for people who suffer from depression to admit the problem and seek help, so it's important for their friends to acknowledge how their own childhood programming sets them up to be codependent. In my case it was my mother's mood disorder and both my parents' alcoholism.

Alicia and I developed the Uplift Program for healing depression together; at the same time I have developed a set of rules for those who care about the disorder's victims.

Guidelines for Coping with Someone Else's Depression

It may come as a surprise that your way out of this situation is not to try to cure the other person's illness. That, for you alone, is an impossible task. Even if you are a trained therapist, you are too close to a good friend to use therapeutic techniques. Your own program will be triggered and the depression will have won. Instead, the solution lies in following these basic guidelines. If you have read the information in this book and followed our suggestions you will already be doing much of this. If so, you will have become an important part of the sufferer's relationship environment that will ultimately defeat the depression.

1. **Understand the disorder.** Take time to find out what depression is and is not. So many popular misunderstandings about the illness and so much denial about its origins exist. If you haven't read it already, you may find Chapter 3, "The Truth About Depression," especially helpful in this regard.

2. **Keep in mind that he can't "snap out of it."** Remember that the other person has a real illness. Like someone with cancer, he can't simply "get over it." Try not to express your frustration or anger in ways you'll regret, but don't suppress your own feelings either. You can say, for example, "I know that you can't help feeling down, but I feel frustrated."

   If the person is an unrelenting pessimist, as so many people with depression are, try to point out the positive things that are happening. His program will probably prevent him from seeing these for himself. The illness has a vested interest in the lie that nothing will go right.

3. **Ask about his feelings and his program.** Encourage your friend to discuss his feelings with you. Your ability to listen nonjudgmentally will be helpful in itself. It will also give you the opportunity to learn about his childhood patterning and what role you are playing in regard to it. Who do you represent to him from his early life? What actions of yours may be triggering depressive episodes? If he has done the exercises in this book, ask him to share with you what he has learned about himself.

4. **Admit your own powerlessness against the disorder.** Many people believe they can cure someone they love just by the sheer force of their love, as if that feeling alone should be enough to effect permanent change. It isn't.

   The first stage to avoiding guilt over someone else's depression is to acknowledge that you are not responsible for it. It's not your fault, and you alone can't cure it. You can offer support, you can show friendship or love, whichever is appropriate, but you are probably too close to be able to solve the problem. Step back, admit that you alone are powerless against the disorder. Seek support for yourself from friends and perhaps a psychotherapist. The first stage toward helping the other person is to get help for yourself.

5. **Do not try to rescue.** A person suffering from a mood disorder will probably be a slave to his program. The disorder will infantilize him, and he may well put pressure on you to fix whatever he perceives to be the problem. Sometimes the pro-

gram can be temporarily assuaged in this way and the depression will lift. But it will come back and the program will make even more demands. You may be forced into trying to play the role of omnipotent parent and feel guilty when you fail to provide what is demanded of you.

One solution is to ask him to identify his real needs for you, as we've described in Chapter 7, "Discover Your Real Needs," and elsewhere. Following these instructions will enable you both to distinguish between functional needs and those dictated by the dysfunctional program.

6. **Don't make excuses for him.** Never become part of the depressed person's denial. Don't lie for him. Making excuses or covering up for a friend or colleague only prevents him from getting timely help. In the addiction field, this is called "enabling." In the case of Brian, my making excuses for him probably did him harm and delayed his recovery.

7. **Encourage him to seek help.** Many sufferers from depression deny that they have the disorder or try to self-medicate with alcohol (as my mother did) or overwork or shopping—all of which are depressives in the long run. Part of your self-preservation is getting the depressed person in your life to seek professional help. This is true whether you live or work with him.

8. **Discover your own program.** It's important to realize that the other person's depression is playing a role in your inner saboteur's game. In clinical terms, you may be getting a "secondary gain" from his disorder. His behavior may seem to give you an excuse to vent angry feelings, or an opportunity for you to play the knight in shining armor, or perhaps a reason to excuse your own real or imagined shortcomings. If you find yourself having relationships with a number of people who are depressed, there's probably a reason in your own past. Seek help in dealing with those emotions and fears.

9. **Tell him what you need.** The depressed person in your life may be ill, but you still have needs of him. All relationships are based on the mutual meeting of needs.

If you aren't honest about what you're getting from the relationship, or what you want to get, you will make the other person feel even worse about himself. If you follow the guidelines in this book, you'll learn how to identify your own needs and boundaries and be true to them. You'll also know when it's OK for you to compromise and when it's not. Be honest about what you can and cannot do, and about what you will and won't do. Never promise what you can't fulfill. You may often be asked to.

On the other hand, going through the process of exchanging real, functional needs with the depressed person can be a very powerful healing tool for both of you.

Above all, remember that even the worst depression is curable, even if you alone can't cure it. The turning point can come at any time, maybe without your even realizing it. If you and your friend do what we suggest, the real person you chose to live with or to work with will come back to you for good.

NOTES

◉

1. This is true even if you do have a genetic or prenatal predisposition for depression. Most researchers believe that such genes (nature) are influenced by environment (nurture). Apparently, genetically we inherit a temperament that, under the right (or wrong) environmental conditions in childhood, can trigger depression.

2. We will talk a great deal about hunter-gatherers because we have not changed biologically since their time. Their genetic makeup is our genetic makeup, and it evolved to suit their lifestyle. The more we diverge from that lifestyle the more stressed we become and this stress leads to societal and individual abuse of us and to depression. We do not mean to glamorize hunter-gatherers.

3. We are not saying that cognitive-behavioral therapy, in particular, is useless, far from it. It is a valuable tool that we ourselves make use of. What we believe is that this method is not sufficient because it does not take into account recent advances in neurobiology, does not trace individual "schemas" back to the past to externalize them, and does not adequately factor in the importance of relationships as both a cause and cure of depression.

4. Hunter-gatherers lived in small bands (maximum size around fifty). With population growth in some places such as North America, these gradually federated to become tribes who shared a common culture and language. In this book, when we refer to hunter-gatherer "bands" or "tribes," we are referring to the smaller, more ancestral unit. We can learn a lot about the lives of these people through studying modern hunter-gatherers in Africa and South America, as well as through archaeological and biological research.

5. The world's population at the beginning of the Stone Age agricultural revolution is estimated at somewhere around five million. At one period of mankind's history, you could have fit all of us onto a couple of commuter trains and had a few seats to spare. There was a real danger of extinction. (Many other hominids, including the Neanderthals, went that way.)

6. We use the term "genetics" a bit loosely. The word has two meanings. The first regards characteristics that all humans share, as in the phrase "men (or women) are genetically (or biologically) wired to fulfill certain roles." The second refers to inherited individual characteristics that are passed down from generation to generation, as in "X inherited the genetic propensity for anxiety from her mother," or "your genes don't determine your destiny." It is, we hope, clear from the text which meaning is appropriate.

7. If young men don't find danger and camaraderie in work or school, they will seek these out in less functional or even illegal ways, which is very largely why they take drugs and play chicken in cars (auto accidents are, with suicide and homicide, the top killers of young American males). They may also become violent and abuse each other and those who are vulnerable.

8. Studies have shown that too much sit-still class work and not enough play are major factors in the development of ADD/ADHD. Many U.S. schools have replaced playtime with more academic classes, which, these studies claim, may promote ADHD.

9. Early childhood adversity, particularly fighting between parents, has been shown to be a causal factor in ADD/ADHD. That this stress can begin in the womb and continue to adulthood is confirmed by research done at Emory University by Prof. Paul Plotsky and presented to the American Association for the Advancement of Science on 15 February 2003.

10. Chimps don't look after their older brethren. Several researchers have pointed out that there are no postmenopausal female chimps to be found in the wild.

11. It is our view that depression is, in a sense, a dissociative disorder. It is a way for the brain to escape from an intolerable situation. We have often heard

clients tell us that "I just wasn't there" when abuse was happening to them. Other clients can be amnesiac about whole periods of their early life.

12. Not all therapists or physicians accept this viewpoint. Some even deny that child abuse exists. Bob remembers talking to an Australian psychiatrist a few years ago who stated, with an edge to her voice, that "sexual abuse doesn't happen in Australia." We have also had conversations with psychotherapists in the United Kingdom and elsewhere who said that child abuse was "an American phenomenon." Some psychologists take the view that although abuse happens, it has no effect in adulthood and therefore need not be addressed. Yet all the evidence, from Freud to modern neuroscience, says that this is simply wrong.

13. Preliminary research published in *Science* in July 2003 has shown that a variant of the serotonin transmitter gene 5-HTT may predispose those who have the "short," or stress-sensitive, version of it to depression. However, the researchers, led by Terrie Moffitt, strongly emphasize that even if you do, depression will probably not occur unless you suffered from events in an early adverse environment.

14. Of course, serotonin is not the only neurochemical implicated in the depression syndrome. Imbalances of cortisol (especially during illness) and noradrenaline (which is closely related to anxiety) also play their part.

15. Very recent studies indicate that behavioral therapies can bring about neurobiological change and reverse the harmful effects of drug addiction. And we believe the same can be said of other forms of trauma that lead to depression.

16. Any process that has the goal of eliciting buried memories will create misunderstanding at best and retraumatization at worst. Each time the client is urged to dredge up a "memory," more neurons are brought to bear around a traumatic experience. Whether true or false, the event becomes solidified in the person's mind and the trauma is increased.

17. In a paper presented to the 2002 annual conference of the British Psychological Society, psychologists who worked with various sports teams

and individuals, including golfers and marksmen, claimed that sports people practicing their game in their imaginations achieved real improvements of up to 57 percent (reported in *BBC News Online*, 13 March 2002).

18. In the professional Feldenkrais training Alicia graduated from, there was almost no mention of emotions, although obviously people in the training were having emotional reactions to the intensive experience. Ruthy Alon, a well-known Feldenkrais trainer and longtime Israeli student of Moshe Feldenkrais, told us that our work represented the direction Moshe "might have taken had he lived longer" in incorporating both emotional and spiritual elements into his work. Other Feldenkrais trainers and practitioners may now be teaching Feldenkrais in a more inclusive way.

19. Alicia's audiocassette tapes containing Repatterning Movements and meditations in movement are available at upliftprogram.com.

BIBLIOGRAPHY

◉

New research in the fields covered by this book is constantly becoming available. This list is limited to those studies and books that we directly refer to or use as primary sources. More information and research can be found on our website upliftprogram.com.

INTRODUCTION

Kaptchuk, Ten, et al. "Pondering the Placebo Effect." *Newsweek*, 2 December 2002.

Ono, Utaka, et al. "Dimensions of Temperament as Vulnerability Factors in Depression." *Molecular Psychiatry* (2002) 7(9).

CHAPTER 1

Bailey, Geoff. Ed. *Hunter-Gatherer Economy in Prehistory: A European Perspective*. Cambridge: Cambridge University Press, 1983.

Barash, David, and Judith Lipton. *The Myth of Monogamy: Fidelity and Infidelity in Animals and People*. New York: W. H. Freeman, 2001.

Becker, Daniel F., et al. "Diagnostic Efficiency of Borderline Personality Disorder Criteria in Hospitalized Adolescents: Comparison with Hospitalized Adults." *American Journal of Psychiatry* (2002) 159:2042–2047.

Biederman, Joseph, et al. "Differential Effect of Environmental Adversity by Gender: Rutters Index of Adversity in a Group of Boys and Girls with and Without ADHD." *American Journal of Psychiatry* (2002) 159:1556–1562.

Bird, Douglas W., et al. "Mardu Children's Hunting Strategies in the Western Desert, Australia." Paper for CHAGS, University of Maine, 2000.

Bronfenbrenner, Urie. Ed. *The State of Americans: This Generation and the Next.* New York: Free Press, 1996.

Danner, Deborah, et al. "Positive Emotions in Early Life and Longevity: Findings from the Nun Study." *Journal of Personality & Social Psychology* (2001) 80:804–813.

Gijswijt-Hofstra, M., and R. Porter. Ed. *Cultures of Psychiatry and Mental Health Care in Postwar Britain and the Netherlands.* Amsterdam: Wellcome Institute, 1998.

Gilbert, Paul Raymond. *Human Nature and Suffering.* New York: Guilford, 1992.

Goldman, David, and Anil J. Malhorta. "The Dopamine Receptor Gene and Novelty Seeking." *American Journal of Psychiatry* (2000) 157:1885.

Harkness, Kate L., and Scott M. Monroe. "Childhood Adversity and the Endogenous Versus Nonendogenous Distinction in Women with Major Depression." *American Journal of Psychiatry* (2002) 159:387–393.

Hawkes, Kristin, et al. "Antiquity of Postreproductive Life." *American Journal of Human Biology* (2002) 14:184–205.

Hayward, John. *Illustrated History of Early Man.* London: PRC, 1995.

Heim, C., et al. "The Role of Early Adverse Life Events in the Etiology of Depression and Post-Traumatic Stress Disorder. Focus on Corticotropin-Releasing Factor." *Annals of the NY Academy of Science* (1997) 821:194–207.

Kaplowitz, P., et al. "Earlier Onset of Puberty in Girls: Relation to Increased Body Mass Index and Race." *Pediatrics* (2001) 108:347–353.

Klerman, G. L., and M. M. Weissman. "Increasing Rates of Depression." *JAMA* (1989) 261:2229–2235.

Licinio, J., and M. L. Wong. "Brain-Derived Neurotrophic Factor (BDNF): From Maternal Deprivation to Manic Depressive Illness." *Molecular Psychiatry* (2002) 7:579–593.

Lott, Deborah. "Childhood Trauma, CRF Hypersecretion and Depression." *Psychiatric Times* (1999) 16(10).

Maier, Gary J. "Understanding the Dynamics of Abusive Relationships." *Psychiatric Times* (1996) 13(9).

McGuire, Lynanne, et al. "Depressive Symptoms and Lymphocite Proliferation in Older Adults." *Journal of Abnormal Psychology* (2002) 111(1):192–197.

Morris, Desmond. *The Human Zoo.* New York: Jonathan Cape, 1969.

Narzroo, James. "Exploring Gender Difference in Depression." *Psychiatric Times* (2001) 18(3).

Palmer, Jack, and Linda Palmer. *Evolutionary Psychology: The Ultimate Origins of Human Behavior*. Needham Heights, Mass.: Allyn & Bacon, 2002.

Price, Richard H., et al. "Links in the Chain of Adversity Following Job Loss: How Financial Strain and Loss of Personal Control Lead to Depression, Impaired Functioning and Poor Health." *Journal of Occupational Health Psychology* (2002) 7:302–312.

Rank, Michael, et al. "A Comparative Study of Trauma Survivors: Nicaragua, Dominican Republic, South Florida." Report presented to the U.S. Center for Disaster Management and Humanitarian Assistance, 24 June 2002.

Rose, Frederick G. G. *The Traditional Mode of Production of the Australian Aborigines*. Sydney: Angus & Robertson, 1987.

Seligman, Martin. *Helplessness: On Depression Development and Death*. New York: W. H. Freeman, 1975.

Stevens, Anthony, and John Price. *Evolutionary Psychiatry*, 2d. ed. London: Routledge, 2000.

Turnbull, Colin. *The Forest People*. 1961 reprint. London: Pimlico, 1993.

Twenge, Jean M. "The Age of Anxiety? Birth Cohort Change in Anxiety and Neuroticism, 1952–1993." *Journal of Personality and Social Psychology* (2000) 79:1007–1021.

Weich, Scott, et al. "Mental Health and the Built Environment: Cross-Sectional Survey of Individual and Contextual Risk Factors for Depression." *The British Journal of Psychiatry* (2002) 180:428–433.

Williams, Kristi, et al. "Violent Behavior: A Measure of Emotional Upset." *Journal of Health and Social Behavior* (2002) 43:189–206.

Wright, Robert. "Evolution of Despair." *Time* magazine, 28 August 1995.

CHAPTER 2

Barker, Sandra B. "Therapeutic Aspects of the Human-Companion Animal Interaction." *Psychiatric Times* (1999) 16(2).

Brissette, Ian, et al. "The Role of Optimism in Social Network Development, Coping and Psychological Adjustment During a Life Transition." *Journal of Personality and Social Psychology* (2002) 81:102–111.

Clay, Rebecca. "Green Is Good for You." *Monitor on Psychology* (2001) 32(4).

Dehaene, Stanislas, et al. "Sources of Mathematical Thinking: Behavioral and Brain Imaging Evidence." *Science* (1999) 284:970–974.

Dunbar, Robin. "Coevolution of Neocortical Size, Group Size and Language in Humans." *Behavioral and Brain Sciences* (1993) 16(4):681–735.

Dunbar, Robin. "Neocortex Size as a Constraint in Group Size in Primates." *Journal of Human Evolution* (1992) 20:469–493.

Kahn, Peter H. *The Human Relationship with Nature: Development and Culture.* Cambridge, Mass.: MIT Press, 2001.

MacCallum, Robert, et al. "Avoiding Pessimism May Be More Important Than Being Optimistic." *Journal of Personality and Social Psychology* (1997) 73:1345–1353.

Martin, Paul. *The Sickening Mind.* London: Flamingo, 1997.

Miserandino, Marianne, et al. "Children Who Do Well in School: Individual Differences in Perceived Competence and Autonomy in Above-Average Children." *Journal of Educational Psychology* (1996) 88(2):203–214.

Reiss, Stephen. "Secrets of Happiness." *Psychology Today*, Jan/Feb 2001.

Schwartz, Michael Alan, et al. "The Crisis of Present-Day Psychiatry: Regaining the Personal." *Psychiatric Times* (1999) 16(9).

Seligman, Martin. *Learned Optimism.* New York: Alfred A. Knopf, 1991.

Sheldon, Kennon M., et al. "What Is Satisfying About Satisfying Events? Testing 10 Candidate Psychological Needs." *Journal of Personality and Social Psychology* (2001) 80(2):325–339.

Winter, Deborah DuNann. *Ecological Psychology.* New York: Harper Collins, 1995.

CHAPTER 3

American Psychiatric Association. *Diagnostic and Statistical Manual of Mental Disorders*, 4th ed. Washington, D.C.: American Psychiatric Association, 1994, p. 424.

American Psychological Association. "New Report on Women and Depression: Latest Research Findings." APA release, 15 March 2002.

Brake, W. G., et al. "Effects of Neonatal Maternal Separation on Gene Expression and Adult Behaviors in Mice." Society for Neuroscience, Abstracts 27 (2001).

Burns, David, et al. "Rumble in Reno: The Psychosocial Perspective on Depression." *Psychiatric Times* (2000) 17(8).

Editorial. "Take Comfort in Human Neurogenesis." *Nature Medicine* (1998) 4:1207.

Fava, Giovanni A., et al. "Cognitive Behavior Approach to Loss of Clinical Effect During Long-Term Antidepressant Treatment: A Pilot Study." *American Journal of Psychiatry* (2002) 159:2094–2095.

Gilbertson, Mark W., et al. "Smaller Hippocampal Volume Predicts Pathologic Vulnerability to Psychological Trauma." *Nature* (2002) 5:1242–1247.

Healy, David. *The Antidepressant Era*. Boston: Harvard Books, 1998.

Ivey, Allen E. *Counseling and Psychotherapy*, 4th ed. London: Allyn & Bacon, 1997.

Kessler, R. C., et al. "Posttraumatic Stress Disorder in the National Comorbidity Survey." *Archives of General Psychiatry* (1995) 52:1048–1060.

Kirsch, Irving, and David Antonuccio. "Antidepressants Versus Placebos: Meaningful Advantages Are Lacking." *Psychiatric Times* (2002) 19(9).

Kramer, Peter. *Listening to Prozac*. New York: Viking Penguin, 1987.

Moffitt, T., et al. "Influence of Life Stress on Depression: Moderation by a Polymorphism in the 5-HTT Gene." *Science* (2003) 301: 386–389.

Munoz, D. P., et al. "Human fMRI Evidence for the Neural Correlates of Preparatory Set." *Nature Neuroscience* (2002) 5:1345–1352.

Nemeroff, Charles. "The Persistent Neurobiological Consequences of Early Untoward Life Events: Treatment Implications." Lecture reported by Deborah Lott. "Childhood Trauma, CRF Hypersecretion and Depression." *Psychiatric Times* (1999) 16(10).

Nesse, Randolph. "Is Depression an Adaption?" *Archives of General Psychiatry* (2000) 57:14–20.

Novac, Andrei. "Traumatic Stress and Human Behavior." *Psychiatric Times* (2001) 17(4).

Resnick, H. S., et al. "Effects of Previous Trauma on Acute Plasma Cortisol Level Following Rape." *American Journal of Psychiatry* (1995) 152:1675–1677.

Self, David, et al. "Extinction-Induced Unregulation in AMPA Receptors Reduces Cocaine-Seeking Behavior." *Nature* (2003) 421:70–75.

Silver, Roxane Cohen, et al. "Nationwide Longitudinal Study of Psychological Responses to September 11." *Journal of the American Medical Association* (2002) 288:1235–1244.

Teicher, Martin. "Wounds That Time Won't Heal: The Neurobiology of Child Abuse." *Cerebrum* (2000) 2:50–67.

Tomb, D. A. "The Phenomenology of Posttraumatic Stress Disorder." *Psychiatric Clinical Journal of North America* (1994) 17:237–250.

Venter, Craig. "The Sequence of the Human Genome." *Science* (2001) 293:498–506.

Vythilingam, Meena. "Childhood Trauma Associated with Smaller Hippocampal Volume in Women with Major Depression." *American Journal of Psychiatry* (2002) 159:2072–2080.

Wessely, Simon. "Metanalysis of Trials Comparing Antidepressants with Active Placebos." *British Journal of Psychiatry* (1978) 172:227–231.

Wessely, Simon. "Mostly in the Mind." *New Scientist*, July 1998.

CHAPTER 4

Azar, Beth. "How Do Parents Matter, Let Us Count the Ways." *Monitor on Psychology* (2000) 31:62–66.

Borkowski, John G. *Parenting and the Child's World: Influences on Academic, Intellectual, and Social-Emotional Development.* Mahwah, NJ: Erlbaum, 2001.

Garbarino, James. *Lost Boys: Why Our Sons Turn Violent and How We Can Save Them.* New York: Free Press, 1999.

Joines, Vann, and Ian Stewart. *TA Today: A New Introduction to Transactional Analysis.* Nottingham: Lifespace, 1987.

Joseph, Stephen. "Peer-Victimization and Posttraumatic Stress in Adolescents." *Personality and Individual Differences* (2003) 29:815–882.

Paoloni-Giacobino, A., et al. "Identification and Analysis of New Sequence Variants in the Human Tryptophan Hydroxylase (TpH) Gene." *Molecular Psychiatry* (2000) 5:49–55.

Tolman, Deborah. "Adolescent Girls' Sexuality: Debunking the Myth of the Urban Girl." In *Urban Girls: Resisting Stereotypes, Creating Identities.* Ed. B. Leadbetter. New York: New York University Press, 1996.

CHAPTER 5

Andrews, B. "Bodily Shame in Relation to Abuse in Childhood and Bulimia: A Preliminary Investigation." *British Journal of Clinical Psychology* (1997) 36:41–49.

Barsky, A. J. "Somatization and Medicalization in the Era of Managed Care." *Journal of the American Medical Association* (1995) 274:1931–1934.

Bass, Christopher, and Stephanie May. "Chronic Multiple Functional Somatic Symptoms." *British Medical Journal* (2002) 325:323–326.

Blomhoff, Svein, et al. "Phobic Anxiety Changes the Function of Brain-Gut Axis in Irritable Bowel Syndrome." *Psychosomatic Medicine* (2001) 63:959–965.

Blumenthal, J., et al. "Effects of Exercise Training on Older Patients with Major Depression." *Archives of Internal Medicine* (1999) 159:2349–2356.

Bose, Joerg. "The Inhumanity of the Other: Treating Trauma and Depression." In *Review of Interpersonal Psychoanalysis* 3. New York: William Allenson White Institute, 2001.

Cooper, Z. "The Development and Maintenance of Eating Disorders." In *Eating Disorders and Obesity*. Ed. K. D. Brownell and C. G. Fairburn. New York: Guilford Press, 1995:199–206.

Dubovsky, Steven. *Mind Body Deceptions: The Psychosomatics of Everyday Life*. New York: Norton, 1997.

Escobar, J. I., et al. "Somatization in the Community." *Archives of General Psychiatry* (1987) 44:713–718.

Fried Ellen, Elizabeth. "Treating the Patient as a Whole Person." *Psychiatric Times* (2001) 17(6).

Gallo, Joseph. "Major Depression and Cancer: The 13-Year Follow-Up of the Baltimore Epidemiologic Catchment Area Sample (United States)." *Cancer Causes and Control* (2000) 11(8).

Glasser, D. "Child Abuse and Neglect and the Brain: A Review." *Journal of Child Psychiatry* (2000) 41:97–116.

Goldstein, Jay A. *Betrayal by the Brain: The Neurologic Basis of Chronic Fatigue Syndrome, Fibromyalgia Syndrome, and Related Neural Network Disorders*. Binghamton, N.Y.: Haworth Medical Press, 1996.

Grayson, B., and M. I. Stein. "Attracting Assault: Victims' Nonverbal Cues." *Journal of Communication* (1981) 31:68–75.

Hippisley-Cox, Julia, et al. "Depression as a Risk Factor for Ischaemic Heart Disease in Men: Population Based Case-Control Study." *British Medical Journal* (1998) 316:1714–1719.

Jankowiak, Janet. "Depression May Be Another Risk Factor for Alzheimer's Dementia." *Neurology* (2002) 59:E2–E5.

Kessler, David, et al. "Cross Sectional Study of Symptom Attribution and Recognition of Depression and Anxiety in Primary Care." *British Medical Journal* (1999) 313:436–440.

Kurtz, Ron, and Victor Prestera. *The Body Reveals: How to Read Your Own Body*, 2d. ed. New York: Harper Collins, 1984.

Lipowski, Z. J. "Somatization: Medicine's Unsolved Problem." *Psychosomatics* (1987) 28:294–297.

Loewenstein, R. J. "Dissociation, Development and the Psychobiology of Trauma." *Journal of the American Academy of Psychoanalysis* (1993) 21:581.

Lustman, Patrick J., and Ryan Anderson. "Depression in Adults with Diabetes." *Psychiatric Times* (2002) 19(1).

Rejeski, W. J., and A. Thompson. "Historical and Conceptual Roots of Exercise Psychology." In *Exercise Psychology: The Influence of Physical Exercise in Psychological Processes*. Ed. R. Seraganian. New York: John Wiley and Sons, 1993.

Salerian, Alen. Reported by Cecilia Capuzzi Simon in "A Walking Cure." *Washington Post*, 11 June 2002.

Schurman, A. D., et al. "Increased Risk of Parkinson's Disease After Depression," *Neurology* (2002) 58:1501–1504.

CHAPTER 6

Baumeister, R. F., and M. R. Leary. "The Need to Belong: Desire for Interpersonal Attachments as a Fundamental Human Motivation." *Psychological Bulletin* (1995) 117:497–529.

Conger, Rand D., et al. "Competence in Early Adult Romantic Relationships: A Developmental Perspective on Family Influences." *Prevention & Treatment* (2001) 4(11).

Morris, Lois B. "She Feels Sick. The Doctor Can't Find Anything Wrong." *New York Times*, 24 June 2001.

Schwartz, Michael Alan, and Osborne P. Wiggins. "The Crisis of Present-Day Psychiatry: Regaining the Personal." *Psychiatric Times* (1999) 16(9).

CHAPTER 7

Bateson, Gregory. *Steps to Ecology of Mind*. New York: Ballantine, 1972.

Gottman, John, and Nan Silver. *The Seven Principles for Making Marriage Work*. London: Orion, 1999.

Maslow, Abraham. *Motivation and Personality*. New York: Harper & Row, 1954.

Rosenberg, Marshall. *Non Violent Communication.* Center City, Minn.: Pud-
dledancer Press, 1999.

CHAPTER 8

Johnson, G. Norine, et al. Ed. *Beyond Appearance: A New Look at Adolescent Girls.*
Washington, D.C.: American Psychological Association, 1999.
Pipher, Mary. *Reviving Ophelia.* New York: Ballantine Books, 1995.
Tannen, Deborah. *You Just Don't Understand: Women and Men in Communication.*
New York: William Morrow, 1990.

CHAPTER 9

Lefkowitz, Eva S. "Negative Expression and Positive Involvement During Conver-
sations Between Women and Their Mothers." Presented 5 November 2001 at
the Gerontological Society of America.
Lewicki, Roy, et al. "Ethical and Unethical Bargaining Tactics: An Empirical
Study." *Journal of Business Ethics* (1998) 17:665–682.
Ryan, R. M. "Psychological Needs and the Facilitation of Integrative Processes."
Journal of Personality (1995) 63:397–427.

CHAPTER 10

Bornstein, Robert F., and Joseph M. Masling. *The Psychodynamics of Gender and
Gender Role.* Washington, D.C.: APA Books, 2002.
Cortesi, David E. *Secular Wholeness: A Skeptic's Path to a Richer Life.* New Bern,
N.C.: Trafford, 2002.
Eaker, Elaine. "House Husbands at Greater Risk of Heart Attack than Workers."
Study for the American Heart Association, 2002.

Friedan, Betty. *The Feminine Mystique.* New York: W. W. Norton, 1963.

Fulghum, Robert. *From Beginning to End: The Rituals of Our Lives.* New York: Ivy Books, 1995.

Ridley, Matt. "Were Chimps the First Socialists?" *New Statesman,* 12 July 1999.

Shapiro, Kenneth. *Animal Models of Human Psychology.* Cambridge, Mass.: Hogrefe & Huber, 1998.

Stanford, Craig. "Chimpanzee Hunting Behavior and Human Evolution." *American Scientist,* June 1995.

Van Gennep, Arnold. *Rites of Passage.* Chicago: University of Chicago Press, 1960.

CHAPTER 11

Christian, Diana Leafe. *Creating a Life Together: Practical Tools to Grow Ecovillages and Intentional Communities.* Gabriola Island, BC: New Society, 2003.

Kelling, George L., and Catherine M. Coles. *Fixing Broken Windows: Restoring Order and Reducing Crime in Our Communities.* New York: Touchstone Books, 1998.

Schaub, Laird. Fellowship for Intentional Community: RR 1, Box 156, Rutledge, Missouri 63563 USA, fic@ic.org, 660-883-5545. Website ic.org.

Sustainable Communities Network.
    URL: sustainable.org/creating/community_index.html.

CHAPTER 12

Arkin, Robert, et al. "Materialism as an Attempt to Cope with Uncertainty." *Psychology and Marketing* (2002) 19:389–406.

Brown, Jonathon. *The Self.* New York: McGraw-Hill, 1998.

Brown, Jonathon, et al. "Self-Esteem and Emotion: Some Thoughts about Feelings." *Journal of Personality and Social Psychology* (2001) 5:575–584.

Burns, David. *Ten Days to Great Self-Esteem.* London: Vermilion, 1993.

Giesler, R. Brian, et al. "Self-Verification in Clinical Depression: The Desire for Negative Evaluation." *Journal of Abnormal Psychology* (1996) 105:3.

Greenberg, J., et al. "Toward a Dual-Motive Depth Psychology of Self and Social Behavior." In *Efficacy, Agency, and Self-Esteem*. Ed. M. H. Kernis, 73–99. New York: Plenum, 1995.

Heine, S. J., and D. R. Lehman. "The Cultural Construction of Self-Enhancement: An Examination of Group-Serving Biases." *Journal of Personality and Social Psychology* (1997) 72:1268–1283.

James, William. *Principles of Psychology*, vol. 1. New York: Henry Holt, 1890.

Josephs, Robert A., et al. "Self-Esteem Maintenance Process: Why Low Self-Esteem May Be Resistant to Change." *Personality and Social Psychology Bulletin* (2003) 29:920–933.

Kasser, T., and R. M. Ryan. "Further Examining the American Dream: Well-Being Correlates of Intrinsic and Extrinsic Goals." *Personality and Social Psychology Bulletin* (1996) 22:281–288.

Kernis, M. H., et al. "Fragile Self-Esteem in Children and Its Associations with Perceived Patterns of Parent-Child Communication." *Journal of Personality* (2000) 68:225–252.

Leary, M. R. "Making Sense of Self-Esteem." *Current Directions in Psychological Science* (1999) 8:32–35.

Ryan, Richard, and E. L. Deci. "To Be Happy or to Be Self-Fulfilled: A Review of Research on Hedonic and Eudaimonic Well-Being." In *Annual Review of Psychology* (2001) 52:141–166.

Salzinger, Kurt. "Take Back Psychology." *Monitor on Psychology* (2002) 33(4).

Seligman, Martin. "The American Way of Blame." *Monitor on Psychology* (1998) 29(7).

Staub, Erwin. "Aggression and Self-Esteem." *Monitor on Psychology* (1999) 30(1).

Weiss, Alexander, et al. "Subjective Well-Being Is Heritable and Genetically Correlated with Dominance in Chimpanzees." *Journal of Personality and Social Psychology* (2002) 83(5).

CHAPTER 13

Beauregard, Keith S., and David Dunning. "Turning Up the Contrast: Self-Enhancement Motives Prompt Egocentric Contrast Effects in Social Judgments." *Journal of Personality and Social Psychology* (1998) 74: 606–621.

Brown, Stephanie, et al. "Providing Social Support May Be More Important than Receiving It: Results from a Prospective Study of Mortality." *Psychological Science* (2003) 14(3).

Csikszentmihalyi, Mihaly. *Flow: The Psychology of Optimal Experience*. New York: Harper and Row, 1990.

Deci, E. L., and R. Flaste. *Why We Do What We Do: Understanding Self-Motivation*, reprint. New York: Penguin USA, 1996.

Deci, E. L., and R. M. Ryan. "The What and Why of Global Pursuits: Human Needs and the Self-Determination of Behavior." *Psychological Inquiry* (2000) 11:227–268.

Dweck, Carol S., and Claudia M. Mueller. "Praise for Intelligence Can Undermine Children's Motivation and Performance." *Journal of Personality and Social Psychology* (1998) 75:33–52.

Eccles, Jacquelynne, et al. "Self-Evaluations of Competence, Task Values and Self-Esteem." In *Beyond Appearance: A New Look at Adolescent Girls*. Ed. Norine G. Johnson, et al. Washington, D.C.: APA Books, 1999.

Holden, E. Constance. "Behavioral Addictions: Do They Exist?" *Science* (2001) 294:980–982.

Goleman, Daniel. *Emotional Intelligence: Why It Can Matter More than IQ*. London: Bloomsbury, 1996.

Goleman, Daniel, et al. *Primal Leadership: Realizing the Power of Emotional Intelligence*. Boston: Harvard Business School Press, 2002.

Pomerantz, Eva M., and Karen D. Rudolph. "What Ensues from Emotional Distress? Implications for Competence Estimation." *Child Development* (2003) 74(2).

CHAPTER 14

Arkin, Robert, et al. "Materialism as an Attempt to Cope with Uncertainty." *Psychology and Marketing* (2002) 19:389–406.

Bower, Julienne E., et al. "Impact of Cognitive Processing on Discovery of Meaning and Natural Killer Cell Cytoxicity in Bereaved Women at Risk for Breast Cancer." *Annals of Behavioral Medicine* (2003). In press at time of writing.

Dawkins, Richard. *The Selfish Gene*. Oxford: Oxford University Press, 1989.

Jenkins, Rachel, et al. *Prevention of Suicide*. London: HMSO, 1994.

McKhann, Guy M., and Albert, Marilyn. *Keep Your Brain Young: The Complete Guide to Physical and Emotional Health and Longevity.* Hoboken, N.J.: John Wiley & Sons, 2002.

Morris, Joan K., et al. "Loss of Employment and Mortality." *British Medical Journal* (1994) 308:1135–1138.

Peteet, J. R. "A Closer Look at the Role of a Spiritual Approach in Addictions Treatment." *Journal of Substance Abuse Treatment* (1993) 10:263–267.

Price, Christine. "Retirement for Women: The Impact of Employment." *Journal of Women and Aging* (2002) 14:41–57.

Pulkids. Pulteney Grammar School: 190 South Terrace, Adelaide, South Australia 5000 Australia, pulkids@student.pulteney.sa.edu.au, 61-8-8216-5555. URL: pulteney.sa.edu.au/Student%20Pages/pulkids/whoarepulkids.htm.

Ridley, Matt. *Origins of Virtue: Human Instincts and the Evolution of Cooperation.* New York: Penguin Viking, 1996.

Rilling, James K., et al. "A Neural Basis for Social Cooperation." *Neuron* (2002) 35:395–405.

Smuts, Barbara. Quoted by Natalie Angier. In "Of Altruism, Heroism and Nature's Gifts in the Face of Terror." *New York Times*, 18 September 2001.

Trobe, Yaacov, et al. "Time-Dependent Gambling: Odds Now, Money Later." *Journal of Experimental Psychology: General* (1992) 131:364–376.

Walker, Alan, and Tony Maltby. *Aging in Europe.* London: Open University Press, 1997.

CHAPTER 15

Abdullaev, Nabi. WHO study quoted in "Russia Remains a Dangerous Place." *Prism* (2002) 8(2).

Coleman, Peter. "Spiritual Beliefs and Existential Meaning in Later Life." Paper for the Economic and Social Research Council, released 2002.

Headey, Bruce, et al. "Pet Ownership Is Good for Your Health and Saves Public Expenditure Too: Australian and German Longitudinal Evidence." *Australian Social Monitor* (2002) 5(4).

Heaton, T. B., and E. L. Pratt, "The Effects of Religious Homogamy on Marital Satisfaction and Stability." *Journal of Family Issues* (1990) 11:191–207.

Ikeda, Daisaku. *Unlocking the Mysteries of Birth and Death: . . . And Everything in Between, A Buddhist View of Life*, 2d ed. Santa Monica: Middleway Press, 2003.

Jacobs, Gregg. Quoted in "Scientists Find Biological Reality Behind Religious Experience." *Boston Globe*, 10 May 2001.

Koenig, H. G., et al. "Modeling the Cross-Sectional Relationships Between Religion, Physical Health, Social Support, and Depressive Symptoms." *American Journal of Geriatric Psychiatry* (1997) 5:131–143.

Newberg, Andrew, et al. "The Measurement of Regional Cerebral Blood Flow During the Complex Cognitive Task of Meditation: A Preliminary SPECT Study." *Psychiatry Research: Neuroimaging* (2001) 106(2).

Newberg, Andrew, et al. *Why God Won't Go Away: Brain Science and the Biology of Belief.* New York: Ballantine Books, 2002.

Ramachandran, Vilayanur. "The Neural Basis of Religious Experience." Paper delivered at the annual meeting for the Society for Neuroscience, October 1997.

Wilson, David Sloan. *Darwin's Cathedral: Evolution, Religion, and the Nature of Society.* Chicago: University of Chicago Press, 2002.

Wright, Keith. *Religious Abuse: A Pastor Explores the Many Ways Religion Can Hurt as Well as Heal.* Kelowa, BC: Northstone, 2001.

INDEX

⊙